The Church seems to have increasing numbers of pastors who are under spiritual attack or who are failing in the ministry. *Pastors at Greater Risk* is an exceedingly helpful book that brings significant hope and practical solutions to the major challenges faced by so many pastors today. I highly recommend it.

PAUL CEDAR
CHAIRMAN, MISSION AMERICA COALITION

There are far greater risks and hazards in the ministry today than in previous years. *Pastors at Greater Risk* addresses these changes and the problems that ministers face. This is a great handbook for all who are in the work of the ministry.

DAVID YONGGI CHO
CHAIRMAN, CHURCH GROWTH INTERNATIONAL

As a minister/psychologist who specializes in working with clergy who have crossed inappropriate sexual boundaries, I recommend this book highly to both clergy and laity as a resource that provides up-to-date information and very practical, hands-on suggestions in terms of making appropriate changes. One important area covered in the book is Internet pornography, which unfortunately is an epidemic problem for both clergy and laity. The good news is that there are resources to provide help; and this book is one of those important sources.

RALPH H. EARLE, M.DIV., PH.D.
PRESIDENT, PSYCHOLOGICAL COUNSELING SERVICES, LTD., AND NEW HOPE EDUCATIONAL FOUNDATION

The ferocity of the spiritual battle and the intensity of
the times are blurring the vision and sapping the spirit of good and
godly church leaders. If unaddressed with the wisdom of the
Word and the power of the Spirit, the battle will increase the number
of casualties already tallied. But there's hope and honest guidance
here. Read and be strengthened, fellow-shepherd.

JACK W. HAYFORD
CHANCELLOR, THE KING'S COLLEGE AND SEMINARY

Drs. H. B. London and Neil Wiseman have done both
pastors and churches a great service by revising and updating their
classic work. The book is right on target. Never before in my entire
ministry have I ever seen the devil as alive and well in the work of
men of God as I have today. Pastors are at risk—and they have too
much to risk to lose. This book will help every pastor to build a hedge
of protection around his life and enable every church to know how
to better pray for their pastor. I endorse it enthusiastically.

DR. JAMES MERRIT
PASTOR, FELLOWSHIP OF JOY, SNELLVILLE, GEORGIA

Pastors at Greater Risk is a must-read for all pastors and the
congregations who support them. London and Wiseman share the
gut-wrenching reality of the pastor's world. This is one of the
most comprehensive books offering biblical and practical steps in
overcoming many of the pitfalls of ministry. Rather than
becoming a statistic, you, your family and your congregation
can be a light for Jesus Christ in your community.

BOB RECCORD
PRESIDENT, NORTH AMERICAN MISSION BOARD

Pastors at Greater Risk highlights the dangerous challenges
to the ministries of those who serve Jesus Christ. Ministers have more
stress, more burnout, more problems, more temptations, more tasks
and more expectations than ever before. The authors understand
this and have attempted to point out the problems and point pastors
to solutions. All pastors would do well to read and heed this book.

ELMER L. TOWNS
DEAN, SCHOOL OF RELIGION, LIBERTY UNIVERSITY

H. B. London and Neil Wiseman have extended a practical
lifeline for church leaders who daily face the threats of turbulent
ministry in the twenty-first century. *Pastors at Greater Risk* is a clarion
reminder that a shepherd's personal health and identity are the
centerpieces of effectiveness. For too long, pastors have focused on
the *doing* of ministry to the exclusion of *being*. This is a book
about being; it could be your first step in recapturing the
personal values, disciplines and skill you may have lost in the
wake of contemporary pastoral ministry.

E. GLENN WAGNER, PH.D., D.MIN.
SENIOR PASTOR, CALVARY CHURCH, CHARLOTTE, NORTH CAROLINA

PASTORS AT 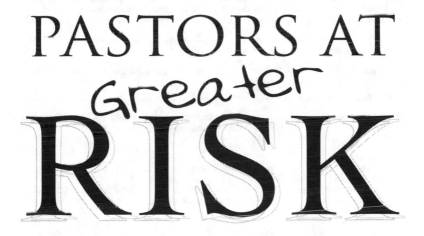Greater RISK

H. B. LONDON, JR.
NEIL B. WISEMAN

Regal

From Gospel Light
Ventura, California, U.S.A.

PUBLISHED BY REGAL BOOKS
FROM GOSPEL LIGHT
VENTURA, CALIFORNIA, U.S.A.
PRINTED IN THE U.S.A.

Regal Books is a ministry of Gospel Light, an evangelical Christian publisher dedicated to serving the local church. We believe God's vision for Gospel Light is to provide church leaders with biblical, user-friendly materials that will help them evangelize, disciple and minister to children, youth and families.

It is our prayer that this Regal book will help you discover biblical truth for your own life and help you meet the needs of others. May God richly bless you.

For a free catalog of resources from Regal Books/Gospel Light, please call your Christian supplier or contact us at 1-800-4-GOSPEL *or* www.regalbooks.com.

All Scripture quotations, unless otherwise indicated, are taken from the *Holy Bible, New International Version®*. Copyright © 1973, 1978, 1984 by International Bible Society. Used by permission of Zondervan Publishing House. All rights reserved.

Other versions used are
THE MESSAGE—Scripture taken from *THE MESSAGE.* Copyright © by Eugene H. Peterson, 1993, 1994, 1995. Used by permission of NavPress Publishing Group.
NLT—Scripture quotations marked *(NLT)* are taken from the *Holy Bible,* New Living Translation, copyright © 1996. Used by permission of Tyndale House Publishers, Inc., Wheaton, Illinois 60189. All rights reserved.
Phillips—*The New Testament in Modern English,* Revised Edition, J. B. Phillips, Translator. © J. B. Phillips 1958, 1960, 1972. Used by permission of Macmillan Publishing Co., Inc., 866 Third Avenue, New York, NY 10022.
RSV—From the *Revised Standard Version* of the Bible, copyright 1946, 1952, and 1971 by the Division of Christian Education of the National Council of the Churches of Christ in the U.S.A. Used by permission.
TLB—Scripture quotations marked *(TLB)* are taken from *The Living Bible,* copyright © 1971. Used by permission of Tyndale House Publishers, Inc., Wheaton, IL 60189. All rights reserved.

Originally published as *Pastors at Risk* by Victor Books, 1993.

Cover and interior design by Robert Williams
Revised edition edited by Brad Lewis

Library of Congress Cataloging-in-Publication Data
London, H. B.
    Pastors at greater risk / H.B. London, Jr., Neil B. Wiseman.—Rev. ed.
        p. cm.
Rev. ed. of: Pastors at risk. 1993.
    ISBN 0-8307-2903-8 (hardcover)   ISBN 0-8307-3237-3 (paperback)
    1. Clergy—Office. 2. Pastoral theology. I. Wiseman, Neil B. II.
London, H. B. Pastors at risk. III. Title.
    BV660.3.L66 2003
    253—dc21
                                                                    2002154770

1   2   3   4   5   6   7   8   9   10   /   09   08   07   06   05   04   03

Rights for publishing this book in other languages are contracted by Gospel Light Worldwide, the international nonprofit ministry of Gospel Light. Gospel Light Worldwide also provides publishing and technical assistance to international publishers dedicated to producing Sunday School and Vacation Bible School curricula and books in the languages of the world. For additional information, visit www.gospellightworldwide.org; write to Gospel Light Worldwide, P.O. Box 3875, Ventura, CA 93006; or send an e-mail to info@gospellightworldwide.org.

CONTENTS

SECTION 3: OVERCOMING THE RISKS IN YOUR PERSONAL LIFE

CONFRONTING THE CRISES

It is impossible to overstate how deeply I feel about the importance of upholding the men and women who serve us through
the ministry of the church. They and their families need our support and understanding! H. B. London, Jr., and Neil B. Wiseman
are on the cutting edge of a movement that seeks to provide that
support. Every concerned and conscientious Christian will want
to benefit from their insights.

The pastor has an incredibly significant and difficult job. The
implications and ramifications of his responsibilities at church
are more extensive than most parishioners realize. A strong
church is the first line of defense for healthy families; and healthy
families are the building blocks of stable communities. But there's
a complicating catch. The pastor, in addition to carrying this
heavy responsibility for the church and society, usually has a family of his own at home. All too often time spent in ministry equals
time away from spouse and kids. If family stability isn't attacked
and eroded at one end of the scale, it seems it will be at the other!
This is a serious and delicate situation. And caught in the middle
of it all, trying (frantically, sometimes) to keep both ends of the
candle burning, is that person we know as the professional minister—a human being like the rest of us, who increasingly finds himself working against a legion of obstacles, unrealistic expectations
and stresses and strains unique to his position in the world.

I have another very personal reason for being concerned
about the pastor's family—I grew up in a preacher's home myself!

And though my memories of my dad and mom and their tireless dedication to the Lord's work are positive, I do know something about the struggles and hardships encountered by those who serve God's people in that capacity. In spite of a few megachurches and media ministries that make the ministry look like a fairly comfortable calling, the fact remains that, in financial terms, the pastorate is no more promising today than it was when my dad preached his first sermon back in 1935. He received 55 cents as compensation for that initial labor of love and averaged $8 per Sunday for the next 52 weeks. His total earnings for that first year in the ministry were $429.82 and, remarkably, he gave $352.00 back to the church. He and my mother lived on a small inheritance that came to them after my grandfather died in 1935 and throughout their lives together gave more than they could afford to the cause of Christ or to anyone who appeared to be more needy than they. Obviously, inflation has jacked up the figure; and yet I'm well aware that many of our pastors today are floundering on the modern equivalent of that $8.00 per week and $429.82 per year. That kind of budgetary restriction just has to place family life under an incredible financial strain!

I am committed, then, to the welfare of pastors and their families. But the question bears even greater significance for society as a whole. For if the pastor's family suffers, the entire church suffers. And if the church fails to be what it should be, society goes a little further adrift. That, I'm convinced, is exactly what we see happening all around us today. Focus on the Family's desire to reach out to pastors where they live is part of our overall plan for building a stronger moral and spiritual foundation for our culture as a whole. This book has arisen out of that concern. The authors are themselves experienced pastors. They know their subject from firsthand experience. H. B. London, Jr., shepherded congregations for three decades before joining the staff of Focus on the Family, the most recent of his charges having been a large and prominent church in Pasadena, California. Neil B. Wiseman has served in a variety of roles—pastor, professor, magazine editor and clergy educator. Both men can teach us a great deal about strengthening the church and society from the ground up by supporting the people who provide us with spiritual leadership. We think it's sound strategy!

Dr. James C. Dobson
President, Focus on the Family

ACKNOWLEDGMENTS

IN GRATITUDE

to

OUR HEROES—PASTORS
for meeting contemporary
challenges with grace and faithfulness

OUR PARTNERS—THE PUBLISIIING TEAM
Bill Greig III, Kyle Duncan,
Kim Bangs, Deena Davis, Brad Lewis,
and behind-the-scenes copyeditors,
artists, designers,
marketers and presspersons

OUR COLLEAGUES—WHO JOINED US IN DIALOGUE WITH READERS
Dr. James C. Dobson,
Gordon and Gail MacDonald,
Archibald Hart, Jerry Bridges, Bob and Sandy Sewell,
Ted Roberts, Dr. Richard A. Swenson,
Linda Riley, Janell Repp, Linda Swanson,
Kandy Veenker, Kay Warren, Pam Farrel, Jane Rubietta

OUR SUPPORT TEAM
Beverley London, Bonnie Wiseman,
Sue McFadden

INTRODUCTION

Welcome to the twenty-first century, pastor. If it doesn't already feel like it, you're about to embark on the most amazing roller-coaster ride of your life.

Yes, you get to ride, but before you climb aboard, you need to take care of some maintenance. The book you hold in your hands is our best shot at an owners' manual for that roller coaster. Ten years ago we published a book titled *Pastors at Risk*. Now we've updated, revised and added to that book to create this one, *Pastors at Greater Risk*.

The first question you might ask is, Why bother? The answer is found in the new title. The risks in ministry are greater than ever. Pastors are working harder in a world that's more corrupt. They wonder why their parishioners expect them to squander energy on trivial matters when evil threatens to wreck the human race. Fatigue shows in the eyes of pastors. Worry slows their stride. Vagueness dulls their preaching.

This struggle takes a terrible toll, as pastors wrestle with crammed calendars, hectic homes, splintered dreams, starved intimacy and shriveled purpose. Some quit in utter hopelessness.

Others lapse into passivity. And many of the rest just hold on by their fingernails.

But the good news is that something can be done. *Pastors at Greater Risk* is our authentic attempt to listen to the anguish of pastors, to scrutinize their frustrations and to propose some answers. Of course, we don't have all the answers, and neither do the fine men and women who contributed to this book. But we do know that we're making a sincere effort to help pastors find fulfillment in their future ministries. The goal is for them to become whole individuals who balance being and doing, family and church, person and profession, worship and work—wounded healers who allow themselves to be healed.

A Bit of Housekeeping

According to preeminent researcher George Barna, more than 9 out of 10 senior pastors are men (95 percent), are married (94 percent) and have been in full-time ministry for 17 years, including 5 at their current church.[1] We recognize this group of pastors as largely the readers of this book. Of course, we know that many women faithfully and effectively serve God in churches as do many singles. Yet because the overwhelming majority of pastors are married males with families, we write with a mostly masculine point of view and we offer a good dose of guidance about marriage and family relationships. If these statistics don't describe exactly who you are, we hope that you'll still glean information from the book; however, for simplicity we're writing to the vast majority.

Also, we face the same obstacles that many teams of authors face. How do we refer to ourselves as we're writing? Again, for the sake of simplicity, H. B. is the "I" in this book, and we refer to Neil in the third person. Of course, both of us contributed completely to what you're reading.

Finally, here's what you'll find as you read on. We've divided the book into three sections that deal with the risks that pastors tell us they face. In section 1, we explore in detail where these risks come from. In section 2, we investigate the risks pastors face right in their own families. In section 3, we look at the risks confronting pastors in their inner, personal lives. Throughout, we and experts on these subjects try to offer solutions for avoiding or overcoming the risks.

In the midst of all the crises that pastors face, we take comfort in a wonderful promise: victory. The gospel message of Jesus Christ offers hope, healing, recovery and wellness. You've probably offered this message to many people throughout your ministry. Now we're offering the same promise to you. Instead of being a victim of the high demand of ministry, you can be a triumphant victor as a minister of the gospel.

H. B. London, Jr., and Neil B. Wiseman

RECOGNIZING THE
RISKS IN
YOUR MINISTRY

A Personal Word from H. B. L.

Be Aware of God's Small Wonders

As a pastor to pastors, I see a lot of pain and discouragement. One pastor said to me recently, "If it were just a jungle out there, I could handle that, but it's worse than a jungle!" He was probably having a pretty rough day. But the truth is, many things in the ministry do take a toll on us. If we're not careful, we can miss the blessings and overlook the joy.

In *The Return of the Prodigal Son*, Henri Nouwen writes,

I am not accustomed to rejoicing in things that are small, hidden and scarcely noticed by people around me. I have become accustomed to living with sadness, and so have lost the eyes to see the joy.[1]

Life will do that to us if we are not careful. We can easily become callused and cynical. When that happens, we need to step back, take a look at our motivation and ask God to forgive us.

The roads I travel take me to places where fellow pastors struggle with the what ifs more than the why nots. They've allowed the naysayers and the "joysuckers" to influence their emotions and responses. They've overlooked their blessings.

Be aware of God's small wonders. Look around you with eyes open and hearts ready to receive even the simplest pleasures. When you do, you become a vessel of happiness to those you encounter.

"Rejoice in the Lord always. I will say it again: Rejoice!" (Phil. 4:4).

CHAPTER ONE

WARNING: CRISIS IN PROGRESS

A CONVERSATION BETWEEN DR. JAMES C. DOBSON AND H. B. LONDON, JR.

- 50 percent of all congregations in the United States are either plateauing or declining.[2]
- 33 percent of pastors confess "inappropriate" sexual behavior with someone in the church.[3]
- 90 percent of pastors work more than 46 hours a week.
- 80 percent believe that pastoral ministry affects their families negatively.
- 33 percent say that being in ministry is an outright hazard to their family.
- 75 percent report they've had a significant stress-related crisis at least once in their ministry.
- 50 percent feel unable to meet the needs of the job.
- 90 percent feel they're inadequately trained to cope with ministry demands.
- 40 percent report a serious conflict with a parishioner at least once a month.[4]
- 53 percent of Americans say the nation's moral problems are greater than the nation's economic problems. 78 percent of Americans rate the state of moral values in the United States as weak or very weak.[5]

Even a quick glance at the risk factors on page 20 shows how pastors today are feeling and the tough life they're leading.

Do you see yourself in these numbers? More important, what can you do about it?

As part of the answer to that question, let me tell you how a ministry for pastors and their families started. During a family gathering, James Dobson and I had a casual conversation. As we talked, we began to realize the need for someone to become *a pastor to pastors* to help ministry professionals cope with these unique stresses they live under. We sensed a need for someone to plead the cause of pastors and families to parishioners across North America.

You probably know that Dr. Dobson is founder and president of Focus on the Family. And I served as a pastor for 31 years. But you may not know that Dr. Dobson and I are first cousins. We're both the only sons of ministers, and we were born just nine months apart. We've been close friends since childhood.

That's not all we have in common. We're both immensely interested in the spiritual health and emotional wellness of pastors and their families everywhere. We believe that if we can help pastors and their families, they'll in turn multiply ministry to families in their churches.

Our casual conversation in Jim's den led to prayer and thoughtful discussions about how Focus on the Family might respond to the unique needs of pastors who serve 350,000 churches across the United States.

The outcome was a commitment by Focus on the Family to assist pastors who face the difficult daily dilemma of meeting the needs of their families while trying to be faithful to the obligations of a contemporary pastorate.

To help pastors build healthier homes, Focus on the Family tries to offer a compassionate heart that seeks to understand their unique stresses; a noncondemning listening "other" for ministers and spouses; and topflight strategies and imaginative resources for spiritual renewal, family-life strengthening, time management and financial stability.

THE CRISIS

I can't recreate the original conversation I had with Jim, but I can let you listen in on another conversation—a Focus on the Family radio program originally heard on 1,900 radio stations—that shows how building awareness among pastors and lay church leaders is the first step in untangling some of the stresses and trials pastors face.

Defensive Line

Dobson: H. B., I believe the Church is the first line of defense for the family. It must not be permitted to flounder. Since the local pastor is the most visual person who represents the Church, he carries most of the load.

He's the one people call when they have a family emergency in the middle of the night. He's the one who puts his arm around someone's shoulder to offer comfort in crises and spiritual support when it's needed the most. The pastor's role is vital. His work is absolutely essential in our society.

Unfortunately, few people stop to think about how much difficulty, how much depression and how many obstacles he faces to serve in this way.

London: That's right, Jim. In many ways, the first line of defense for the family is the Church. But it can only be strong when the pastor is emotionally stable and spiritually solid. That's why

I believe that if we can strengthen pastors and their families, we can be a catalyst for spiritual renewal in many churches across the nation. But it's an uphill battle: We live in a culture of increased religiosity but decreased morality. Pastors have never had to work harder to serve people than they do now. The pressures are incredible and brutal.

Dobson: Describe the pastors we're talking about.

London: There are 350,000 churches in the United States served by pastors who head families, so I assume that's the size of our problem. Families in pastors' homes face all the pressures every family faces, plus unique demands pastoral ministry makes on them. These pastors need help with their families as much as they need to be able to do ministry well.

I want to encourage these faithful pastors. I want to serve those with deeply felt spiritual commitments who give themselves every hour of every day to ministry. I want to help

Balance is the principal issue; everyone wants it but few seem able to make it work for them.

those ministers whose families sacrifice to keep their husband or father in the pastorate. The church couldn't exist without these families.

Dobson: What are the main difficulties the average pastor faces?

London: Their most pressing problems relate to time, money and family. I think we must help pastors balance these areas. Balance is the principal issue; everyone wants it but few seem able to make it work for them. They ask, "How do I minister effectively to my family and still be fair to my congregation?" There's always more to do than time allows.

Dobson: It's a bottomless pit—they never get done. The burden of unfinished work is probably greater in the pastorate than in any other vocation.

London: The terrible tyranny of the unfinished is always with them. But like all strong family units, pastors' families need to make it specific—they need to stop and talk to each other and take time to understand what's happening in each other's lives. Then if something is amiss, they need to take time to fix it.

Dobson: Still, if you're a pastor and you get a call at 3:00 in the morning—if someone has a heart attack—you go to the hospital. If someone has a serious automobile accident, you go. And if a family has a runaway teenager, you go to offer support in any possible way.

London: That's it exactly. You answer the phone. You get up. You stagger into the shower. You go. You pray all the way. You minister however you can for as long as you're needed. Then you pick up your day wherever you can find it.

Something Must Change

Dobson: But that pace takes a terrific toll—emotionally, spiritually, even physically. Faithful ministers must live in a perpetual state of fatigue.

London: Something has to change—that's the message I hear often these days from the letters pastors write about their frustrations in ministry.

Dobson: Let's talk about what your mail says. When you first came to Focus on the Family, I think you wrote 5,000 pastors to see what they were thinking and feeling.

London: Yes, I randomly selected 5,000 pastors from our mailing list. I asked three questions:

1. What's the greatest danger facing pastors and their families today?
2. What's your number one challenge as you serve your congregation?
3. If it were possible for me to do so, how could I personally assist you through utilizing the resources of Focus on the Family?

Dobson: What a list of questions. I guess you had a blizzard of responses and the phones started to ring. What conclusions have you reached after reading hundreds of letters?

London: Second to the balance issue is the difficulty of motivating people to live consistent lives and to help the Church accomplish the Great Commission. Pastors are frustrated because people seem apathetic. They're experiencing a lack of people willing to do acts of Christian service.

I don't want to overgeneralize unfairly, but these pastors are saying that the good people in their churches seem centered on their own comforts, achievements and happiness rather than on the needs of others. Of course, the laity have many of the same pressures pastors have in their families and on their jobs.

Dobson: You've told me that about 40 percent of pastors say they have considered leaving their pastorates in the last three months.

London: That's what our surveys indicate. And though most of them will never leave the ministry, it does reflect an agonizing dissatisfaction that's largely unrecognized by those outside the profession.

Dobson: That's frightening when you calculate how important the church is to the family and the community. The Church is the essence of the Christian movement and the cornerstone of everything we believe and stand for. Yet 40 percent of its leaders say they're thinking about bailing out. Why are 40 percent ready to give up?

RISK FACTOR

50 percent of all congregations in the United States are either plateauing or declining.

London: It's a buildup—an overload or even a soul-breaking accumulation—of all we have been discussing. Pastors feel victimized because the work is harder and more complicated than ever before. They work harder now yet see less response and fewer results.

People are easily enticed by cultural nonvalues. Many people in the Church place more value on success and show than on spiritual reality and wholehearted repentance and authentic holy living.

Many pastors of churches of all sizes also feel pressured to be like the megachurches. For most, it's an impossible dream, but they hear about it often and some of their church members talk about it often.

Then, too, I think there's a disheartening message that trickles down from superchurches through books, tapes, conferences and religious TV programs; so pastors want to be like the biggest churches. But that creates unbelievable frustration because they can't be like megachurches.

The reality is that most pastors will never pastor churches of more than 100 members. Somehow, pastors need to hear that it's pleasing to God and important to the Kingdom if they do their work well in whatever size church they serve.

Dobson: I realize my qualifications to speak on some of these issues are limited, but I believe an emphasis on numbers is mistaken. It's upside down. The priority is wrong. Put the spiritual needs of people first, and numerical increase will be the natural outgrowth.

London: But some small churches have neither quality ministry to people nor increased numbers; some have not had a visitor in church in months or maybe even years. It's hard for a pastor to keep up his morale in those situations.

Moving Beyond Survival

Dobson: What about the health of those churches? I think I saw a statistic that 90 percent of churches are in survival mode. In other words, they are hanging on for dear life and trying to make ends meet. Do you agree?

London: Yes, and many of those churches have tried everything they can think of to break out of that, but they've failed. So some change pastors every three or four years. They're frustrated by nonproductive activity and tired of preaching that judges their lack of spiritual commitment. And we need to be aware that the secularization of society wounds them greatly because it encourages sporadic attendance and irregular giving.

Dobson: That constant moving tears up pastors' families, too.

London: Sure, and they can't even begin to develop trust between pastor and congregation in such a short time—to say nothing about trust in the community for the church.

Dobson: And did you tell me more than half of the pastors' wives are severely depressed?

London: Yes. And their wives often have reason to be depressed. They're expected not to express themselves. They're supposed to sit in the corner while their husbands run the show. And they slowly die when they see their husbands come home, sit in a chair and stare into space. They ask, "Is it worth it all? Are we doing any good? Does anyone care? Will it ever change?" And most of the obvious answers are even more frightening than the questions.

Dobson: I have to admit that you're giving me a new perspective on the local congregation and how much the pastorate has changed. I also have to admit that I'm a little convicted in the way I deal with pastors. I've often asked why the church isn't fighting abortion and pornography and why the church isn't reaching out to single mothers. Now I see that many pastors are hanging on by a thread. It changes my perspective and makes me believe something has to be done to change these situations.

London: You speak often about pastors having full plates. That word picture is amazingly accurate. Their plates are running over with so many demands and causes that they just throw up their hands when a new one comes along. One more challenge to take up a new cause, however noble, is just too much for them. Any additional expectation can push them over the edge.

One pastor writes that he feels like an old-fashioned wagon with the wheels coming off after someone removes the toggle pin from the axles. When the wheels come off, it either turns over or ends up in the ditch. That illustrates how many pastors feel today.

Dobson: How widespread is this problem, and what can be done?

London: All I can say is read my mail, answer my phone, hear what pastors tell me in conferences, and then you know pastors are in pain—everywhere. More than anything else they need the love, encouragement and prayer support of the people they serve.

That's why I believe our mandate is to encourage spiritual restoration and renewal and then help pastors better manage their time, money and personal lives. I think our first responsibility is to initiate spiritual renewal and restoration in the life of the pastor's family. We are going to do it every way we can—through books, tapes, magazines, pastor gatherings and conferences.

In the years I have left, I want to be available to speak with pastors and help them extend their ministries to families—especially their own families. I also want to be able to help those who are burned-out or depressed. I want pastors the world over to feel loved and valued.

HOPE IN THE ASSAULT

The prevailing crisis among pastors is crystal clear. Contemporary spiritual leaders are under a twofold assault—one within and one without.

Inside the Church, the snares of secularism entrap many believers. Daily, pastors deal with diluted dedication, family disintegration, superficial commitments and an accepted churchly consumerism no longer interested in sacrifice, suffering or servanthood. People still use the well-worn, friendly old words, but the new meanings refer to a Jesus who provides comfortable happiness and makes no demand on conduct or money. The enemy has secularized the Church without a shot being fired by anyone.

RISK FACTOR

90 percent of pastors work more than 46 hours a week.

Outside the Church, pastors face a new dark age where success is king and real faith issues are far down the average person's priority list after the PTA meeting, latest video release, Little League game or weekend diversion.

However, Charles Colson lights a hopeful sunrise in this dark night, "History pivots on the actions of individuals, both great and ordinary."[6] If Colson is right, every pastor needs to hear and heed the ancient question asked of Queen Esther, "Who knows but whether you have not come to the kingdom for such a time as this?" (Esther 4:14, *RSV*).

Who knows? God knows. Every individual pastor makes a difference; the *Church* and the *world* need every pastor serving at their best for such a time as this.

A Personal Word from H. B. L.

Pastor, You're Special

I saw it first on the front of a worship folder—a simple verse by Rebecca Barlow Jordan titled "God Made Pastors":

God gave them tender hearts, to hold the hurts of others. He gave them gentle hands, to reach out with compassion and love. God gave them eyes, to see the beauty and worth of a single soul. He gave them feet, to move swiftly, to pursue justice, restoration and peace.

God had His hand upon them—and breathed hope into their spirits.

He filled them with His strength and placed a message of urgency around their lives. God challenged them to greater works than He had ever done. Then, with His own hand of blessing, He wrapped them up in His mantle of love . . . and called them pastors.[1]

Nice, huh? Probably easier read than done. But the truth is that God called you. He asked you to fill a post of duty, to carry a cross, to respond to an assignment that is exclusively yours. Thank you for your response.

Paul wrote to the church in Ephesus, "It was he who gave some to be . . . evangelists, and some to be pastors and teachers, to prepare God's people" (Eph. 4:11-12). That verse has your name all over it. Please don't overlook the fact that what you are doing for Christ and the church is no accident. Live like the called-out one God created you to be.

CHAPTER TWO

MINISTRY KEEPS GETTING TOUGHER

RISK FACTORS

- 40 percent of American adults gave nothing to churches in 2000; one-third of born-again adults said they tithed, but a comparison of their actual giving and household incomes reveal that only one-eighth did so.[2]
- 19 percent of pastors indicated that they'd been forced out of ministry at least once during their ministry; another 6 percent said they'd been fired from a ministry position.[3]
- The typical pastor has his greatest ministry impact at a church in years 5 through 14 of his pastorate; unfortunately, the average pastor lasts only five years at a church.[4]
- The average number of adults attending services at a Protestant church during a typical week is 90.[5]
- Church attendance in the United States is 43 percent of all adults in a typical week; however, fewer than one out of three adults attends church services every week.
- Only half the adults who say they're Christians contend that they are "absolutely committed" to the Christian faith.
- 44 percent of Americans who declare themselves to be Christians believe that Jesus sinned during His time on Earth.[6]
- 64 percent of adults said that truth is relative to the person and their circumstances.
- 31 percent of adults say that their most common basis for moral decision making is doing whatever feels right or comfortable in a given situation.[7]

Pastoral service is harder now than ever before. What's going on?

Unprecedented shifts in moral, social and economic conditions are battering congregations. These changing circumstances and declining values directly affect pastors and their way of life. Many of these difficulties were almost unknown in earlier periods of history. These changes seem to be taking the Church in the wrong direction at breakneck speed.

At the same time, pastors' concepts of ministry are in flux. Now, clergy expect personal fulfillment and meaning where former generations seemed satisfied with sacrifice and even expected suffering. Clearly, this new breed of pastors views their world, their work and themselves differently than their preaching parents and grandparents did. Not better or worse—just different.

At the same time, contemporary people—the reason for ministry—are harder to reach. Their preferences and priorities are shifting more profoundly and swiftly than at any time since the rugged agrarian and individualistic ideals of the early pioneers and settlers.

Church marketing expert George Barna summarizes the new realities: "In two national surveys . . . one among adults and one among teenagers, people were asked if they believe that there are moral absolutes that are unchanging or that moral truth is relative to the circumstances. By a 3-to-1 margin (64 percent versus 22 percent) adults said truth is always relative to the person and their situation. The perspective was even more lopsided among teenagers, 83 percent of whom said moral truth depends on the circumstances, and only 6 percent of whom said moral truth is absolute."[8]

Barna summarizes the implications of these findings in the same report. He notes:

Substantial numbers of Christians believe that activities such as abortion, gay sex, sexual fantasies, cohabitation, drunkenness, and viewing pornography are morally acceptable. Without some firm and compelling basis for suggesting that such acts are inappropriate, people are left with philosophies such as "if it feels good, do it," "everyone else is doing it" or "as long as it doesn't hurt anyone else, it's permissible." In fact, the alarmingly fast decline of moral foundations among our young people has culminated in a one-word worldview: "whatever."[9]

As a result, pastors are feeling and talking about bewilderment or even disorientation about ministry. While discussing pastors under his supervision, one church leader said, "Morale is at an all-time low in our geographic area; so many people have lost their jobs and moved away that our pastors are working harder than ever and showing smaller gains."

A third-year seminary student questions if investing his future in service through the church is good stewardship of his life.

Pastors worry about parishioners and prospects. Recent surveys reveal only 43 percent of adults attend church on a given Sunday, and 34 percent can be considered unchurched because they haven't attended a church service in the past six months.[10] This isn't encouraging news for the church or pastors.

One veteran observer said, "The church is beyond change—what it needs is intentional revolution."

One pastor trying to accept these challenges said, "The work is harder than ever before, but the difficulties mean they need us more. In the long run, I hope that makes the difficulties beneficial to us."

To begin understanding what's going on in this profession in the middle of spiritual war zones, we need to look at the hazards of ministry. When we recognize the threats, we can take the first step toward disarming our frustration. Then in response, we can design effective strategies to meet and solve our difficulties.

One veteran observer had it right: "The church is beyond change what it needs is intentional revolution." Perhaps pastors need to see the Church and themselves that way, too. Then the message becomes, "Ministry is vastly different from what it used to be—I must retool my ministry with strategies to meet effectively the challenges I'm facing."

HAZARD 1:
WALK-ON-THE-WATER SYNDROME

Most of us have a story about a friendly stranger in the next seat on a plane who stops talking when he learns his fellow traveler is a pastor. Most of us have been served by a waitress who puts a spiritual spin on the conversation when she learns her customer is a preacher. At other times, conversations shut down completely when a pastor walks up and someone warns, "Clean up your act; the pastor is here."

I experienced walk-on-the-water syndrome when my sons were teenagers. The church's college department bought me a new, bright orange bike. My sons, Brad and Bryan, were so excited that they begged, "Dad, come home and go riding with us."

So I dropped my work, went home, put on my sweatshirt, shorts and tennis shoes and took off. As we neared home after a fun filled ride, a red pickup driven by our neighbor made an abrupt turn in front of me. As an inexperienced bike rider, I reached for the nonexistent foot brake. Then my hand slipped off the handlebar brake, and I went crashing into the truck. The bike crumpled into a mass of spokes and steel. I didn't crumple, but I did hit my head, skin my shins, bloody my forehead and—most of all—injure my pride.

My sons immediately began acting like Secret Service agents, checking every house and vehicle, hoping no one saw me on the ground.

The nervous driver inquired as he came around the back of his truck, "Are you okay?"

I responded, "Are you kidding? I'm in pain. My bike is broken. My kids are embarrassed. And besides that, why didn't you signal?"

The environment changed radically and the embarrassment increased when the driver's wife came out of her house screaming, "Pastor, Pastor, Pastor." Then she stuck a bony finger under the driver's nose and said, "See there. You couldn't just hit a kid. You had to hit a pastor."

I remember thinking, *I always knew people thought I was different because I was a pastor. But I never realized I was in a distinct grouping even when it comes to accidents.*

This ministerial mystique often makes pastors feel ill at ease. And though laypeople may not realize it, pastors have accidents, eat at McDonald's, father children, fret about bills and misunderstand their kids. Some even worry about their marriages and feel bone weary. No holy aura makes them perfect or extraordinary, and they know it.

RISK FACTOR

The typical pastor has his greatest ministry impact at a church in years 5 through 14 of his pastorate; unfortunately, the average pastor lasts only five years at a church.

Sadly, walk-on-the-water syndrome triggers in a few pastors an obnoxious, pseudoholy, prideful opinion of themselves. They allow themselves to believe the nice things parishioners say about them. They think they're always right. They resist accountability. They think they deserve every privilege they can manipulate. But the apostle Peter left a dazzling show-and-tell message for such egoists—anyone who tries to walk on water either does a lot of sputtering or drowns.

To find satisfying effectiveness, a pastor's view of himself and his ministry must resist all these delusive images. He must cultivate an accurate awareness of reality about himself and about his environment.

Hazard 2:
Disastrous Personal Problems

Every day I receive heartbreaking letters from pastors and their spouses. They detail the consequences of secret sins, describe emotional brokenness and explain stress that one pastor called a "boiling inside that feels like I swallowed burning sulfur."

Pastors also express their fear of changing environments for ministry. Such changes are like a gigantic iceberg, where individuals see only a tiny tip of the threatening menace. Overwhelmed, they feel isolated when misery comes.

You'd expect that any occupation dealing with stressful issues would cause casualties. Pastors aren't any different. And the stress is multiplied over and over as problems grow and snowball. An unsatisfactory reaction or terrifying circumstance in one area significantly impacts other aspects of a pastor's life and ministry. A big fight with his spouse on Saturday night shows up in Sunday morning's preaching.

Hazard 3:
Church Member Migration

Like wild geese, church members are on the move. They're not leaving Christianity; they just move to another congregation.

This superficial lack of loyalty puts pastors on edge. Long-held assumptions about doctrinal devotion and congregational commitments no longer seem significant. Fewer and fewer people choose a church or continue to attend because of biblical teaching or theological conviction.

Member migration is a widespread problem that reaches across denominational lines. In spite of the efforts of churches to win new converts, it's estimated that as much as 80 percent of church growth is a result of people moving from one congregation to another.

Like wild geese, church members are on the move.

This migration has created substantial losses in mainline churches. Smaller churches of various affiliations lose members in droves to larger, multiple-program churches. In the wake of this volatile mobility, small churches increasingly feel inferior, and that leads to a survival mentality. Laypeople and ministers who continue to serve in small churches are left to sink or swim as they mourn the losses of members and money.

Occupational mobility and employment downsizing increase the displaced-person problem even more. When faithful members move to new locations, they leave volunteer ministry assignments vacant. In a small church, it can take years to nurture others to replace the loss of even one stable, involved family.

As pastors worry about this member migration, they can lose their spiritual focus. Then they begin to go about their work more out of duty than calling, performing tasks of ministry but with no spiritual passion. As they constantly dress old wounds in the congregation and go through the motions of empty routines, nothing happens. They feel frustrated because they're not making a difference. It's all so different from the idealism they enjoyed when they started on their pilgrimage of ministry.

These feelings of futility shrink the soul. Inspiration dries up. It's hard to keep going. As a result, many pastors are convinced nothing will ever happen. So this conviction becomes a self-fulfilling prophecy—nothing does happen.

Finally, the loss of relationships caused by member migration further feeds pastors' discouragement and loneliness. As a pastor finds himself in such a situation, he examines his limited resources and then begins to believe that he has no human chance to make a difference—that's a longhand description of ministerial depression. To say it more concisely, spiritual burnout comes from believing there's no reason to try because the situation is always going to be the way it is, or worse. Limited opportunities and the pastor's frame of mind create a treadmill of hopelessness. In light of these pressures, many pastors settle into dreary monotony, withdraw altogether or hate the status quo they settle for. These grim realities can terrorize a pastor and hypnotize a declining congregation.

HAZARD 4: TECHNOLOGICALLY SHAPED PREFERENCES

Top-notch television and religious radio bring the most accomplished musicians and capable preachers into our family rooms. When church members have firsthand experience with flawless performances, is it any wonder they believe such programs should be models for their churches?

Most of us remember Sundays when we felt totally anointed as we preached, only to have a worshiper say at the door, "Pastor, did you hear Robert Schuller (or some other television pastor) preach this morning? What a message!"

The result of this accumulated technological excellence is that pastors preach to people who watch TV religious services with jammed sanctuaries, polished musicians and skilled speakers. Think of the adjustments church members must make when they come to a church of 50 where the air conditioning is broken, the kids are noisy, the music is amateurish or a fly or two is buzzing overhead.

No matter how hard they try, these individuals find it difficult not to think their church is inferior—even though their pastor, perhaps after working at a second job all week, does his best to open the Word. And it's even worse in situations where the pastor feels discouraged and functions only at a maintenance-mode level. This all produces an unspoken hopeless despair. Uncertain how to cope, faithful pastors push ahead, doing their best and invoking holy words long after optimism is gone.

HAZARD 5: DISTRACTED PEOPLE

People in the early twenty-first century live at a hectic pace, and they're far busier than many pastors realize. Some have acrobatic schedules that keep their children involved in school and sports activities. Others have overtime far beyond the traditional 40-hour workweek, workouts at the health club and jobs that require moms and dads to work different shifts. Distractions stress people all day, every day.

When people are bombarded by commitments, church can become just another event on the calendar.

When people are bombarded by commitments, church can become just another event on the calendar. Church certainly isn't the center of family life that it once was. There was a time, likely gone forever, when a revival captured the attention of a whole town.

As a result of these distractions and overcommitment to such a variety of activities, getting people to attend church more than once a week is an uphill struggle. Sometimes it's a battle to get them to attend even once a week, as the weekend becomes family time. All of these distractions also undermine active involvement and stewardship.

HAZARD 6:
CONSUMER MENTALITY

Consumer mentality saturates life today. Shopping malls have become centerpieces of community life. People can purchase whatever they want, whenever they want. They expect to find an abundant selection of sizes, colors and prices.

When these same people come to church, they naturally expect programs and ministries to appeal to their widely varied interests. However, they frequently have little commitment to make things happen or to help fund the cost of this smorgasbord kind of ministry.

This reality means that when people move to a new community, they choose a church on the basis of what it does for them rather than what they can do for it. Few choose a new church for its biblical teaching or theological soundness.

This consumer mentality also prompts people to change to churches within their communities. They simply move to a place with better children's programs, more appealing music, larger facilities, more convenient parking, more exciting preaching or more energetic services. Like changing

RISK FACTOR

Only half the adults who say they're Christians contend that they are "absolutely committed" to the Christian faith.

supermarkets or gas stations, the customer moves down the street to the next church.

As a result, they also dodge serving. They don't want to teach Sunday School, work with the youth group or "baby-sit" in the nursery. They simply want a church that provides inspiration and encouragement for them. They may even feel uncomfortable with the biblical language of sin and salvation.

HAZARD 7:
SUFFOCATING EXPECTATIONS

Pastors are facing a juggling act as they deal with mushrooming expectations from congregation, denomination, community, spouse, children or even self. In the church, for example, members sometimes say straightforwardly, "Pastor, you are paid to do church work, so you unravel the problems and care for the details." Even emotionally robust pastors find it takes energy and patience to cope with whining traditionalists, demanding visionaries and lethargic church members all at the same time.

To confuse the issues even more, the expectations often conflict with each other—at church, at home and in the greater community. As a result, dehumanizing fatigue becomes a way of life for pastors, so even the strongest feel their stamina wearing thin.

Perhaps a freeing insight comes from author Hugh Prather when he suggests that expectations are enslaving judgments we make of each other. He thinks expectations are often so far off the mark from reality that they drive wedges between people who formerly had fine relationships before one of them got carried away with an impossible ideal. As a solution, he suggests, "Expectations, like cataracts, must be removed because there is no way around them."[11]

Thinking how to remove unrealistic expectations is a stimulating exercise for an overburdened pastor. Amazingly, in the process he may discover that his expectations of his parishioners and his family may be as unrealistic as their expectations of him. Or even more amazing, he may discover that the expectations are in his head—that is, his expectations are mostly self-induced.

HAZARD 8:
DECIMATED ABSOLUTES

Our permissive society has trashed absolutes. *Sures* have been bartered into *maybes*. The Ten Commandments have been rejected as the code of conduct. It's almost as if society is committing suicide by inches because self-control, compassion, tolerance, faith, integrity and respect for authority are all in such short supply.

Even believers routinely substitute an "I'm not so sure" for "thus saith the Lord." Church people don't run their lives by biblical truth any more than secular people do. Everyone does what's right in his own eyes. Researcher George Barna sounds like a prophet to the Church:

> When a majority of Christian adults, including three out of four born again Baby Busters, as well as three out of four born again teens proudly cast their vote for moral relativism, the Church is in trouble. Continuing to preach more sermons, teach more Sunday school classes and enroll more people in Bible study groups won't solve the problem since most of these people don't accept the basis of the principles being taught in those venues. The failure to address this issue at its root, and to do so quickly and persuasively, will undermine the strength of the church for at least another generation, and probably longer.[12]

Regrettably, this problem involves more than a collapse of moral absolutes in society. It also shows in subtle shifts where clergy and local lay leaders have loosened their personal commitments to biblical teaching and holy living.

Whatever the reasons, biblical absolutes have deteriorated into mere personal opinions. Consequently, many laypeople view

biblical and doctrinal matters as a theological smorgasbord where they choose what truth they want to govern their lives. Apparently, many join the church these days by a socializing osmosis rather than as a result of a supernatural transformation.

Whatever the reasons, biblical absolutes have deteriorated into mere personal opinions.

The devaluing of virtue and fading moral absolutes can make pastoring difficult and biblically based preaching nearly impossible.

HAZARD 9: MONEY STRUGGLES

Contemporary money problems force churches to revise their funding priorities radically. Giving is down and costs are up. In most households, including the pastor's, two paychecks are the norm. And young pastors often carry staggering educational debts into their ministries.

Other problems complicate a church's giving and spending. The graying of members also means many of them need ministry well beyond their peak earning and giving years. Middle-income jobs are being eliminated throughout society. And health insurance for everyone, including pastors, has skyrocketed to unbelievable levels.

All these factors impact a pastor's pocketbook. At the same time, many pastors find themselves locked into a middle-class standard of living by their tastes, their level of education and the expectations of their congregations. Low pay and middle-class tastes do not create economic stability.

To meet or solve financial burdens, the pastor often becomes bivocational, or his wife goes to work. This means the couple struggles to find time for church responsibilities and for each other. Her commitments at work can also hinder the family's ability to move to a new assignment, so some pastors continue in current pastorates well after their work is finished. In the struggle of being locked in, they become more bone weary, lose their challenge or self-destruct emotionally.

HAZARD 10:
DYSFUNCTIONAL PEOPLE

The breakdown of the modern family has greatly complicated pastoral care. In addition to new complexities, the need for pastoral care has increased. One pastor, serving his first church that he describes as an average-sized rural/resort church, summarizes the overloads dysfunctional people cause for pastors: "I spend enormous time rescuing people from their sins—sexual problems of every kind (rape, child abuse, surrogate parenting, shattered marriages, homosexuality, sexual addiction), addictions to drugs and alcohol, addictions to laziness and work, anorexia, anger and rage, stunted personality development, low self-esteem and hopelessness." What a list.

The church attracts dysfunctional people like these because—at least ideally—it represents acceptance, love and belonging. It's like the family they never had. When those people come to Christ, they bring their problems with them, and they look to the church for hope and healing. When churches ignore these pains from people's pasts, the unresolved issues pop up in strange and unexpected ways. Like poison ivy, the crop gets bigger and bigger when it's ignored.

Fallout from dysfunctional homes accelerates when pastors bring unresolved emotional baggage from childhood to their own ministries. The result is that many churches have dysfunctional pastors leading congregations of dysfunctional people. What an explosive minefield!

One pastor notes that he has six extended families. Both his parents had divorced twice and remarried a third time. He tries to maintain civil relationships with all of them—which isn't easy. Imagine the problems he brings into his ministry from his past.

If pastors don't intentionally resolve their past personal problems, the demands dysfunctional people bring to them will create personal burnout, stress and depression. Helping dysfunctional people uses up lots of any healer's energy, but it's more difficult when the leader has to deal with his own problems at the same time.

Consequently, the personal and family crises pastors face every day with people in their churches terrify them. They wonder if ministry actually harms their own children, shortchanges their own marriages or damages their own wholeness. Since they fear what burnout can do, many revisit ministry decisions that in prior generations were settled for life. Others desperately try to deal with their long-buried emotional difficulties. To make matters worse, many pastors don't seek professional help because they don't know who they can trust with their inward secrets.

HAZARD 11:
PASTORAL DEFECTION

Pastoral AWOL is on the increase. As we explored a bit in chapter 1, frontline pastors desert because they're frustrated by growing worldly values inside the Church and overwhelmed by cultural chaos on the outside. The problem is so large that some church leaders fear that not enough battle-ready soldiers will be available to influence this new century. No one knows how large the defection rate will be when the fight becomes fiercer. And the battle fatigue of those who remain will likely thwart their effectiveness.

Even the most rudimentary demands like sacrifice, selflessness and service fly in the face of current values. And this only baffles new potential recruits. Armchair pessimists, even some inside the Church, goad prospective pastors with questions about how preposterous their

The future of the Church is in crisis because fewer exemplary candidates are answering God's call to ministry.

occupational plans seem from a practical point of view. Accurately, the doubters suggest that ministry requires forsaking family roots, submitting to rigorous training and committing to lifelong low pay. They argue: "Why pay such a high price for a cause which may be losing its soul?"

The future of the Church is in crisis because fewer exemplary candidates are answering God's call to ministry. Both quality and numbers have tapered off.

HAZARD 12:
SEXUAL TEMPTATION
AND INFIDELITY

Our society seems to be drenched with sometimes explicit sexual information. As a consequence of the sex scandals sweeping the Roman Catholic Church, people distrust clergy more than ever. Television brings visually stimulating smut into our family rooms. Internet pornography is as near as the modem on the family computer.

Further, each week seems to bring heartbreaking news about another moral failure among pastors. In fact, infidelity by pastors may be the bottom line of an accumulation of a thousand small things that go wrong in a marriage that no one takes time to fix. When ignored, what seems to be unimportant flares into an emotional or moral earthquake.

Could it be that an overly fatigued pastor doesn't recognize the spiritual withering of his own soul? Spiritual depletion shows in this minister's letter: "Pastors often carry a sense of futility about ministry into their homes when they're not effective in facilitating Spirit-directed, positive change in the lives of those they serve. This creates an edginess at home that easily casts a negative shadow on family relationships. The pastor then has a temptation to resent the emotional necessities his wife and family place upon him." More important, he may miss the overwhelming joy and satisfaction those primary relationships at home can provide.

Don't miss this important reality: Pastors are especially vulnerable to outside emotional support during seasons of fatigue, frustration and hopelessness. That's why they must nourish every possible prevention dynamic that flows from a happy marriage. Whatever the tempting circumstances, infidelity is sinfully wrong and it completely sabotages the work of God. One morally bankrupt pastor ruins the credibility of a thousand and makes their work immeasurably more difficult. And those closest to the fallen minister in the family or the local church usually carry scars forever.

For these reasons and more, every pastor should weigh two often-overlooked truths: (1) infidelity by one minister may turn someone away from Christ forever, and (2) a satisfying marriage energizes ministry. Why not renew your marriage now? Rekindling an old love at home is a thousand times more sensible and pure than participating in a scandalous fling.

HAZARD 13: LEADERSHIP CRISES

Major institutions from medicine to military to ministry suffer from a crisis of leadership these days. The lack of integrity in the upper echelons of major corporations illustrates this problem. In a similar way, the contemporary church is adrift in many places, without the vision or purpose of competent, Christ-centered leaders.

At least part of the leadership crisis may be a character issue as some pastors quietly abandon principles of integrity and devoted service. Then a quest for personal privilege and professional advancement replaces abiding values and the servant model of Jesus.

We all know someone who uses the church for personal gain. As a result, we grieve. But perhaps we're too intimidated or frightened to raise a protest. And we may even be too fooled to face these issues in ourselves.

Regardless of the size of his church, every pastor is tempted to use power inappropriately sometimes—often every day. A self-centered craving to be in control—a problem that generally nauseates pastors in laypeople—is even more poisonous to a shepherd of souls. Embers of spiritual vigor never burst into a flaming passion in many congregations because a continuous civil war for control is in progress.

Maybe it's time to recall that the remedy for the control issue is absolute loyalty to the lordship of Christ, from the least to the greatest.

The apostle Paul's description of a leader is "fellow servant." It's not executive pastor or CEO. Perhaps it's time to change the climate in churches where pastors seek prominence and power.

In its place we need leadership energized by a pastor's personal devotion to Christ, by his frequent encounter with biblical truth and by his efforts to motivate laypeople to competent service. The Church needs spiritually vigorous and exceptionally enabled individuals to lead it out of leadership gridlock into a glorious future of holy achievement.

HAZARD 14: LONELINESS

Like a chronic virus, loneliness troubles many pastors. When someone asked Mother Teresa what she thought the worst disease facing the world was, she responded, "It is not AIDS, leprosy or cancer, but loneliness."[13]

One pastor said, "Loneliness feels like God is gone and has taken everyone who mattered with Him." Loneliness is an occupational hazard for pastors because so much of their work—like sermon preparation, administrative details and personal prayer—is done alone behind-the-scenes.

Pastors can even feel lonely during times of pastoral care. When a pastor supports people in crises at an accident scene or in a hospital room, he's left alone with his own questions about the ultimate issues of life and death.

Pastors often reside great distances from their college and seminary classmates, extended families, and childhood friends, so geographic isolation contributes to loneliness. Special treatment by the people in their churches—though well-intended and often-appreciated—also tends to leave pastors feeling isolated from "common people." Some never allow themselves to be human—only "Pastor" or "the Reverend."

On the other hand, those at the top of any organization—including churches—also create isolation for themselves when they assume, "I'm better than the people I serve . . . better than my neighbors . . . better than anyone in the church," or "I don't know how to react to common people." Many others keep themselves emotionally isolated because they fear someone might see their weaknesses.

In moments of candid insight, some pastors admit they don't know how to cultivate friendships. In fact, some even think that living in isolation makes them faithful to their training that friendships are a sacrifice pastors make to avoid feelings of jealousy among church members.

How silly! Think again. What person is jealous of his doctor's, lawyer's or teacher's friends? Still the long-perpetuated myth lives on.

Author Elizabeth Skoglund offers helpful insight for living beyond loneliness in ministry:

In moments of candid insight, some pastors admit they don't know how to cultivate friendships.

The solution is not to bury one's feelings in busyness or to run to an exotic resort . . . . [But living beyond loneliness] is to be found in the positiveness of a task and the reality of one's Taskmaster. It is to be found in quietness in one's own backyard. It is not for sale, cannot be bartered for or negotiated. Yet, to live beyond loneliness is a state for which kings would exchange their power and fortunes.[14]

HAZARD 15:
INSTITUTIONAL BABY-SITTING

Churches, like all buildings, businesses and organizations, have unlimited needs for maintenance or improvement. A light bulb burns out. A carpet needs cleaning. The five-year-old faded missionary poster needs replacing. The senior adults need a van driver for one of their activities. Equipment breaks down. And clutter accumulates.

Pastors can allow direct-mail promotions, telemarketing and administrative trivia to choke the life out of personal soul care and sermon preparation. Baby-sitting a church and a congregation gets even more difficult to bear when members complain—and they will—about inconsequential matters or tattle to the minister about gossip they hear or start.

Pastors need to look for ways to get others to shoulder maintenance and improvements. And they need to teach members of the family of God to solve petty relational issues. It's not that the pastor is too good to care for institutional details or to keep spiritual infants satisfied. Rather they need to be investing their time, energy, imagination, creativity and hard work in more essential, eternal dimensions of evangelism, faith and nurture.

HAZARD 16:
SELF-SATURATED MINISTRY

L. Gregory Jones, dean of Duke Divinity School, opens an essay with these two sentences:

"You know, Mom, the trouble with our new pastor is that he needs us to love him so much that we can't see God anymore." This was the assessment of a thirteen-year-old boy talking with his mother about the struggles they were having at the church.[15]

The boy was on to something.

When a pastor focuses on self-centeredness, becomes obsessed with personal needs or engages in self-aggrandizing talk about sacrifice or humility, he draws a congregation's attention away from Christ.

Such foolishness—often rooted in an excessively high estimate of past achievement, professional competence or even personal piety—represents a failure to recognize that the New Testament standard is self-sacrifice. Sometimes this kind of attitude comes from a deeply buried sense of weakness and inadequacy; the pastor feels some need to be the center of attention and to receive truckloads of affirmation.

After taking the picture of an ego-driven pastor, a photographer friend of ours remarked, "He's so set on himself that I could have taken his picture without film."

One retired pastor was right when he noted, "One of the biggest problems of ministry is that we always have to take ourselves to every new assignment, which tends to make new places seem a lot like the places we left."

HAZARD 17:
EMERGING EVIL IN SOCIETY

Who would ever imagine ministry would be done in a society where airplanes are turned to missiles, where a sniper kills random victims and terrorizes suburban Washington for days and where school shootings have become common?

Who would believe a time when millions of people have no Christian memory? Who would believe the American family would experience such widespread moral collapse? Who would believe the Church would experience worship wars and that the government would look favorably on support for faith-based initiatives for the homeless?

But this complex environment for doing ministry is our present reality. Our culture needs us more than ever. God has providentially placed us in the here and now for some important purpose. And we need to offer effective ministry in spite of complexity and confusion.

While the environment for ministry has changed, God hasn't. The Lord of the Church is still beside us, offering us assurance that He will be with us, even unto the end of the age.

HAZARD 18:
LOST CHURCH MEMBERS

Church research specialist George Barna discovered the shocking fact that half of all adults who attend Protestant churches on a typical Sunday morning aren't born-again Christians. Campus Crusade reports similar findings: "Our surveys suggest that over 50 percent of the hundred million people in church here in the United States every Sunday are not sure of their salvation." Barna also reports the staggering statistic that 90 million Americans assume they're Christians but don't regularly attend church and they're confused about their eternal destiny.[16]

Think of the implications of these amazing studies for the ministry of a local congregation and the frightening possibility that these people who don't know Christ personally will fill official positions that control the work of the church.

HAZARD 19:
UNEMPOWERED MINISTRY

Physicians and lawyers can do their work based on education, practice and the goodwill of their patients or clients. But pastors need more—more than education, experience, consultants and goodwill. To minister effectively, pastors need vital and up-to-date contact with Jesus Christ.

Being so close to religious issues, it's possible for pastors to operate as if their continual spiritual development and growth came by a sort of spiritual osmosis. Pastors who leave the ministry say it all started when they became dry or empty and they didn't work to replenish or connect with the source.

Pastors who travel around the religious block a few too many times can try to live without the power of the living Spirit. And nothing can be more frustrating as trying to lead a church without the power of the head of the Church.

HAZARD 20:
CLERGY ABUSERS

Most churches are made up of wonderful, caring laypeople who love their pastors. These are individuals who are gracious, tender, loving and generally generous. However, some congregations have an individual or a small group of people who wound pastors and cause horrendous damage in the life of the congregation.

Some pastors who've suffered at their hands call these people clergy killers; psychologists might call them pathological antagonists. Generally, they're part of a vocal or controlling minority that causes such chaos that the abused pastor leaves and the congregation is left to pick up the broken pieces.

Veteran pastor Guy Greenfield shares his painful experience:

> I am a recent trooper from the battlefield of bloody confrontation who tried to be pastors, loving, understanding, reconciling, and redemptive, yet ended up being shot down and left to die on the battlefield of the church, and there are thousands just like me.[17]

The reality is that such abusers are real. They do their destructive work over and over again. Even their own congregations don't know what to do with these people, so they're free to repeat their destructive behavior. These abusers create long-standing problems that lock some congregations into never-ending patterns. Perhaps the only response is for pastors to avoid going to these churches.

FACE DOWN THE HAZARDS

You've read about the hazards. Now I want to challenge you to rise above them. Make your ministry happy work. Keep the long view of Christ in mind. Give yourself in service to Christ, so He can rescue people from the enslavements of sin. Help those you minister to become established in a Christ-saturated life. Immerse yourself in greatness. Keep remembering that love outlasts everything else.

Confront the hazards with God-provided courage, creativity, imagination and faith.

What needs to be done can be done.

Remember, the Lord called you. He honors you with a partnership with Him. You're a unique and extraordinary trophy of grace that God gave to your congregation. But that's not what makes you special. Rather, God's power at work in you is greater than any weapon in the world's arsenal. Don't ever forget it.

The energizing spirit of Christ makes high-achievement ministry possible—even in the toughest of times and in the hardest of places.

When the saints go marching in to heaven, the procession will be headed by faithful spiritual leaders of all generations, followed by those they introduced to the Savior. Close to them will be the people of God who were served by a faithful company of

Spirit-enabled pastors who took the gospel into the culture of our time. Of them the whole company will say for eternity, "Never was so much owed by so many to so few."

Be one of those few. Keep faithful. Keep encouraged. Keep believing Keep working. Always remember that the world depends on you even though it doesn't know it.

A Personal Word from H. B. L.

LEADING YOUR CHURCH TO HEALTH

I recently read *Excellent Protestant Congregations* by Paul Wilkes. The author examined 311 congregations—of every type and style—over a two-year period. He listed the factors that he concluded describe "excellent" churches.

- Evidence of a joyful spirit
- Awareness of members' diversity
- Welcoming attitude toward all in the church community
- Emphasis on true spirituality and a deep relationship with God
- Innovative and thoughtful worship
- Collaborative decision making among pastor, leaders and lay members
- Awareness of Christian tradition
- Scripture-based teaching and preaching
- Confrontation of real problems with members and the church's community[1]

How does your church do at matching these criteria?

For several years, I've been preaching the message of church health. I believe every body of believers can be healthy if they're willing to look honestly at themselves. These guidelines might be a start.

CHAPTER THREE

WHO DECIDES WHAT YOU DO?

- 86 percent of pastors said they'd choose ministry as their career if they had it to do over again.[2]
- 87 percent of pastors say a strong sense of God's call is why they chose ministry as a career.[3]
- Churchgoers expect their pastor to juggle an average of 16 major tasks.[4]
- Pastors who work fewer than 50 hours a week are 35 percent more likely to be terminated.[5]
- 31 percent of pastors indicated that conflict management was lacking in their seminary or Bible college training.[6]
- 87 percent of Protestant churches have full-time paid pastors.[7]
- Two-thirds of pastors reported that their congregation experienced a conflict during the past two years; more than 20 percent of those were significant enough that members left the congregation.[8]

The scene is a pastor's support group in a small town 90 miles from Chicago. Four pastors make up the group—a Methodist, a Baptist, a Roman Catholic and a charismatic. In this setting, Roger Gendron signals a cry for help.

"Professional pastoring has me weary to the bone," he says. "When I allow so many expectations from many different directions to crowd Christ out of my ministry, I feel devoid of His life-changing power that should flow through me into my work for God."

As Roger speaks, tension mounts in the group—each member suffers from ministerial energy depletion. Members of this group, like most pastors, feel harassed by expectations, especially those that have little to do with ministry.

"Christ crowded out" is slow but certain suicide for ministry. Can expectations really crowd Christ out of ministry? Whose expectations are worth such a high price? Ministry without Christ describes the most draining of all human activity.

Who sets the agenda may be the most pivotal issue of ministry. Most ministers have too many bosses and wear too many hats. In many cases, congregations expect their pastors to do whatever task anyone dreams up; after all, no one knows exactly what a pastor's real job is. This may be the primary reason many churches stand still and stagnant—the pastors are overwhelmed with trivia and have no time left for what matters most.

This soul weariness shines through a few lines of sarcasm one minister wrote in his journal:

> If I wanted to drive a manager in the business community up the wall, I'd make him responsible for the success of an organization but give him no authority. I'd provide him with unclear goals, ones the organization didn't completely agree to. I'd ask him to provide a service of

an ill-defined nature, apply a body of knowledge having few absolutes and staff his organization with only volunteers who donated just a few hours a week at the most. I'd expect him to work 10 to 12 hours per day and have his work evaluated by a committee of 300 to 500 amateurs. I'd call him a minister and make him accountable to God.[9]

URGENT LESSONS ABOUT EXPECTATIONS

Over the years, I've received a blizzard of letters recounting mind-boggling confusion about unreal expectations in hundreds of local congregations. While many pastors seem willing to settle for efforts to balance expectations, others insist they no longer want the job they're educated to do. The distress is painfully real.

- *Salary*—a missions pastor: "It's almost as if the church members resent paying our salary because it competes with things they would like to have for our church. Only through months of waiting on God have we stayed in ministry at all."
- *Strain on pastor's marriage*—a minister's wife: "Unrealistic expectations from our church members pull my husband and me away from each other and many times hinder our walk with God."
- *Ministry received but nothing given*—a flip side of expectation is a congregation's willingness to take ministry but give nothing in return. Such a situation was described by a pastor from the South Central United States: "It seems that so many of our members are more than willing to have ministries so long as someone else does the job."

- *Burnout blamed on expectations*—a pastor's wife from California: "We wear so many hats. From our family we provide preaching, directing the choir, pianist, special music, Sunday School teachers, bookkeeper, women's ministries and many more. Burnout from sheer physical exhaustion is just around the corner most of the time."

- *Manipulation*—an insightful pastor from Hawaii: "I felt manipulated and guilty when a nonmember who came for spiritual counsel threatened suicide. She intruded on our family time, called at all hours of the night and made outrageous time demands at the study. She assumed she had a right to do this, and I allowed it because I didn't know what else to do."

- *Many things needed for churches to prosper*—a pastor who serves seven rural churches: "A pastor needs to do too many things well in order for the church to prosper, including administration, biblical scholarship, counseling, youth work and pastoral calling. The results are either a dysfunctional family life or divorce at home."

- *Outreach dissatisfactions*—a pastor's wife from the Northwest: "Our high-energy outreach efforts tend to generate little response. And our leaders blame my husband because the church doesn't grow."

- *Self-imposed expectations*—a pastor from the Northeast: "Pastors need to set boundaries. The pastor and the people need to realize that the pastor can't solve all their problems. Without good boundaries, we take blame when things go wrong even when we had no responsibility in the matter."

- *Counseling misfired*—a pastor's wife from Maine: "My husband is not a bad pastor just because a couple he's working with went ahead with a divorce."

- *My expectations or theirs*—a minister from the Southwest: "I'm not sure if the expectations come from the church or from me. Either way, they have the same effect on my mental and physical health.

RISK FACTOR

Churchgoers expect their pastor to juggle an average of 16 major tasks.

How sad if we pastors order our lives by expectations we think the congregation has, when we're actually driven by our own inner need to succeed."

- *Self-imposed requirements*—a youth pastor from Sacramento: "I am my own pusher and worst critic. I need to learn to walk with God intimately, invest in my family and still work hard in ministry. I don't know how to find a balance. Can you help me?"

- *Abused priorities*—a pastor from Michigan: "I abuse priorities and blame it on the church. It's easy to allow ministry demands to make me reschedule family responsibilities. Unfortunately, years have slipped by before I recognized this error. But I now must face the truth that the church would be happy for me to put my family at a higher priority. Since I can, why don't I?"

- *Downward spiral of expectations*—consider a portion of this letter in which a pastor recaps three crippling backlashes that flow from unbalanced, unrealistic and unmet expectations:

Unrealistic expectations in a church are like a downward spiral, and they harm everyone.

First, the people become passive and dependent. Believing their pastor's education is what qualifies him to minister, they conclude from this erroneous premise that they're unable to minister. The responsibility for ministry, therefore, falls completely on the pastor.

The second step is to see the pastor as a professional who gets paid for ministering. So they reason, *Why should we do his job?* They falsely reason that the responsibility for ministry falls totally on the pastor.

A third destructive attitude springs from their passivity and dependence. Passive, dependent individuals often become demanding people who heap increasing loads of responsibility for ministry on the pastor.

The preceding observation hits right on target in much of contemporary church life. Uninvolved, demanding people often unknowingly create churchwide discontent at times when the pastor is too fatigued or too fed up to challenge the disruption. As a result, it seems easier to do what everyone expects. In the process, the pastor becomes a pawn of unrealistic people, and his own spirituality stagnates.

Another serious fallout evolves when laypeople or pastors put a professional spin on the pastorate. Yes, pastors—by education and credential—are true professionals, when precise definitions are used. Yet they

A faithful pastor can make a life-changing and eternal difference in people's lives.

do their work best when they view themselves as servants of Christ and shepherds of souls. More influential than a board chairman of the largest corporation or the most prominent political leaders can ever be, a faithful pastor can make a life-changing and eternal difference in people's lives.

WHO DECIDES WHAT PASTORS DO?

Where do expectations start? According to one overworked pastor, the answer is "everywhere and with everyone."

Think about how many people formulate expectations for a pastor's ministry: church members, official documents, colleagues, theological educators, secular literature, ecclesiastical superiors, role models and even TV talk-show hosts. And in a discussion of the matter, a seminary professor added, "Don't forget Jesus and Paul." That many sources make expectations so muddled that even legitimate demands become confusing or downright contradictory. Consider how expectations from so many different places can affect a pastor's ministry.

Amateurs

Well-meaning "amateurs" who possess limited knowledge of ministry frequently form and express their expectations. Though these expectations may be good-natured and intend no harm, they often irritate pastors. Every seasoned minister can recite a long list of things people have expected of him.

A mechanic extends a pseudocompliment following a service, "That was a wonderful sermon. I'm glad you have that old sermon file where you can grab a good sermon and preach it to us. Pretty soft job, Pastor, working one day a week." The pastor thinks that the mechanic means, "I like you, but you sure don't work very hard compared to the rest of us." The pastor stands speechless because he knows he'll never change this man's ideas about ministry. For weeks, a flashback of this conversation makes the minister mildly miserable.

Or a retiree murmurs to a fellow church member, "I haven't seen the pastor for a month. I feel like he's neglecting me. What does he do with his time?" When the criticism reaches the pastor, as it will, he thinks the retiree means, "The pastor doesn't take care of old people like he should." The retiree is really saying, "The pastor is among the most important people in my life, and I count on his attention."

Or a church usher grumbles to a lay leader, "I told the pastor we needed new light bulbs in the hallways, but they're still burned out today." The pastor thinks the usher means, "The pastor is responsible for maintenance, so why doesn't he get on the ball and replace the bulb?" Perhaps the usher really wanted the lay leader to give higher priority to church maintenance needs and take this load off the pastor's mind.

Everyone has definite opinions about what the pastor should do. Many people even think God gives them a right to tell the pastor what they expect and to make sure he does it. Unfortunately, some churches pass many unworthy or impossible expectations from one generation to the next without much thought or evaluation.

Troubled People

More than ever before, a new set of rising expectations comes from troubled people who want something better than broken marriages, dysfunctional families and destructive lifestyles. When people turn to Christ, they discover joy and many answers to life's riddles. But they then view the pastor as the key person in this new relationship with the family of God. Much like combat victims, these wounded victims of sinful battles require warmth, direction, guidance, conversation, counseling, discipleship, healing and a lot of time. Their needs are monumental and their expectations overwhelming. While the pastor seems willing to befriend them, they sometimes stretch his skills and availability to the breaking point. And when the pastor isn't available, they feel rejected.

Family

Highly influential and outspoken formulators of expectations often reside at the pastor's own address. His wife and children may not understand why it takes so much time and effort to be a faithful pastor. They ask, "Why do you go to work so early in the morning when no one is expecting you?" "Why did you get home so late last night?" "Is it necessary to visit sick people in the hospital every day when no one else in the church does it?"

Community

Sources of expectations in the community include civic duties, hospital visitation policy, school activities, social service agencies and ministerial associations. While the level of involvement varies from one pastor to another, there's always some level of expectation for pastors to be involved in their communities.

Church Organizational Structures

Congregational structures and denominational commitments also contribute to the dilemma of expectations. Pastors serving independent churches often have constraining demands of their local congregations shaped by constitutions, traditions and the views of powerful lay leaders. Conversely, pastors with denominational connections may be overinvolved in the life of their family of churches. Even if these expectations are unwritten, understated or subtle, they're still real expectations pastors must face.

The Pastor Himself

Because ministry is a faith issue at its core, pastors must reconcile their call to ministry with what they think God expects in their present assignment. In other words, a pastor often places unrealistic expectations on himself. His wife, children and church aren't the only sources of his confusion. He himself is often the source of unrealistic demands.

These self-induced expectations may come from a perfectionistic tenacity to do too many things, too often and too well. This inner problem may be rooted in unrealistic goals for life, for ministry and for the present setting. Too often the pastor doesn't face the fact that he's more of a generalist than a specialist, which means he's probably not able to do everything as well as the best he's seen.

Sad but true, a pastor's own expectations make him apprehensive about how he spends his time, energy and money. These annoyances can easily goad pastors to second-guess even their best efforts.

Such distractions can make a pastor wonder if the tone of his voice in his sermons was sufficiently pastoral. Later, while working at being a good parent, he may experience self-doubt that someone needs him more somewhere else. And during a competent administrative presentation, he can find himself musing about how to arrange the biggest wedding of the year or about someone with a terminal illness.

Inner Agitator

The inner agitator is an inner voice of doubt. It claims to be a trusted confidant, but it's actually an inner antagonist—an accuser—who arouses fears of failure and reminders of unfulfilled obligations. Like a critical prompter in a play, the inner agitator tries night and day to correct every real and imaginary fault.

This inner agitator holds the pastor hostage, presents itself as an enlightened conscience and sometimes claims to speak for God. A preacher friend calls this harsh companion a taskmaster within who drives him like a slave before the Emancipation

Proclamation. The resulting bondage produces a dismal ministry. More often than not, the inner agitator holds the pastor captive to a load of accumulated expectations from his past that have little to do with his present assignment. In this buildup, the pastor should be aware that he's dealing with an accumulation that didn't originate from one congregation, one church leader or even a handful of people in the local church. The pastor needs to throttle this inner agitator so he doesn't blame all his challenges about expectations on the present congregation. His present concerns could have started half a lifetime ago by someone who's been in the cemetery for years. It is heartbreaking when a pastor or spouse is riveted on issues that no one in the present setting cares about because of the expectations stirred by their inner agitator. How sad to fight such unnecessary battles in the soul.

It is heartbreaking when a pastor is riveted on issues that no one in the present setting cares about.

DEBILITATING EFFECTS OF EXPECTATIONS

Whether real or assumed, expectations choke the vitality out of a pastor's spirit. Then what *others* think or what *they* want tortures him with worst-case scenarios of what might happen. As a result, disquieting fears nag every expression of ministry, and pastors become so spooked that they can't see the difference between a pesky mosquito and a ferocious lion.

These occupational hazards extend into every dimension of a pastor's life, including his home. For example, pastors often think the community and church expect their families to be perfect. This bafflement shows in the comment, "Our church has the stereotypical belief that pastors' kids are going to be the worst or the best. Ours don't measure up either way."

A pastor's wife summarizes this strain: "It seems everyone wants to have a piece of us and of our time. It's smothering us." And another pastor observes, "My wife struggles to be seen as herself and not as the last pastor's wife."

Without extreme care, these debilitating feelings shut a pastor off from two energizing forces for ministry—intimacy with Christ and tenderness with family. A mature minister warns: "In this overload frame of mind, a pastor often gives up on a fruitful devotional life and a robust, satisfying family life. As a consequence, many wrestle with empty souls and a loss of family through divorce or rebellious children."

Because of these hypnotic expectations, it's easy for a pastor to barter— trading the important to concentrate on the immediate. Describing his frayed emotions, a veteran spiritual leader writes about the complicated demands he is experiencing: "Exhaustion comes from just thinking of the many

RISK FACTOR

Pastors who work fewer than 50 hours a week are 35 percent more likely to be terminated.

more complex predicaments people bring to me these days, let alone trying to help them with the problem." Like cancerous cells in the human body, left unchecked, these priorities and unrealistic expectations will multiply and feed on themselves.

Is this what God intended for ministry? The answer is a resounding no. Rather, all this agitation about expectation is a contradiction of the faith we preach.

One pastor opens windows of grace for others while criticizing himself: "To a great extent, I'm a victim of expectations, my own and others. Many of us who preach grace as a way of life do not practice it in relationship to our ministerial tasks. We're more eager to please the people than we are to rest in the fact that God wants to use us the way we are. We preach grace, but we practice a theology of works."

A serious attempt to reconcile grace with expectations and to balance dependence on God with duty to others may provide the much-needed answers we seek. What liberating freedom comes to a pastor's mind when he realizes his best self and his noblest efforts are good enough for God.

SUGGESTIONS FOR RESHAPING YOUR CHURCH'S EXPECTATIONS

Why not start a one-person campaign to reshape the concepts of ministry among opinion shapers in your congregation? Include yourself in this revolutionary exercise. Maybe you see existing expectations as fixed and unmovable, but they can be changed. Since so many people shape these expectations, the key is to begin changing them bit-by-bit—among lay leaders, committees, individuals and church members.

Think of the payoff of truly visionary expectations. You might consider the following strategies for reshaping expectations in the church you serve.

Develop Expectmanagement Skills

"Expectmanagement" is as old as ministry itself. It simply means the ability to use expectations to create an exciting church and cultivate fulfillment for yourself as the pastor. In the process, you give benign neglect to unrealistic expectations.

Expectmanagement means that you recognize beneficial expectations and ignore unrealistic ones. Of course, you don't simply ignore all expectations as notions of impractical dreamers. Instead, you respond to the heart cries of committed Christians who want their church to be better, recognize an idea whose time has come and anticipate what may be needed tomorrow. You simply focus on productive expectations and then respond positively to them.

Define Ministry for Yourself

A few pastors have such a foggy view of their work that they call everything ministry. However, while playing ball with their children, mowing the lawn and visiting a neighbor are worthwhile activities, they're probably not ministry. Other pastors feel confused by a collision of roles and division of labor between pastor and laypeople or between pastor and spouse. Some pastors have unclear concepts on the location of ministry, so they wonder if it's done on the street or in the study. Others have a murky notion of the time required to build a profession, so they either are involved every waking moment or handle time like a wealthy country gentleman with no schedule to keep and no place to go.

A gap exists between lay and clergy perceptions about what constitutes effective ministry. That's why you must ultimately define and implement the meaning of ministry for yourself. To know what you're doing and why you're doing it solves many questions and clarifies how ministry affects individuals in your congregation.

Defining ministry doesn't mean that it's arbitrarily determined only by your personal preferences, prejudices or perspectives. Rather you'll be informed by Scripture, congregational and/or denominational understanding of the doctrine of the Church, lay and clergy church leaders, theological training and colleagues in ministry.

Once you've grasped data from these sources, you must then define ministry for yourself, making sure it is acceptable to God and appropriately accountable to your church. In this process, you'll do yourself a favor to recognize that the church is a voluntary organization where people vote approval or rejection with attendance as well as financial support.

The next step in defining ministry is for you to articulate clearly your concepts of ministry to your decision makers and your congregation, both individually and collectively.

This kind of forthright discussion needs to make room for adjustment and input from your congregation, because they've entrusted their spiritual development to you. In the secular workplace, this dialogue is called negotiating. In the church, it's more of a congregation-wide clarification of what ministry really is. Your role as pastor is best negotiated when you're forming relationships in your church.

You must define ministry for yourself, making sure it is acceptable to God and appropriately accountable to your church.

All of these processes will help your congregation develop a new understanding of what ministry should be and will allow them an opportunity for valid input. They have a right and a need to be heard. Their concerns can inform your understanding of your church, your community and the world where your ministry takes place. At the same time, this dialogue helps shape congregational views of ministry.

The main purpose for defining ministry isn't to draw battle lines or cause conflict, but to provide in-depth communication that can strengthen the church, inspire the laity and build vital relationships that will help you. Through this dialogue-defining effort, you and key lay leaders can build a strong foundation for wholesome future expectations by the whole people of God.

Evaluate Expectations by the Golden Rule

It's easy to spot absurd expectations in others, but it's more difficult to detect these in ourselves. While a pastor usually considers his expectations as visionary and right, he may view expectations by others as unreasonable or even preposterous.

This two-way process of creating and receiving expectations can be tricky. I once heard a pastor expounding utopian concepts for his congregation while openly scorning something someone expected of him. Too bad churches don't have umpires to call "Foul ball."

You need a healthy dose of charity and grace when your church's only frame of reference for ministry is a universalizing of their past experience. For example, a family from rural Ohio now living in metropolitan Miami expects their pastor to do his work the way their grandfather's pastor did 50 years ago in a rural setting. Of course, ministry in such a different context simply can't be done the way they remember it being done. Their stubborn stand on methodology is regrettable, but the pastor's response should be effective ministry to all people, even those who don't appreciate his style.

Exhibit a Christ-Saturated Life

A Christ-saturated life means that you live and serve on such a high plane that you go well beyond your expected or legal obligations in marriage, finance and use of time. John Wesley said of early Methodists, "Our people die well."[10] Why not give the church reason to say, "Our pastor lives well—better than anyone we've ever known. We want a similar quality of life."

Reasonable people notice when you allow Jesus Christ to enrich the details of your life, and they'll more readily come to your defense when others are overly critical about unmet expectations. In fact, those same supportive people may adopt your model as their pattern for Christlike living in a secular world.

Commit to Excellent Ministry

A miraculous cure for unrealistic expectations is to provide distinguished ministry, especially in highly visible areas such as preaching, worship or pastoral care. Word then gets around that you do your work as well as or better than any previous pastor. Excellence means doing the work God has given His Church well and in an exciting, interesting manner.

Such an excellent expression of ministry can give you a line of credibility that you might need to weather tougher times. Many congregations overlook a pastor's faults when they know he serves competently in other important phases of ministry.

Realize that you can't meet all expectations. You can't be all things to all people. Sure, you want to give high priority to emergencies. Emergencies aren't always the obvious things: major illness, death, emotional crises. They may be passages: death of parents outside the congregation, extended joblessness or ordinary illnesses. When you serve your people well in times of crises, they'll be more forgiving and gracious when you don't meet all their expectations. Get control of your time, so you can maximize your achievements; then leave the rest to God.

Accept the Reality of Unfinished Work

A pastor's work is never totally completed. That means some unfinished tasks will hound you at the end of every day and wait for you the next morning.

The pressing concerns are those you should leave undone and those you'll give priority to tomorrow. Not every demand has equal importance and urgency. You must constantly attempt to prioritize demands on your ministry.

Focus on the Meaning of the Term "Pastor"

Why are you a pastor? Many enjoy the title or position without embracing the tasks and relationships. For them, being a pastor

is a professional attainment rather than a life-changing opportunity, a profession rather than a calling to serve Christ's
Church. Pastoral work always comes into clearer focus through
a self-talk question: *What does the Father want me to do as pastor in
this assignment today?* This focus will bring your ministry to life.

To cope fairly with expectations, you need an organizing center to give direction and focus to your work. This is a transforming insight. You must seek God's priority in each ministry situation as your centering focus. Above everything else, you must
deliberately care for the spiritual needs of your people; their spiritual maturity is never automatic, nor does it come by osmosis.

Know the Difference Between the Few and the Many

Don't allow a minority to determine your perspective or set your
ministry agenda. Always consider who says what. The word of a
faithful saint needs to carry more weight than a grumble from a
recreational complainer. Don't judge your entire congregation by
the attitudes and actions of an unfair and inaccurate few. Try not
to confuse the whole with the part. One grousing member isn't a
reason to preach a fiery sermon or a
cause to resign. The majority of people in your congregation will probably be fair-minded in their expectations. Trust the evaluation of the
many over the judgment of the few.

Try not to overgeneralize about
either the critic or the affirmer. Set
aside the notion that one vocal person speaks for several or many. More
often than not, they speak only for

**Remind yourself that
even difficult people
have no pastor but you.**

themselves and almost never for God. At the same time, remind
yourself that even difficult people have no pastor but you, so
they need your acceptance and forbearance.

Follow the Father's Agenda

The appropriate pattern for determining the pace and priorities for ministry is to find and follow God's plan for you.

In far too many instances, a pastor feels obligated to listen to so many voices and tries to please too many people. The pastor hears conflicting expectations at home and church. Denominational leaders and ministerial peers add their advice. And so does the 16-year-old clerk behind the counter at the convenience store. Even a street beggar has his say: "Good preachers always give to people like me—you can't be much of a pastor."

All this confusion needs clarification. Even if you could accomplish everything that everyone wants done—an impossible assignment—you still might not please the originator of your ministry. Since God inaugurated your call to Christian service, He must have something important in mind for you to achieve in your present setting. The ultimate issue is to discover what He wants for you by implementing the mandate of Scripture.

The dense fog that conflicting expectations cause starts lifting when you lead your church into genuine spiritual achievement based on a biblical agenda. Use the Bible to establish the agenda for authentic ministry. Saturate your thinking with Scripture, and then communicate the mission you see and hear from God by every possible means. The Lord's ways lead to simplicity, achievement and fulfillment.

Dietrich Bonhoeffer gives this clear challenge to find direction for the Church from Scripture:

It is not our heart that determines our course, but God's Word. . . . How often we hear innumerable arguments "from life" and "from experience" put forward as the basis for the most crucial decisions, but the argument from Scripture is missing. And this authority would perhaps point in exactly the opposite direction from which we are going.[11]

Faithfully activate the biblical mandate in your church. Then stop stewing about what all the novices and specialists say about methods, marketing, expectations, obligations, cultures and opinions. For 2,000 years, people have been magnetically drawn to Christ's mission for the Church and the world. They still are, even in our setting.

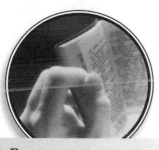

R E N E W A L   S T R A T E G I E S

DISCOVERING SOLUTIONS

✓ Develop expectmanagement skills.
✓ Define ministry for yourself.
✓ Evaluate expectations by the Golden Rule.
✓ Exhibit a Christ-saturated life.
✓ Commit to excellent ministry.
✓ Accept the reality of unfinished work.
✓ Focus on the meaning of the term "pastor."
✓ Know the difference between the few and the many.

Conquering the Risks in Your Family Life

A PERSONAL WORD FROM H. B. L.

CHERISH YOUR MARRIAGE

In an interview I did on *Viewpoint*, the radio arm of Save America, host Chuck Crismier cited some statistics that startled me: 20 percent of pastors say they view pornography at least once a month, 33 percent of pastors confess "inappropriate" sexual behavior with someone in the church, and 20 percent of pastors admit having had an affair while in the ministry.[1]

A study of 4,400 clergy from 10 Protestant denominations found: "Those in ministry 'are equally likely to have their marriage end in divorce' as general church members."[2]

While these might seem a bit overstated, the conclusions of Save America are:

- Pastors are risking holiness in pursuit of personal and parishioner happiness.
- When those manning the "lighthouse" of the nation participate in turning out the light, shipwreck is inevitable.
- Pastors must restore authority of God's Word in their own house before we can ever hope to see righteousness in the Church House.
- Pastors must repent . . . in openness and brokenness . . . before we will truly see oneness and brokenness among the people.[3]

In this day of moral free fall, the words of Paul are very pertinent: "Among you there must not be even a hint of sexual immorality, or of any kind of impurity" (Eph. 5:3).

Stay pure. Pray for one another.

CHAPTER FOUR

AVOIDING THE HAZARDS IN MINISTRY MARRIAGE

A CONVERSATION WITH GORDON AND GAIL MACDONALD

- 25 percent of pastors' wives see their husband's work schedule as a source of conflict.[4]
- 13 percent of pastors have been divorced.[5]
- Those in ministry are equally likely to have their marriage end in divorce as general church members.
- The clergy has the second highest divorce rate among all professions.
- 24 percent of pastors have received marital counseling.[6]
- 80 percent of pastors say they have insufficient time with spouse.[7]
- 48 percent of pastors think being in ministry is hazardous to family well-being.[8]

Her honest question deserved an honest answer: "Why do I hear so much about pastors' marriages going bad? Even before we came to school, we had a great marriage that I rated a 10. Now I wonder if we will face unusual pressure next year."

The questioner, a 31-year-old mother of two and an expert computer programmer, married a plumber eight years ago, long before he thought about ministry.

Their family made an amazingly positive adjustment while the husband-father attended Bible college. However, as he finished pastoral preparation, she was bothered about possible marriage pitfalls in the church.

She continued, "I have a friend whose husband has been a pastor for five years. She half-jokingly says that every couple going into ministry should have two identical signs artfully lettered with the message, *Warning: Ministry May Be Hazardous to Your Marriage*. She'd put one sign in the pastor's study about eye level with his desk and the other in their bedroom. She says the office sign would remind her husband of potential problems in counseling and overwork, while the bedroom sign would remind both wife and husband that, without persistent commitment to each other, ministry competes for priority, sensitivities and intimacies in marriage."

We responded to this future pastor's wife, "Most marriages of couples in ministry are strong and healthy. You just don't hear about them because good marriages don't make for particularly interesting conversation." That led to a long chat about how a pastor and his wife can give each other a satisfying marriage.

It does seem that there is little middle ground—ministry either strengthens or stresses marriage. Difficulties drive some couples to blame normal marriage and family problems on the ministry. Others turn their difficulties into adventure, and they strive for a fulfilling relationship where both husband and wife are more fun to be with as they share in a cause worth living for. One commonsense key seems to make the difference—a deliberate decision to build a strong marriage. Then fragile marriages become solid; get-by marriages become special; and great marriages become grand.

THINGS HAVE CHANGED IN PASTORS' MARRIAGES

The role of women in our culture leaves many pastors and wives confused and challenged about their marriages, often compelling them to renegotiate their relationships with each other and with the church. In their insightful book *Clergy Families,* Paul A. Mickey and Ginny Ashmore accurately depict the way it used to be:

> In an earlier era of clergy marriages, we find unambiguous, stylized roles and behavioral expectations. The early portrait is of a family in which the minister is male, the spouse is a faithful Christian homemaker who reflects the virtues of the Virgin Mary, works with the spiritual industriousness of the mystics, and is willing to martyr herself on behalf of her pastor-husband and "his" church.[9]

While you might be able to cite contrary examples and stormy exceptions, these words largely depict this bygone era.

In earlier times, it was somewhat common for pastors' wives to feel victimized as unpaid servants of the church. They were married to imperfect husbands whom others imagined to be carbon copies of the Lord. Sadly, the wife knew better about her human husband. Either willingly or grudgingly, she was cooperative or even subservient while at the same time being lonely, troubled, angry and often aloof.

Society, the church and women have irrevocably changed, even though traditional thinking still prevails in some congregations. Consequently, new roles for men and women have called into question long-held assumptions regarding marriage, parenting and church connections. But a constructive opportunity to improve relationships rather than ruin them can emerge from this fierce societal debate.

The issues, however, are much deeper than liberation from rigid expectations. Rather, true freedom to grow healthy marriages begins when a pastor and wife discover and nurture the quality relationship they wish to have with each other. A high-satisfaction marriage starts with a shared willingness to help the other be his or her best self. Such an exceptional marriage takes time, insight, sensitivity, priority, mutuality and practice.

There's also a church issue that needs dialogue and negotiation. Pastors and churches must be sensitized to the fact that the health of a pastor's marriage and the well-being of the church depend on each other.

A high-satisfaction marriage starts with a shared willingness to help the other be his or her best self.

A pastor with a troubled marriage seldom does his work well. And a problem church seldom ministers effectively to its pastor or his family. A weakness in one injures the other.

Competition between marriage and ministry must cease. Every personal effort a pastor makes to strengthen his marriage is a gift he gives himself, his spouse and the church. These efforts also protect the couple from the moral dilemmas that surround them in contemporary society.

PAIN IN PASTORAL MARRIAGES

Incidents of emotional and legal divorce, separation, immorality and loss of intimacy are exploding through the roof. Listen to the anguish that arrives almost daily in my mail.

- *Temptation:* "In my marriage, almost daily I'm tempted to succumb to the lust of the flesh, the lust of the eye and the pride of life."
- *A statistic:* "I feel as if I'm a statistic waiting to be counted, that at any time I might fall to immorality. These thoughts don't consume me, but they do get my attention often."
- *Cycle of pain:* "I need help to get out of the biting, picking and bickering cycle in my marriage. We do destructive things to each other."
- *Suffering children:* "One morning after her dad resigned from the pastorate and moved in with another woman, my little girl was crying so hard that I told her to be strong; and she said, 'Mommy, my strong is broke.'"
- *Divorce:* "I've been a workaholic concerning ministry and it cost me my family. Recently my wife filed for and obtained a divorce, taking our children with her. My life is lonely and empty now."
- *No emotional support:* "In reality, congregations neither value nor affirm a pastor who seeks to be a faithful family person as well as a faithful pastor. I sometimes wonder if they know what I feel."
- *Guilt for family time:* "I wish some organization would speak to the issue of people—particularly those who are committed to Christian ministry—who feel guilty when they enjoy their family. Can't I enjoy both ministry and family?"

- *No affirmation:* "I get sidetracked into thinking ministry takes priority over home caring because I don't get much affirmation from home like I do when I'm ministering to people."
- *Need for love:* "The burden of a critical, fault-finding, lukewarm church is pulling our marriage down fast. Is it wrong to want to feel loved and valued by our church?"
- *World's system:* "We hear the world saying it is okay to bail out once the going gets rough, and it's tough to counteract that."
- *Greatest needs:* "Our greatest needs are communication, tolerance and patience between my wife and me! It feels like she's unsupportive of me. We lack time together because we have separate ministries plus a three-year-old, a one-year-old and a third child due in three months."
- *Fear:* "I feel a danger of the cooling of the love relationship between my wife and me. I'm afraid a fatal attraction—one that could kill our marriage—could arise."
- *Emotional separation.* "Many clergy couples are married but separated in heart."
- *Waste:* "We've both tried so hard and failed so grandly. How many people will this hurt and how many souls may not be won because of this adultery? It's such a waste and I can't bear it."

RENEWAL PRINCIPLES FOR STRONG CLERGY MARRIAGES

Gordon and Gail MacDonald are well-known Christian leaders and authors. In our conversation with them, they offer principles any couple in ministry can use to strengthen their marriage—renewal for troubled marriages, prevention for healthy marriages and advice for new marriages.

London/Wiseman: Thanks for your willingness to share insights about brokenness and restored marriage relationships. Both of you have contributed so much to so many pastors and their wives, especially through your writing. What's the favorite of all your books?

RISK FACTOR

The clergy has the second highest divorce rate among all professions.

Gail: That's a tough question—a little like trying to decide the favorite among your children. *Ordering Your Private World* is special to me because it was such a surprise the way God used it.

Gordon: I think my two favorites are *Christ Followers in the Real World* and the one that Gail and I wrote together, *Till the Heart Be Touched.*

Is Intimacy Being Starved in Pastors' Marriages?

London/Wiseman: *Till the Heart Be Touched* discusses intimacy and relationships, doesn't it?

Gordon: Yes. We deal with the question, In a world that is saturated with sex, is intimacy actually being starved?

London/Wiseman: How do you define intimacy?

Gordon: Intimacy is a passionate connection between two people. Though it's most intense in a marital relationship, it's also involved in a broader sense in friendship. The whole book deals with qualities that make intimacy possible and satisfying.

London/Wiseman: And you also wrote *Rebuilding Your Broken World,* in which you describe ways to mend a broken world. How does that idea relate to intimacy, especially in marriage?

Intimacy is a passionate connection between two people.

Gordon: It's about intimacy in many ways. It's no secret that *Rebuilding Your Broken World* was written out of a time in my life where I personally experienced total, humiliating failure.

London/Wiseman: What special lessons did you discover in that broken place?

Gordon: In that dark night of failure, I was forced to ask: "Does God have grace enough to squeeze restoration out of the worst a person can do by choice?"

I learned that we *choose* to sin. But our choices are surrounded by environments or conditions we allow or accept. Then we make choices, do things and hold attitudes that wouldn't be possible if we didn't allow the environment or conditions to exist. So it's important for us to recognize, reject and correct troublesome environments where we might make those bad choices.

Gail: It's also important to recognize that some people suffer a broken world because of the rippling effect of evil and not because of their own choices. So they need to rebuild their broken world as well, just like I needed to rebuild our broken world, along with Gordon. We needed to do this in tandem because we loved each other.

Deceit Makes You a Sitting Duck

London/Wiseman: Gordon, you wrote a powerful sentence: "Evil must be named and sin must be hated."

Gordon: I believe that. I've begun to realize that all sin begins with deceit. We lie to ourselves or someone else lies to us. In that spiritual fog—a definite blurring of truth—we come to believe that a lie is the truth. Many sinful acts in the Bible are prefaced by glaring deceit.

London/Wiseman: How does that affect ministry and a pastor's marriage?

Gordon: For the sake of a healthy marriage, every pastor and his wife need to realize that our contemporary climate communicates many deceitful messages. In those settings, you can be tricked into believing that the consequences of your choices will not be as bad as you once thought. You'll think, *I'll get away with this*; *Everybody's doing it*; or *Maybe God doesn't care about my being a bit slippery at this point.*

The first thing every man or woman in leadership needs to realize is that the minute you allow deceit to enter your life, you're a sitting duck for some sinful impulse.

London/Wiseman: Do you think Bible personalities had a broken-world experience?

Gordon: Many did. The number of people who didn't have some crushing, shaming experience is a short list compared to those who did.

A Broken World Portrayed

London/Wiseman: Can we make a clear connection between brokenness in the Bible and a pastor's marriage?

Gordon: Let me be specific. By broken world, I mean anything that has a catastrophic result that threatens or destroys a marriage, a ministry, a relationship or a lifestyle.

Gail: It's important to recognize that relationships are among our greatest strengths. Gordon and I spent all these years working on relationships with each other, with our family and with our Lord. Yet relationships can be destroyed in an unguarded moment of fatigue or disillusionment.

We need to face the fact that about an inch beneath our Christian skins is a barbarian inside.

Destructive Lifestyle: Above Criticism and Correction

London/Wiseman: You once mentioned three lifestyles that lead to choices that produce broken worlds. Do you think those apply to pastors and their marriages?

Gordon: They especially apply to pastors. One is the leader who places himself above criticism, so he won't accept counsel from others. He won't listen to rebuke, beginning first with his spouse and then close friends and working colleagues. This happens easily, because if you head a church or religious organization, you're likely to be a strong-willed person. You'll tend to ward off others who want to erode your will and plan. This strength in a leader—which is so necessary for a clear-focused ministry—becomes a terrible hindrance.

London/Wiseman: How does that cause a broken world?

Gordon: The downside of this strength is that you stop letting people get through to you. You start out with something admirable, but you end up in a trap with calluses on your soul and your mind. Then you refuse to hear when people try to talk to you about the state of your soul, your moral condition or your toxic attitudes that are eroding your spiritual condition.

London/Wiseman: I heard of a pastor whose church members and staff say, "He has no one to say no to him."

Gail: That's sad and scary. No one can possibly know it all, and being head of an organization doesn't make a leader smarter or more spiritual than other team or family members. It's easy for a pastor to be fooled by his own propaganda because he's supposed to be right.

RISK FACTOR

24 percent of pastors have received marital counseling.

Gordon: I can illustrate from my own experience how much real effort it takes to be able to listen to criticism or correction. I've stood at the door of a sanctuary and had hundreds of people tell me that my sermon was the greatest they've ever heard. Then when I go home and my family wants to criticize some dimension of my life, it's hard to listen and even harder to believe what they say.

London/Wiseman: Then you believe your own press and wonder how those criticizing you could possibly be right.

Gail: Yes, and you flow toward where you get strokes rather than toward reality or what might be helpful.

Destructive Lifestyle: No Familiar Boundaries

Gordon: That's exactly right, and the second destructive lifestyle that encourages a broken world is what I call a traveling lifestyle.

London/Wiseman: How does that apply to a pastor whose ministry is mostly in the local setting?

Gordon: One of the greatest restraints to sin is a fixed community like a neighborhood, village, small town or even a church where people know you well. This is a place where you commit to the norms and behavior patterns of this group of people day by day. I grew up in a community like that where the neighbors took the responsibility for rebuking or correcting you. So you were a pretty good kid under those constraints.

London/Wiseman: But in our transient culture, it becomes a question of who cares or who will know, doesn't it? How is this being played out in pastoral ministry?

Gordon: We need to face the fact that about an inch beneath our Christian skins is a barbarian inside us who is desperately wanting to get out and express himself. The moment we have no restraints, even passive restraints, we're vulnerable—open to a destructive response to an alluring temptation.

Destructive Lifestyle: Addicted to Success

Gordon: The third lifestyle that contributes to a broken world has to do with success in any dimension of life such as money, prominence, power or even marriage.

Gail: Successful people begin to feel indestructible, so they try to possess their ministry rather than manage it for Christ. They become oversensated by life so they can't center down, be still, get redirected or gain perspective. Everything starts to seem larger than life, and they begin to run on natural energy instead of divine enablement. In error they reason, *I didn't pray, and I didn't seem to need it.*

London/Wiseman: That seems to trap all pastors, regardless of the size of their church. They think what they're doing is the most important thing in the whole world. Since God gave them this dream, they think, *I must be great. I must be good if He trusted me with this.*

Gordon: Let me push this idea to another dimension. Gail and I have been blessed on occasion by the generosity of friends who have done things for us we could never afford. Many pastors, even in much smaller churches, have a similar kind of relationship with their congregations.

Recently, we were treated like a king and a queen. Both of us quickly realized that anything that lifts you out of the realities of an average human being affects you so that you feel special and pampered. This can be a severe problem for a pastor.

You begin to think of yourself as untouchable by all the things that do other people in. You're convinced you're immune to failure and that nothing is ever going to go wrong. Wow, is that a wrong attitude!

London/Wiseman: So you start to think that you're even beyond moral breakdown?

Gordon: Yes. And that kind of feeling of success can drive you to a sort of addiction—not addiction to alcohol or drugs or sex, but addiction to excitement and activity.

Gail: Addiction to sensation, really.

Restoration—Start with Repentance

London/Wiseman: Let's talk a bit more specifically about your restored broken world. God gave you a second chance. Now, God is allowing you to touch thousands of people with a message of restoration and healing. Many pastors' marriages need healing like you've experienced. Would you describe the process God used to start your healing?

Gordon: As a starting point, pastors need to take the biblical concept of repentance seriously. You must come to a moment when you realize that hidden in the innermost depths of your person is a foul, stinking mess called evil that defies rational description, and it's waiting to ambush your mind and twist the truth.

London/Wiseman: Is repentance once for all?

Gordon: I think it must be continuous, because you don't repent of just an act, but a condition. That's why all of us stand on level ground before the Cross. It's not because some of us have committed sin number nine and others are guilty of sin number two or three. Instead, we all possess a condition that is potentially destructive. And I mean viciously destructive. Every day with fresh brokenness, I have to go back to recognize that the same evil that betrayed me several years ago may betray me tomorrow in a different way.

Gail: This repentance lifestyle has been an ongoing process. It's made it possible for us to live by the grace and mercy of God and continually extend mercy to each other.

Add Mercy to Repentance

London/Wiseman: How do you make this connection between repentance and mercy in marriage?

Gail: Well, mercy from me toward Gordon is possible because I've seen him offer mercy to me and to others over so many years. Mercy is an important part of ministry for us and also in our relationship with each other.

London/Wiseman: Repentance and mercy—what powerful sources for building strong relationships between pastor and spouse in risky times like ours.

Gordon: Gail gave an enormous amount of mercy to me, but that didn't come easy. Both of us know what it's like to live with real pain. But from pain came a purifying, a presence and a tenderness of God at work in our lives. Now our marriage literally abides in a constant flow of a grace and mercy that makes me love my wife in ways I never loved her before.

London/Wiseman: What about others who serve as accountability partners or as grace givers?

Gordon: Those people are necessary because you can't truly forgive yourself, you can't give yourself grace, and you can't restore yourself. These must be gifts, first from God and then from significant people in your life.

After your family, this comes from men and women who surround you and serve as spiritual splints so that healing can come. The example of a splint from medicine illustrates the healing process that has to take place.

Gail: Regrettably, a lot of people find it difficult to accept discipline. But discipline is necessary for healing to take place.

Add Accountability to Mercy and Repentance

Gordon: Gail's right. The first indication that you're with someone who doesn't understand the need for discipline is when he or she says, "I've failed terribly, but how soon can I get back?" or "What can I do and how long do you think it will be before I can be preaching again?" When someone asks a question like that, you realize they're trying to skip over the steps of healing. They're not interested in having their souls scoured and finding out what went wrong. They're much more interested in how quickly they can get on with business as usual.

You must have accountability people so you can put yourself in their hands and say, "You call the shots right now, and I'll totally submit to you."

London/Wiseman: Somewhere in your writing you said, "Restoration was a result of people who cared."

Gordon: That's the way it is. It can't be "I feel sorry for you; you're my friend; and what can we do to make you feel better?"

One grace giver said, "A player is deeply wounded down on the field and we have to get him help so that he can play again."

Gail: That means you have to listen to things that are hard to hear, do things that are difficult to do and take directives that might not be easy to take. I can remember Gordon poring over the book of Romans as part of this discipline. He was making it a personal book because it was so important to let the Word of God be the basis of his healing.

Evaluate and Renovate the Environment
London/Wiseman: So the process so far involves repentance, mercy and accountability to grace givers. What comes next?

Gordon: For me, I then did a careful inventory of environmental issues that allowed deceit to take place. This made us respectful of fatigue and burnout. In Gail's book *Keep Climbing*, she wrote about disillusionment, which we realized we'd gone through as well.

Gail: As we explored our environment, we realized we didn't pray enough. We had too much work and not enough diversion. We learned that we needed more laughter and friendship. So we now work hard to maintain a friendship network. This has to be proactive because it's easy to lose contact with friends.

London/Wiseman: Gordon, you also wrote that God has put all the pieces for rebuilding in place and the process has been time-tested.

Gordon: I really believe that. The Bible has an endless string of men and women who came out of terrible situations and were restored in the grace and power of God.

Gail: One powerful passage is Galatians 6:1, in which the apostle Paul instructs us to restore each other gently. The concept is the same as mending nets, which are restored so they can be used again in the future.

London/Wiseman: Help us make a clear application for pastors. Put in crystal-clear words the things you've been through that could have destroyed your marriage and that might destroy other marriages. Many pastors are trapped in brokenness that may not have to do with moral failure, but they really need help in putting their relationship back together. What's their hope?

Gordon: Their hope, like ours, is the gospel. If the gospel can't heal the worst situations when people yield, repent and open themselves to the disciplining, restoring grace of God, then the gospel isn't worth much. But we know the gospel is worth everything because Christ provided it through His death and resurrection.

People can sincerely seek healing for brokenness; however, they'll never find it if the Christian community around them isn't committed to healing. And that's one of the tragedies occurring in places where men and women have failed—the Christian community doesn't have the will to offer healthy healing.

Only when the Church commits itself to restorative ministry will men and women stop acting in self-righteousness.

Only when the Church commits itself to restorative ministry will men and women stop acting in self-righteousness and, with the tenderness of Galatians 6:1, start being committed to getting every broken player back on the field again to serve in the Kingdom. Then I think we'll see a revival spirit break out as we begin to act as if we believe restoration is possible and desirable.

London/Wiseman: Building an environment for restoration is something every pastor, especially those with sound, healthy marriages, can do. Everyone can be involved in restoration, either as a giver of grace or a receiver of grace.

Gordon, you've written two paragraphs that have great implications for strong marriages and for quality present-tense Christian living:

> Change comes when we become *reachers*. When I speak to groups of people and tell of the time in my life when I realized that I had become a visionless person, the room grows very quiet. Over and over again I get the

feeling that I am talking to people who have lost their vision, who have forgotten how to dream about a future in which there are growth, achievement in kingdom purposes, and joy at the thought of meeting Jesus. . . .

How much I love to paint the portrait of the *reaching* Paul, who in that prison cell forgot those "things which are behind." He renounced all rights to whine about circumstances, adverse people, and the fear of death. This man who had once worn the uniform of a Pharisee embraced the present reality and squeezed every ounce of opportunity out of it. I am reminded of the comment made by one of America's great marine officers in Korea, "We're surrounded on all sides; we've got the enemy right where we want him."[10]

TOUGH OBSTACLES IN CLERGY MARRIAGE

The MacDonalds underscore the fact that startling shifts in society and pressures in the church put incredible stress on pastoral marriages. Regrettably, too many settle for too little sparkle, too much tradition, too little intimacy and too much concern for their image.

What can you do to help yourself take more initiative? What adjustments, large or small, can you make so that your marriage can enrich your ministry and your ministry can strengthen your marriage?

Start by taking advantage of marriage resources in your community. Look for assistance through community agencies, school districts and units of government. You'll also find marriage materials at Christian bookstores, libraries, counseling services and seminars. And you can probably find a support group for every problem, from loneliness to communication to sexual dysfunction, in your own community or one nearby.

However, in the unique dimensions of a clergy marriage, you and your spouse must also cultivate awareness and develop coping skills to deal with distinctive challenges built into the fabric of ministry. Your goal isn't to struggle at a minimal level of fulfillment, but to create a stable, satisfying marriage that energizes your ministry.

What makes clergy marriages different from other marriages? What points of tension do you need to consider? And how can these differences be positively used to deepen your marriage relationship? Consider several significant stress points:

Competitive Vows

If you're married, think back to your wedding and contrast those commitments with the ones you made at your ordination. In a basic sense, ordination covenants and marriage vows compete because both commitments are exclusive and binding; neither allows much room for the other. H. Newton Malony and Richard Hunt explain this conflict:

> We have seen many variations on the nature of the ordination vow and on the nature of the wedding vow. Nevertheless, at some level the ordained minister will encounter a fundamental conflict between the two.[11]

Incessant Emotional Overload

Your work as a pastor—seldom physical but always bearing spiritual overtones—often involves riding an emotional roller coaster. Within the period of a day, you might rejoice with the parents of a new baby, visit an unwed mother and her grieving parents, and cry with a dying child—perhaps even all in the same hospital. Or, after rejoicing in the faith of new members in a morning worship service, you may be soothing and counseling a battered woman at a shelter that afternoon.

The pain, emotional struggles and declining commitments of others, coupled with your own fatigue, discouragement and despair, take a toll on your whole being and leave you with almost no reserve for your family or yourself.

Then when you get home, you may find the emotional climate different than you expect. With all the demands you encounter, you need home to be a safe sanctuary where you can take your tired body and battered spirit to be recharged by the people you love most. But by the time you get home, your family members may have had all the pressures they can handle for one day—Mom's work schedule, your son's rained-out baseball practice, a mailbox full of bills, a car problem or your daughter's double homework assignment.

One pastor's wife said it better than any outsider could: "I've worried many times about my husband's overload. I'm sorry as I can be, but I have to protect our children from church problems and try to get ready to do my own job tomorrow. I'm ready for him to resign from this madness whenever he's had enough."

An Out-of-Sync Schedule

By this point in your ministry, you've realized that you need to make most contacts with the people of your church on evenings and weekends. And Sunday is probably your busiest day. How could these demands of ministry be more out of sync with the needs of your family and marriage? The times you need to meet with other people are the exact times your family is available and needs you the most. In addition, you need to be with them.

The problem of out-of-sync schedules deepens if your spouse works. Her fixed work schedule plus commute time and your evening and weekend obligations don't leave much common time together.

Get creative and design flexible time schedules. Plan ways to be available when your spouse and family members are. Move ministry activities to other time slots. Begin with small improvements if you can't make major alterations.

Depending on your children's ages, school schedules and calendars, your spouse's commitments and your church's programs, you may need to make specific changes. In the process, evaluate your church's calendar in terms of achievement versus activity— many busy churches don't accomplish as much as they think.

Temptations Resulting from Endless Contacts

Unlike physicians, counselors or lawyers, as a pastor you see parishioners in numerous settings as you serve them in many roles. In a short time frame, you may preach to them, counsel them, visit their homes, serve them Communion, attend or participate in common athletic events, enjoy social contacts and offer comfort in times of loss.

Some therapists who specialize in clergy cases believe this creates a situation where intimate relationships can develop easily, a process that's misunderstood by many pastors. Enticements that result from frequent contact may be especially tempting; for example, if a pastor is counseling a woman and knows her marriage problems. H. Newton Malony and Richard Hunt explain:

> It is difficult to keep one's position clear while becoming involved in a variety of relationships with others There is a decided tendency in such situations to lose perspective, to become grandiose, and to use faulty judgment.[12]

Those three factors—lost perspective, grandiose ideas and faulty judgment—spell potential trouble for any occupation, but especially for ministry.

Diverse Patterns of Marriages

Patterns of pastoral marriages can also be an obstacle. Each of the following patterns have unique intricacies and distinctive time and intimacy demands. Some marriages will look just like the ones described, but others may take elements from more than one of the following models.

Partners in ministry is the conventional pattern where the wife stays home and shares with her husband in as many details of ministry as possible. By definition, this relationship encourages immeasurable interdependency, so the wife's outlook greatly influences the pastor's decision making. The wife in this marriage model is somewhat of an unofficial copastor. She makes calls, leads Bible studies and has high visibility in ministry to women. The flaw is that both partners are sometimes so influenced by the other's viewpoints that they can't accurately gauge reality. They begin to think alike—and some people say they even begin to look alike.

Ministry is his business is an independent relationship where the pastor does his ministry as a profession, and the wife is largely uninvolved in the work of the church. In this pattern, the wife participates in church life at about the same level as an average layperson. Often the pastor explains this pattern by saying, "My wife's ministry is keeping me together."

The wife brings home the bacon is a pattern where a valiant woman works outside her home because of economic necessity. In some small churches, she may carry most of the family financial burden on her shoulders. Sometimes her salary even keeps church doors open; without her job, there would be no church to attend and no pastor to lead. These women are among God's unsung heroes; however, this pattern often produces weary isolation, unresolved hostility and lack of confidence in the husband's ability to earn a living.

The two-career pattern is very familiar on the secular economic landscape and is often chosen by clergy couples. As we noted earlier, this arrangement may mean that the wife's career sometimes takes priority over her husband's ministry. She may make more money than her husband, and the potential of job transfers may complicate the situation. This model can also make it difficult for the pastor to consider a new assignment or can cause dissension if he's called upon to resign to follow his wife in her career.

SUGGESTIONS FOR NURTURING PASTORAL MARRIAGE

As we've seen, cultivating a satisfying marriage is an important part of emotional and spiritual wholeness. A commitment to marriage development provides a significant way to live a quality life that's pleasing to God, fulfilling to both partners and healthy for the church.

In a conversation about what he desires from his marriage, one pastor remarked, "Since we plan to be married for a lifetime, we think it's worth earnest effort to make it all it can be—at least as much effort as getting a good education." He's right. Marriage offers joy, meaning and pleasure.

The intense, demanding dimensions of ministry that many consider harmful to marriage can actually cultivate closeness.

You can actually use the intense, demanding dimensions of ministry that many consider harmful to marriage to cultivate closeness that grows out of sharing thoughts and experiencing service together. One pastor's wife caught the idea: "The more we discuss and the more we do in ministry, the more we discover what we want to do and to talk about. Being married to someone who's not a minister must be a pretty dull life."

What follows is a partial to-do list that can help you maximize the potential in your marriage.

Allow Marriage to Be an Adventure

A satisfying marriage is near the top of all life's joys. While separation or divorce creates immense image complications for any pastor, the larger problem is the emptiness that comes from the loss and the gloom in his inner world of what might have been. You can improve your marriage by making renewed commitments. The challenge is establishing a healthy relationship with the church that allows you to maintain an independent life as a couple and still maintain a loving, available and guilt-free connection with the congregation. Only you can set the limits and enjoy the adventure.

Focus on Process

Much happiness in a good marriage comes from the process of spending years together, in good times and in bad. Like all good marriages, a pastor's marriage is made up of covenants and celebrations—the first date, the proposal, the wedding, the vows, the reception, the honeymoon night, the birth of a child and growing old together. But marriage is also made up of moments when each of you expresses gratitude, works on healing misunderstandings, nurses sick children back to health and observes customary rituals. To have a fulfilling marriage, you need to think of it as much more than a state or condition. Instead, it's a series of moments and events connected by commitments to each other and tightly linked to the grace of God.

Spot Warning Signals

Too many pastors and their spouses believe the work of ministry and the financial support of a congregation have them locked into their present ways of relating to their environment and to each other. Though it will take deliberate effort on your part, become proactive and preemptive regarding any issue in your marriage that presents difficulty or dissatisfaction before you're forced to do so—or worse, before you settle for a dreary, nonfulfilling relationship.

Live by Spiritual Principles

Practice grace, forgiveness and mercy in the details of your marriage. Onlookers will observe something powerfully magnetic about a marriage that puts biblical principles into practice. Such a healthy, wholesome marriage shocks secular people with its durability and quality.

But there's much more. Marriage vows energized by love offer you a gratifying way to live. Christ the enabler helps us create a high standard of communication, friendship and intimacy that others seek to imitate. Pastors and their wives may teach more about healthy marriage by how they live than by all they preach and teach.

Commit to Wholeness

To enjoy a high-octane marriage, you and your wife must constantly tend to two pressing inner issues: spiritual reality and emotional nourishment. Neither of you can minister effectively without these elements in abundant supply. Whatever the cost in money, time or priority, you must work on emotional and spiritual health to make your marriage stronger. Create a caring environment where you nourish spiritual reality and emotional strength in each other. Cherish the fact that someone is at your side who loves you and cares about your well-being more than anyone else on the earth, even through the thick and thin of ministry. Then you'll have each other long after the current crisis is past.

Put Marriage on Your Calendar

You're probably faithful to whatever you write on your calendar or enter in your Personal Digital Assistant. Why not put your wife into your schedule one night each week? If someone asks to meet with you that night, you can simply respond, "I'm sorry, I have a prior commitment. Could we get together another time?"

Then guard that date night with tenacity—let nothing get in the way of that private time.

To enrich a happy marriage investment, plan to spend one evening a week together as a couple. You can bear most burdens together if you set a time to discuss or resolve troublesome issues.

Remember That Pampering Is Never Deserved

Because of appreciation for your ministry, some people will pamper you with special favors they wouldn't give anyone else. If you're convinced that this generosity is simply a gift of appreciation, receive it with kindness and gratitude. But never allow yourself to believe that the people of God owe you anything or that you are really as great as their giving seems to imply. As Gordon MacDonald said in the interview: "You begin to think of yourself as . . . immune to failure and that nothing is ever going to go wrong. Wow, is that a wrong attitude!"

Develop a Small Group of Splint People

Splint people around you are like splints around a broken bone that help it heal straight for renewed usefulness. These people can be members of a small group that hold you accountable or people who love you too much to let you off easily. Give such a group opportunity to hold you accountable and tell you what needs to be fixed, changed or eliminated. Every pastor has some weaknesses, blind spots or liabilities people tolerate. But if you allow people to correct you in these areas, your ministry will improve greatly.

Live a Repentance Lifestyle

Remember that confession, tempered by grace and mercy to yourself and to others, should be a way of life. If you have some attitude or action that needs God's and someone else's forgiveness, make sure you're not too proud or blind to do what you preach. If you don't repent, the results will be broken relationships or people problems that will weaken the church or keep someone from the kingdom of God.

One church lost 10 families in a year because a pastor was caught in a lie. What he could have repaired with four or five sentences of confession never healed. As the years passed, a second generation of many of those families remain completely alienated from any church. That kind of pride costs too much in Kingdom casualties. And think what that infection has done to the pastor's soul for all those years.

YOUR CHALLENGE

MAKE YOUR MARRIAGE STABLE AND SATISFYING

Every marriage can be better. And happily married pastors are more effective pastors. The time is now for you to stand up and get serious about your own marriage.

Haven't you seen enough marriage heartache and brokenness in those you serve? Haven't you observed the horrible results of infidelity in ministry, leading only to perpetual disappointment and misery? And while you may be fully committed to healing and grace giving, you must be able to see that prevention is many times better than the most gracious, wholehearted restoration?

Pay the price to make your marriage solid, satisfying and spiritually sound. Move up on your list of priorities your commitment to emotional, spiritual and physical intimacy with your spouse. Demonstrate in your own marriage all that you preach to others about commitment, integrity, accountability and virtue.

Do it because it's right and fun. Make the Father rejoice. And you'll provide a model of a Christ-centered marriage for those you lead in your church and your community.

RENEWAL STRATEGIES

HELP YOURSELF TO A HIGH-OCTANE MARRIAGE

✓ Allow marriage to be an adventure.

✓ Focus on process.

✓ Spot warning signals.

✓ Live by spiritual principles.

✓ Commit to wholeness.

✓ Put marriage on your calendar.

✓ Remember that pampering is never deserved.

✓ Develop a small group of splint people.

✓ Live a repentance lifestyle.

A Personal Word from H. B. L.

Cutting Down the Worry Load

Whenever I'm with a group of pastors' wives, I'm always amazed at how dedicated they are—but also at how concerned they are for *you*, their husbands. The heartaches they tell me about ring true: insufficient time together, communication difficulties, congregational expectations, child-raising challenges, income level and usage, career concerns and self-image issues.

Recently I spoke with some women troubled over the way people in their congregations had been treating their husbands. They seemed to feel that this mistreatment was only getting worse. Calls to our pastoral care line at Focus on the Family seem to support that conclusion.

As pastors, I think we sometimes dump too much on our spouses about the problems we're facing. Yet at other times we hold everything inside. So what's the solution? We need to realize that challenge is as much a part of ministry as affirmation is. We need to get tougher and not take ourselves quite so seriously. And when we do believe our ideas are clearly God's ideas, we need to *take a risk*.

When possible, we need to remove the worry load from our wives and talk with a colleague instead. Of course, God stands ready to listen, too: "Trust in Him at all times . . . pour out your hearts to him, for God is our refuge" (Ps. 62:8).

CHAPTER FIVE

GOD MADE YOUR WIFE SPECIAL

CONVERSATIONS WITH PAM FARREL, JANELL REPP, LINDA RILEY, JANE RUBIETTA, LINDA SWANSON, KANDY VEENKER AND KAY WARREN

- 58 percent of pastors indicate that their spouse works either part-time or full-time outside the home because the family needs the income; 34.5 percent say their spouses don't work outside the home at all.[1]
- 56 percent of pastors' wives say that they have no close friends.
- 21 percent of pastors' wives want more privacy.
- 60 percent of pastors' wives desire more training to serve better.[2]
- 45 percent of pastors' wives say the greatest danger to them and family is physical, emotional, mental and spiritual burnout.
- 38 percent of pastors' wives say the number one frustration in ministry is time management.[3]
- 53 percent of pastors' wives say they have difficulties raising children.[4]

Great women of faith have had incredible influence across Christian history. The Bible records the noble influence and transforming actions of women such as Ruth, Naomi, Deborah, Esther and Mary—all shining examples of hearts devoted to God.

In the same way, many contemporary women have great influence on the Church—women who also have noble stature and influence and who are married to men in the pastorate. Each one deserves thunderous applause, extravagant bouquets and expressions of thanks that can't be measured.

Many pastors would quit before next Sunday without the love and strength of their wives. These women often work in the secular marketplace subsidizing the family income, so their husbands can serve God through a local congregation. Without such sacrifice, many ministers would find their Kingdom involvement radically curtailed. As we mentioned in the last chapter, many smaller churches would close completely.

Much of the effective work done in local congregations doesn't appear on the front pages of newspapers or in lead articles of pastors' magazines. In thousands of churches, pastors' wives make miraculous contributions to the well-being of the Church and the salvation of the world. Now, as much as ever, the Church depends on the minister's wife for energy and imagination.

Yet pastors' wives are reeling as they strain to do their best with marriage, children, church and career. They're being forced to look at old questions about ministry in new and different ways: What about work outside my home? What about frustrating expectations—others' and mine? What about my husband's long work hours? What about money for pressing needs? Will my children survive the stress?

The Contemporary Scene

Focus on the Family reports that about 5 percent of the letters they receive come from pastors' wives. In the Ministry Outreach/ Pastoral Ministries department at Focus, the figure increases to 20 percent, because we specifically serve pastors and their families. In their letters, pastors' wives share frustrations that run the gamut from loneliness to anger. These concerns well up from the changing nature of ministry and the risks that pastors and their families face.

RISK FACTOR

56 percent of pastors' wives say that they have no close friends.

And pastors' families aren't immune to the severe crises of our times. Here are several summaries of the kinds of calls we receive:

- Pastor's wife called because their son has been sexually abused by an adult church member.
- Pastor called because his wife is having panic attacks and is on medication, but she moved out of the house and says, "Leave me alone." He has full responsibility for their three children. His wife says that she never had the opportunity to experience her teen years, so she wants to live that lifestyle at age 38.
- Pastor's wife called because her husband has abused her and their children. She fled to a shelter in another state, but her husband found them and wants them to return home immediately.
- Pastor's wife called because she just found out there have been many women in her husband's past through the years he's been in ministry. He's looking to start a new

church, and she worries he may be a sexual predator.
- Pastor's wife called and her pastor-husband later called, admitting a need for help because he's struggled for years with an emotional attachment with someone in the church that has gone beyond healthy boundaries.

A DIALOGUE WITH PASTORS' WIVES

Over several years, we've had informative interviews with outstanding pastors' wives and other women actively serving in ministries to pastors' wives. The dialogue here is a collection of several conversations.

Those whom we interviewed are: Jane Rubietta, Abounding Ministries, Grays Lake, Illinois; Linda Riley, Called Together Ministries, Torrance, California; Kay Warren, Saddleback Community Church, Lake Forest, California; Pam Farrel, Masterful Living, San Marcos, California; Linda Swanson, Fairhaven Ministries, Roan Mountain, Tennessee; Janell Repp, Minnesota Renewal Center, Shoreview, Minnesota; and Kandy Veenker, Mountain Learning Center, June Lake, California.

Clergy Marriage and Congregational Health

London/Wiseman: Someone once said that you can gauge the health of a church's ministry by looking at the health of the marriage of the pastoral couple. While that may be an oversimplification, there must be a significant connection. Generally the key balance point for a clergy family rests with the wife and mother. So when she receives encouragement and affirmation, the whole family and church benefit.

We speak to pastors' wives at a lot of conferences, and we find a wide variety of feelings among these spouses. But one thing jumps out: a kind of desperate possessiveness when it comes to their families. Sometimes they feel like they're losing their grasp on their kids and they aren't with their husbands as much as they'd like. They say they also feel like they're living in a world of unrealistic expectations.

Some are thrilled about their roles. Some are harried about their situation. Some are discouraged. Some are angry—almost seething with resentment. But they keep going because they're committed to their husband's ministry.

Jane, tell us about your own experience and what you think pastors' wives need most.

Problems Early On

Jane Rubietta: It's such a big picture, isn't it? As a pastor's wife, I hit bottom right away in our first church—within a few weeks. My husband was pastoring two small churches. We had a new baby born just weeks after we moved in. It was crazy. My husband was working 80 hours a week, and I was trying to be what everybody else thought I should be.

London/Wiseman: All that happened within a few weeks in your first assignment?

Jane Rubietta: Yes. After an especially traumatic day in our home, I remember thinking that I didn't have the faintest idea about who I was supposed to be. It was a painful, confusing experience, but it was the beginning of a long-term healing process that saved our marriage and prepared me for much more effective service for Christ.

Out of desperation I did what I encourage pastors' wives to do: Stop and say, "Wait, who am I? If I separate myself from everyone else's needs and demands—including husband, children and church—who am I without all of that?" I didn't have a clue, but I knew I had to find out. The heart issue is, Who am I in Christ?

London/Wiseman: How does knowing who she is in Christ help a pastor's wife sort out her confusion of roles and relationships? How does it help with the expectations of the people and her husband?

Jane Rubietta: It helps her understand what God calls her to be. Then when she hears the cry about needs in the church, she knows whether that's where God wants her to serve.

Spiritual Giftedness
London/Wiseman: How does that relate to a pastor's wife's spiritual gifts?

Jane Rubietta: That's an interesting component of the whole question of what a pastor's wife does in the church. Try thinking about it this way. If I serve outside my gifts, I am filling a slot that someone else has been called to and designed by the Lord to fill. So when I say yes unadvisedly to a request to serve, I may be keeping someone else from serving and I won't do the work as well as the gifted person.

London/Wiseman: Sometimes wives say, "My husband thinks I should do this." What he may really mean is, "We are desperate for someone to take up this ministry." What then?

Expectations from Within
Jane Rubietta: That's an important part of the whole picture. I often hear pastors' wives say, "My husband thinks I need to do this." At those times, I want to talk to the husband and say, "Expecting your wife to be what everyone else thinks she needs to be isn't faithful to her or to your vows to God." If a wife does step into a ministry role that doesn't really fit her, it should only be for a short time until the person with the right

gift combination for that task comes along.

London/Wiseman: How do you tell the pastor-husband, "Your security, success and upward mobility don't depend on your wife's fulfilling every expectation of people in the church"?

Jane Rubietta: I think we repeatedly have to tell ourselves and our mates that the only upward mobility God is interested in is the upward call in Christ. When we live out that idea, we can give up our need to receive affirmation from our congregations.

The only upward mobility God is interested in is the upward call in Christ.

London/Wiseman: Linda, when you think of your life in ministry, is it different than you expected when you and your husband started?

Linda Riley: I was young when we started—21—and I remember having a prideful feeling of self-importance. I recall thinking it was a privilege and a challenge to be married to a pastor. But I was alarmingly naive. I knew little about people—they can be so strange and unpredictable. I needed a better understanding of people's emotional makeup.

The Value of Mentors
London/Wiseman: In the early years, did you have a pastor's wife you could draw encouragement or guidance from—a mentor or model?

Linda Riley: Yes, the pastor's wife in the church where I first became a Christian. I began my personal relationship with

Christ during the Jesus Movement in 1970 in a congregation led by a pastor who used to be a Kansas farmer. He was as different as night and day from the hippies who came to find Christ in his church. His wife was so caring and sweet. While dealing with people so unlike them must have been confusing, they just stood back and let God do wonderful things in that little church.

London/Wiseman: What was helpful about that pastor's wife?

Linda Riley: Those were fruitful days of harvest; young people would fall on their knees when the name "Jesus" was mentioned. In that setting, the pastor's wife was sort of an old-fashioned type—always lovable and interested. She was very noncontroversial and supportive of everyone, especially her husband. For me, she was a wonderful example of a strong Christian woman.

I'm impressed by almost every pastor's wife I know. They all have commendable strengths—such as perseverance, dedication, commitment and a desire to please the Lord and to serve their families and churches. For the most part, they rise to meet the challenges of ministry and are a great asset to their churches and communities.

London/Wiseman: Kay, tell us your thoughts.

Kay Warren: Pastors' wives are my favorite people. Even though the particular details of our lives differ—the size of our church, where it's located—at heart, we struggle with the same concerns. And so, my heart both aches and rejoices with pastors' wives.

Expectations from Without
London/Wiseman: What are some of the unique problems pastors' wives face these days?

Kay Warren: I believe that pastors' wives get caught in the middle between their own expectations for themselves, the expectations from their husbands and the expectations of the congregation.

London/Wiseman: What happens when the expectations conflict or do not fit the person?

Kay Warren: Typically the expectations don't have a lot of power or clout. But there is a way through them.

A Husband and Wife Team
London/Wiseman: How?

Kay Warren: Here's how it works. I believe the pastor and his wife must be a team—not joined at the hip—but *one* in purpose and intent. I tell pastors whenever I have the chance that their greatest asset is not their own abilities, skills or training, but the wife by their side. If given the opportunity, many pastors' wives will "rise and shine." If she is respected and honored by the pastor—if he celebrates her gifts and unique personality—then the congregation sees her in a new light and often she is given respect and honor by them as well. If he neglects her or disrespects her by disparaging her opinion, viewpoint or advice in front of others, her life will be difficult.

London/Wiseman: So you think the pastor may be partly responsible for the problem? How interesting.

Kay Warren: Yes. So I suppose pastors' wives suffer most from the way their husbands treat them. I don't think pastors do this intentionally; in fact, most would probably deny that this is their pattern. But I've seen it over and over.

London/Wiseman: What can pastors do to help the situation?

Kay Warren: I would like to encourage each pastor to elevate his wife—to view her as a gifted addition to his team, because as a team there is no limit to what God can do through them in a church.

London/Wiseman: We hope every pastor hears your perspective of his being responsible for how the congregation treats his wife and that he can help her soar—"rise and shine" is the way you said it. What special advice do you suggest for wives?

Kay Warren: First of all, learn how God made you. God creates each of us uniquely. He gives us heart and passion. He gives us abilities. He gives each of us a distinctive personality. And He gives us experiences—good, bad, positive, negative. Based on that, look for a place where God can use you in ministry that fits who He made you to be.

RISK FACTOR

53 percent of pastors' wives say they have difficulties raising children.

Constant Pressure

London/Wiseman: Pam, when you talk to pastors' wives, what do they say are their biggest concerns?

Pam Farrel: Well, they're carrying heavy loads, so they are tired. The core issue is they feel their lives are out of control. They feel like they're supposed to please everyone all the time, and they always feel like they're letting someone down.

When you live under constant pressure of feeling you're letting people down, it's easy to become depressed or just give up hope. That affects your kids and your husband and your church.

So the health of the pastor's wife is really important.

Strength from God's Character

London/Wiseman: How can a pastor's wife work through that?

Pam Farrel: Let me tell you how a friend jolted me through it when I called her long distance to have a pity party. After she listened for a while, she asked, "Pam, what character trait or attribute of God are you forgetting?" I answered back, "Oh, pretty much all of them."

Then I took out my Bible. I looked at all the verses that I'd underlined and highlighted. It was as if God sent a love letter straight from His heart to my heart that day. Then He began to take me on a journey. He seemed to be saying, "Let me define you. Let me show you the passion that I've placed inside of you. Let me show you the uniqueness that you have before me, and then you'll be excited about life again."

London/Wiseman: Pam, that's a great thought, this love letter from God. What did God's love letter say?

Pam Farrel: I took all the Bible verses I'd marked. Then I personalized the verses and strung them together, and this is what it says:

> Nothing is impossible for Me. I'm able to do immeasurably more than you can ask or think. In Me all things were created in heaven and on Earth, visible and invisible, thrones, powers, rulers, authorities. All things were created by Me and I am before all things. And in Me all things hold together, even you. Mine is the greatness and the power and the glory and the majesty and the splendor. I am exalted as head over all. Wealth and honor

come from Me and in My hands are strength and power to exalt. Nothing on Earth is My equal. It is not by your might. It is not by your power, but by My Spirit.

I know when you sit down and when you rise. I perceive your thoughts from afar. I'm familiar with all your ways. Before a word is on your tongue, I know it completely. You cannot flee from My presence. If you go up to the heavens, I am there. If you make your bed in the depths, I am there. If you rise on the wings of the dawn, if you settle on the far side of the sea, even there My right hand will guide you. My right hand will hold you fast. Even darkness is as light to Me. I stretch out the heavens like a canopy and spread them out like a tent to dwell in.

I measure the waters of the earth in the hollow of My hand and with the breadth of My hand, I mark the heavens. I'm the creator, the wonderful counselor, the mighty God, the everlasting Father, the Prince of Peace. I'm the alpha and the omega, the beginning and the end. I'm immortal and I dwell in unapproachable light. Yet, I tell you, approach My throne of grace with confidence so that you might receive mercy and find grace to help in time of need.

London/Wiseman: That's so beautiful and helpful. What else did you do?

Strength from a Mentor

Pam Farrel: As Linda Riley suggested earlier, I deliberately searched for a mentor. For me, a mentor is someone with wisdom, strength and experience, someone who

> A mentor is someone with wisdom, strength and experience, someone who believes in you—a coach.

believes in you—a coach. My husband called a professor friend from seminary, Jim Conway. We began having lunches with Jim and his wife, Sally. They began to share their wisdom. Jill and Stuart Briscoe have been recent mentors of ours, too.

London/Wiseman: That concept of mentoring is different than Linda Riley's older and more experienced pastor's wife model. Do you mean mentors don't have to live close by—or even in the same town?

Pam Farrel: Right. Some may be available for only a few e-mails a year. It's amazing because the mentors have been where you are and may be where you are going. Even the busiest Christian leader may agree to exchange a dozen e-mails a year.

Your Kingdom Passion

London/Wiseman: What else did you do to deal with your discouragement and sense of isolation?

Pam Farrel: God took me on a journey to help me rediscover my passion. My passion is equipping women to be all God designed them to be. I believe God wants us to find our passion for His kingdom. Then our service for Him to others is enjoyable— something we feel we were born to do. That is so much more fulfilling for a pastor's wife than filling a slot that no one else wants to do. Passion and giftedness and opportunity and need all came together for me. That makes service that fits a person pure joy.

London/Wiseman: Was there anything else you did?

Priorities

Pam Farrel: Yes, our individual and family priorities were always in disarray—crisis, really. So my husband and I went away for a couple of days to work on establishing priorities for our life and ministry. We made a detailed list of everything important to us and then prioritized each item on the list. Next we listed all our responsibilities to family, church, logistics of living—everything we could think of—on three-by-five cards. We prioritized those cards by assigning an A, B or C to every item. Then we took the Cs and decided that then wasn't the season for those issues—we delayed them indefinitely. Then we looked at all the Bs and asked, Who can we hire or delegate these items to?

Finally, my husband and I negotiated all the A priorities. In that process, we decided that whoever had the responsibility for an A priority could do it in his or her own way and timing. The plan was to do a new set of priorities about every 18 months. We were amazed by the results. Now we spend almost no energy on who does what and when.

Praise

London/Wiseman: That's very practical. Do you have other ways pastors' wives can cut down their stress and increase their joy in living?

Pam Farrel: I remember and practice advice given to me by a missionary. Instead of criticizing and complaining, try praying for creativity. And so I prayed, "God, show me what's good about my life."

I began praising God. That verse in Proverbs is so true: "Above all else, guard your heart, for it is the wellspring of life" (4:23). I find when I protect my heart with praise, I'm able to go forward no matter how badly I want to quit. I start praising, and it gets better.

Competition Between Church and Marriage

London/Wiseman: Linda, what issues are pastors' wives bringing to you?

Linda Swanson: One of the main things I hear is how pastors' wives often feel like their hands are tied. They watch their husbands struggle with pressures of ministry and feel there's nothing that they can do. Sometimes they feel like they have to protect him from the congregation—but they've learned how hard that is to do. So in this no-solution mode, they end up feeling isolated and alone.

London/Wiseman: What about you, Janell? What are pastors' wives saying about their needs?

Janell Repp: I hear wives saying they desperately want to figure out their role in the church. They know that the church called their husbands as pastor. But they're along as a sidekick, and they're trying to figure out what their ministry should be.

One common hazard of the ministry is trying to be a people pleaser.

London/Wiseman: Kandy, what's your take on what pastors' wives are experiencing?

Kandy Veenker: We commonly face two issues. The first is an emotional issue where wives feel that they're in competition with their husband's mistress, the church. And their perplexing emotional question is, How do I compete with God for my husband's affection, his attention and the nurturing of our marriage relationship?

London/Wiseman: Do they fight the demon of perfection, of having to be a role model for the whole world?

Kandy Veenker: Oh, definitely. One common hazard of the

ministry is trying to be a people pleaser. Sadly, people pleasers live in constant fear of rejection. But we're told in Galatians 1:10 to be God pleasers.

London/Wiseman: Janell, what do you hear from pastors' wives?

Janell Repp: I hear that they want their own walk with God. They're seeking God's face and listening to His voice. I think the real key is to keep your eyes fixed on Jesus.

London/Wiseman: Have you figured out a way to help pastors' wives understand they don't have to fulfill everyone's expectations and that they don't have to measure up to their predecessors?

Janell Repp: It's one thing to say I don't have to measure up, but another to believe it. I think wives are hearing this often, and if they are in reasonably good health emotionally, they can learn to abide in peace. I think pastors' wives worry that if they share things with someone in the church or try to break through traditional myths, they'll get their husband in trouble or somehow they'll interrupt his shepherding the flock.

Solutions to the Isolation Problem

London/Wiseman: The issue of isolation and no friends comes up often. Do you have any suggestions?

Kandy Veenker: When I was a teenager, we moved to a small town. I learned if I wanted friends, I needed to go out and make friends. It's the same thing with pastors' wives today. They have to make a choice to phone other pastors' wives from other churches in their area and, if they're safe people, get together with them. By a safe person, I mean someone who—according to Henry Cloud and John Townsend in their book *Safe People*—draws us closer to

God, someone who draws us closer to others and someone who helps us become the person God created us to be.

Linda Swanson: I live in a very isolated place. But as I get involved in the people's lives in my community, God has built some loving relationships. We're different, but we've learned to love and appreciate one another. So if you want a lifetime of friendships, you can't just necessarily look for someone who looks just like you, lives in the same life stage, same children's situation, same educational background.

Janell Repp: I think people do ask, "How in the world do you find a friend?" I've often encouraged pastors' wives to pray for friends. I think that the Lord loves to give good gifts to His children. I think He'll even clue you in when you're introduced to someone or meet someone new: "This is a new friend."

Remember how four friends lowered the paraplegic through the roof to Jesus' feet? I often say that the Lord wants us each to have four corner friends that will get us to the feet of Jesus when we feel desperate and stuck and when we can't get there ourselves. I've counseled people to pray for friends, and I believe the Lord miraculously brings friends our way.

London/Wiseman: If we were sitting here together and a pastor's wife came in and said, "I don't think I can do this anymore. My husband's ministry is going great. God seems to be blessing him. But I don't know if that blessing passed over me, because I am really in an emotional, spiritual hole." What would you say to her?

Jane Rubietta: I'd ask her, "Where along the way did you get lost? And what will it take for you to be found?" Like the father of the prodigal in Scripture, the Shepherd is looking for her. She doesn't have to do it alone.

I'd ask her to set aside some time to be alone before God in silence, in a renewed state of repentance. Then she'd be set free again by that loving, affirming presence of God in her life.

Suggestions for Maximizing Growth in Your Marriage

Who'll read this first—the pastor or his wife? We hope that this conversation offers husband-pastors fresh ways to understand their wives' view of mutual commitment to each other and to the ministry. And we hope ministry wives find practical help offered here. For both, we hope you discuss these concepts and then design strategies for enriching your relationship.

The following guidelines provide growth points for those who want to rescue a failing pastoral marriage or make a good marriage better.

Cultivate a Lifetime of Intimacy with Your Spouse

A newlywed couple returning from their honeymoon cruise, seated across the aisle from Neil on a plane, were a little too loud as they teased each other about an ad in a big-city newspaper— maybe the *New York Times*—titled "Sex Forever."

Though Neil couldn't see the ad they were discussing, he couldn't help overhearing their conversation. It set him thinking about how pastoral couples need to cultivate a life of intimacy together.

Of course, we hope that every married couple, whether clergy or lay, celebrates with joy and even ecstasy the biblical idea of sexual love. And we believe the church needs to do much more to inform and to inspire appreciation for God's gift of human sexuality.

But beyond what needs to be done for the church, every clergy couple needs to work at the joys of growing intimacy across a lifetime. A kiss before dinner. A surprise gift. A touch that says I'll always be here for you. A walk in the park. A visit to the lakeshore or seashore. Work to continuously build your relationship so your spouse knows she is the highest priority in your life.

Marriage is a living, breathing, growing and changing relationship; and you need to feed and nurture yours.

Keep open to the mysteries of how a man and woman can love each other more and more across a lifetime. Talk and touch. Surprise your spouse and best friend. Be willing to be surprised.

Use phrases like "I love you"; "You're special to me"; "I'd marry you again in a heartbeat"; "You're wonderful"; "I'm proud of you." The "one flesh" of marriage is great, but one heart, one soul is even better. Give yourself a fulfilled marriage that gets better with age.

Connect with a Support Person

Find a support person who cherishes your uniqueness and understands ministry—a "soul friend" to help you focus on the meaning of ministry and remind you of its possible fulfillment.

You might consider someone raised in a pastor's home, a pastor's spouse or a key layperson. Or look for veteran ministers or their spouses—especially cheerful people who love Kingdom work. Or consider pastoral retirees experienced at establishing priorities and dealing with the pressures of ministry.

Try to find someone of your own gender with spiritual stamina and emotional resilience. To help you most, they also need a healthy relationship with God, a stable self-regard, a willingness to listen and an ability to question self-imposed myths you have about ministry. The goals for this connection are dialogue, hope, prayer and accountability.

Deprofessionalize Your Faith

Your faith can supply satisfying nourishment for a healthy marriage. However, it's frighteningly easy for anyone who lives close to the day-to-day events of the church to professionalize personal faith. It's also easy to bypass the spiritual disciplines because they sound so familiar. Clergy marriages often wither as a result.

Like everyone else, you need to feed your faith to make life happy and holy.

You need to feed your faith to make life happy and holy.

The Father's provisions are lavish: assorted prayer forms like adoration, confession, thanksgiving, petition and intercession; scriptural saturation that takes the Bible into the details of life; fasting that illuminates motives and intensifies dependence on God; spiritual formation calisthenics; celebration of creation; inspiration of church music; and awareness of supernatural enabling to make ministry authentic and beautiful.

To enrich your marriage, strengthen your personal spiritual development in every possible way. Share your spiritual discoveries with your spouse and allow the interaction to weave Christ into the fabric of your marriage.

Guard Against Perils

Good marriages require rigorous effort. This is particularly true for clergy couples because personal wholeness is a necessary component in the life of authentic pastors. But because of the demands of church ministry, a clergy couple's marriage requires more effort on the part of both partners.

Hear the anguish of a pastor suffering from moral collapse: "My wife and I failed each other. We indifferently starved each other emotionally until our marriage died a natural death from neglect." You can escape perils like this if both you and your spouse work to be best friends and to be life's greatest pleasures for each other.

Like taking a time-out in a basketball game, marriage tensions need instant attention. Always play up the pluses and play down the demands ministry makes on your marriage.

Avoid emotional isolation by creating a weekly time island of spiritual, emotional and physical intimacy that you spend alone together to catch up on all dimensions of your marriage. Stand firm against every temptation. Remove yourself from any circumstance that even faintly compromises your commitments to each other or diminishes the influence of your combined service for Christ. It takes hard work coupled with a willingness to resist every trace of seduction.

Seek Both Satisfaction and Solutions

Most of us have enough problems to make us want to get off this whirling planet. One pastor's spouse angrily announced, "Of course I am an impossibility thinker. The church and my husband made me that way!"

Many pastors can easily identify with a minister who remarked, "I'm planning to have a serious burnout as soon as my schedule allows—I earned it."

Threatening landmines fill many pastoral assignments—bombs waiting to explode in the minister's marriage. Nonetheless, simply highlighting the hardships leads nowhere. Surely you can do more than just criticizing the profession or describing the hazards. Start by facing down the fears and overpowering the obstacles. And don't forget to admit that many marriage aggravations are simply human problems and not distinct ministry issues.

As a Goliath, forward step; initiate a candid discussion of your concerns with your spouse. This strategy will move you both from overly generalized feelings of malaise about your marriage to identifiable issues you can talk through and resolve together.

Accept Love from Your Congregation

Helper types like pastors frequently have difficulty accepting love from those they serve. But your congregation very likely has at least one person who wants to love you and your spouse. Each of you and your marriage will be more healthy if you accept this offer of love and help.

Since love is contagious, you can create a two-way sharing between your congregation and yourselves as a couple. A wise Christian statesman commented, "As laypeople, we only grow as our pastor gives us love and he receives ours." Rejoice in the reality—the Lord reveals Himself in the love of the people we serve.

Refuse to Abuse

Many people don't exactly know what to think about society's broadened concept of abuse. But if abuse actually means emotional or spiritual mistreatment, then it may be epidemic in many clergy marriages. Its many destructive expressions include biting sarcasm, passive dissension, trivial pouting and emotional estrangement.

Any pastor can abuse his marriage by giving so much of himself to the church that he has no energy left for the most important people in his life. He flies under the motive of giving first priority to the church, but it causes him to neglect and harm his family.

Abuse flows the other way when the pastor's spouse resents the church and feels deserted by her husband. She releases her frustration by criticizing his parenting, nagging about his long hours and belittling the congregation. This only builds up the walls of isolation.

When this happens, husband and wife exist in lonely, emotional isolation. Though they may never divorce, they live in two disconnected, miserable worlds. While they eat at the same table, sleep in the same bed and view the same TV programs, they're worlds apart—separated, alone and frustrated.

If this describes your marriage, you can break the bondage within the relationship by asking the Spirit of Christ to come into your marriage. Then you'll both have room to grow as forgiveness, reconciliation and tenderness replace nagging, criticizing and rigidity.

Develop Gentle Assertive Skills

Some churchgoers expect pastors' wives to relay messages to their husbands that people would never say directly to him. If that happens to you, learn to say, "I'm not the pastor, why don't you call him about that issue?" Or say, "You think I know a lot about that issue—but I don't. Please check with the person who carries that responsibility."

Try Extravagant Praise

Increase the affirmation you give your spouse and children. They have hundreds of qualities worthy of your praise. Look for them. Celebrate their specialness. Speak a word of authentic praise and watch your mate burst into bloom. For greater joy in your relationship and for an enduring sense of its specialness, be extravagant with your praise.

Try the Big Four

Remember Pam Farrel's four strategies for simplifying and enriching your life?

1. Pray creatively, "Lord, show me what is good about my life."
2. Seek mentors, even short-time people who may not live near you.
3. Develop a genuine affection for Scripture as God's love letter to you.
4. Work with your mate to prioritize the details of your life seriously.

Surrender Resistance to Ministry

Some clergy couples live in a continuous state of agonizing anguish, believing God messed them up by putting them into the ministry. They feel like victims, believing circumstances beyond their control have locked them into a gloomy existence.

But take a step closer to the facts. Living in a clergy marriage will never be as bad as you expect nor as good as you wish it were. This reality is true of all marriages, regardless of the partner's occupation.

If you want to live authentically in a satisfying clergy marriage, you need to let go of all pent-up resistance to ministry. Resisting ministry hurts everyone. But you can find a safe place in God's grace where acceptance becomes a liberating way of life.

We have a friend whose wife planted a church when she was 59 years old. She studied to be ordained after her six children were grown, about the time her husband retired from a career of service as a postman. When a newspaper reporter asked the husband about this strange set of circumstances, he replied, "God can do what He wants. I want to wholeheartedly cooperate with His plan." His answer is exactly right for every ministry couple—wholehearted cooperation with God's plan. Give up resistance and discover joy in the journey.

Never Forget How Important Pastors' Wives Are

Since God made the gospel so people focused, the relationships in your home are a microcosm of the family of God. Your home is a place where family members can demonstrate, enjoy and even test love. Every bit of time, money or effort you invest in your family is an investment in the health of the church and the kingdom of God. Refuse to allow home and church to compete in your priorities, your spouse's heart or your time with your children.

CHERISH THE JOYS OF A GREAT MARRIAGE

How can you build a great marriage? A Christ-filled marriage starts with less emphasis on self. It requires refocusing from *me* to *we*. And it requires you to increase your care for each other.

But think of the benefits. A genuinely Christ-empowered marriage offers you the brimming pleasures of time-tested satisfactions rooted in fidelity, chastity, honor, truth, integrity, trust, respect and purity.

God made every woman original and unique and special and astounding and unpredictable. Husband and pastor, thank God for how interesting and different your wife is from you. Wife, thank God for the privilege of being your best self for Him, for that's always good enough for God and for everyone else that really matters.

If faith makes every human relationship better, then pastoral marriages offer enormous potential for your lifelong satisfaction. At the same time, a strong marriage can provide a noble pattern for both your congregation and your community—it may be the only fulfilling marriage some dysfunctional people ever see. All that adds up to an impressive combination—individual contentment and laudable modeling for others.

Let's get it straight and enjoy the realities—people in the world and members of your church will be drawn to authentic faith, inner attractiveness, fulfilled marriages and solid families.

Cherish the privileges you enjoy in a clergy marriage. The list is impressive: flexible time, unique opportunities to influence people's lives, an extended family in the church, special people who visit the pastor's home and the opportunity to share in shaping the church's future ministry. Focus on these and other advantages built in to your marriage. Try listing specific benefits of your marriage.

For too long, clergy couples have emphasized what they miss by being in ministry. One pastor even made the foolish mistake of saying from his pulpit, "If I hadn't gone into the ministry, I could have been president of General Motors by now." Someone replied in a whisper that could be heard for at least three pews, "Yes, and you might have been a garbage collector by now, too."

It's time to count the blessings pastoral ministry provides for marriage and family. After counting them, say to your mate, your children and yourselves, "This is a good way to live, and God blesses us with the benefits."

R E N E W A L   S T R A T E G I E S

CHERISH YOUR WIFE ABOVE ALL OTHERS

✓ Cultivate a lifetime of intimacy with your spouse.
✓ Connect with a support person.
✓ Deprofessionalize your faith.
✓ Guard against perils.
✓ Seek both satisfaction and solutions.

✓ Accept love from your congregation.

✓ Refuse to abuse.

✓ Develop gentle assertive skills.

✓ Try extravagant praise.

✓ Try the Big Four.

✓ Surrender resistance to ministry.

✓ Never forget how important pastors' wives are.

A Personal Word from H. B. L.

Cherish Those Who Matter Most

You probably have some type of office—either in your church building or in your home. As I visit colleagues from time to time, I'm fascinated by what I see in their offices—places where they spend so much of their lives.

Looking around my own office, I see a variety of things that hold great value to me: gifts wonderful people have given, books I've read and many I hope to read, the desk and chair I occupy for so many hours each day and a stack of paperwork that's never really caught up. On the walls are my ordination certificate and things that remind me of places I have been, people I have met and my academic accomplishments. On my bookcase shelves are remnants of an elephant collection and the beginnings of a Harley motorcycle set. Many of these keepsakes, mementos and other stuff would mean very little to anyone else. But for some reason, I just keep hanging on to them. Can you relate?

But when I swivel my chair around to the credenza behind my desk, I see pictures of my family: my two sons, their wives and kids. In one of the pictures, Bev and I are standing with our grandchildren—the most important people in the world to us. All of a sudden, the other things in my office pale in comparison.

Do you have pictures of your family in your office? Are they your priority? I pray so.

CHAPTER SIX

SHOWCASE KIDS OR STRONG FAMILIES

- 35 percent of pastors report that their children's walks with God is the biggest concern about their families.[1]
- 52 percent of pastors say that they faithfully take off at least one full day each week to spend with their families.[2]
- 52 percent of pastors say they and their spouses believe that being in pastoral ministry is hazardous to their family's well-being and health.[3]
- 67 percent of pastors believe that their children love—either most of the time or all of the time—being part of a ministry family.[4]
- 61 percent of pastors say that they would begin looking elsewhere if they knew their current pastorate was detrimental to their families; 16.5 percent say they'd resign immediately.[5]
- 41 percent of pastors say that the most stressful time of day in their home is evening.[6]
- 66 percent of pastors and their families feel pressure to model the ideal family to their congregations and communities.[7]
- 52 percent of pastors spend time off from pastors' duties to do activities with their families; 21 percent spend time with hobbies or physical tasks.[8]

What could be more embarrassing to a pastor than a crisis brought on by his wayward children? To take a close look at such a situation, consider this true scenario. The names have been changed to protect the *guilty* and the *innocent*.

Ted Abbott, a pastor highly respected by young ministers and by his parishioners, lives down the road in the next town and sounds like someone everybody knows. Abbott, age 45, helped First Church grow from 225 to 400 members in four years. He's proud of his achievements and boasts of tripling attendance in two previous churches. Honored by his denomination last year as pastor of the year, Ted has reason to be self-confident; and he shows it.

Ted and Pat married 25 years ago while they were students in a Christian college. Both rate their marriage 9 on a scale of 10. Pat, a gifted second-grade teacher, considers herself a career professional. The Abbotts have three children: Josh, 16; Tim, 14; and Sally, 11. Most of the time, the family seems supportive of Ted's ministry. Church members enjoy bragging about their minister's family.

Recently, Josh generated a family earthquake when he was dismissed from school for drinking on the high school campus. Two fellow students accused Josh of supplying them with alcohol during lunch break. The town is full of talk, and Pastor Ted is especially embarrassed.

Though Pat feels humiliated, too, she's consumed with closing a school year and renewing her state teaching credentials. Being a mother, wife, authentic Christian in residence and teacher keeps her plate too full. Deep down, she thinks Josh was experimenting, but blames Ted's emotional and physical absence from the family as the root of the problem. The situation affects the other children, too: Tim is bewildered and Sally won't quit talking about the situation.

Few outside the family know the private Ted who is proud and high-strung. He worries that Josh's actions will tarnish his ministry. Ted wants to control the church at any cost because he enjoys every kind of power. For years, family and church have pampered Ted, so he thinks of himself as something special. Yet deep down, he knows that his inner spiritual resources are dry and brittle.

Josh doubts his father's sincerity about ministry. Some family friends think Josh is unconsciously acting out resentment toward his father.

Ted believes Pat's professional teaching commitment is the real problem. He blames the church for not being more affirming of his family. In fact, this is his pattern: blame is more important than solving a problem.

This incident forces Ted to evaluate relationships with his son, his other children and his church. While hiding his true feelings from Josh, Ted strains to deal with his outrage and chagrin. He really wants the best for his family, but he wonders how he can face the congregation the following Sunday.

His feelings are complicated even more by a wise old church member who reminds him, "You only have two years left before Josh leaves home for college. Make the most of it for his sake."

How can Ted deal with this crisis? As a pastor, he has sterling success, but he feels like a failure as a parent. In this chapter, we'll depart from the interview format we've been using and use both the story of the Abbotts and letters from pastors' families to explore many issues those families face.

FAMILY GROWTH IN MOTION

Because of this crisis, the Abbotts have a rare opportunity to grow together with increased acceptance, forgiveness and insight. If they use this situation for family growth, the natural embarrassment is a small price for the benefits everyone will receive, especially Josh. Above all else, the children must know they are not on display for the sake of their father's ministry.

A Mirror to Check Values in the Family

It's a given of family life that parents, regardless of their line of work, must endure some impulsive behavior by their children.

But Ted and Pat need to make whatever's going on with Josh top priority in this circumstance. As a part of the solution, Ted and Pat must come to terms with blaming each other. In the process, two important principles apply:

1. Kids are more important than reputations.
2. Doing right produces good impressions rather than good impressions producing right.

Unconditional love will help carry Josh to adulthood and teach his pastor-dad several life-changing lessons.

Lay Support: An Unused Resource

In every ministry setting exist some nonjudgmental parishioners who have heartfelt interest in the pastor's children. Their concern grows from the same root as all compassion and grace—Christ Himself. Pastors often overlook their serious desire to help. One group of lay leaders recently reminded their pastor, "We know how to love confused teenagers because we have so many of our own."

The minority that mistreat pastors' families get too much publicity. Horror stories abound; many are true. But generally only one or two church members—not an entire congregation—truly hurt clergy families. Most church members are patient and tender with preachers' kids. The problem of this silent majority is that they don't speak up often enough.

The lesson from Ted's experience teaches pastors that someone in the church has an encouraging word about his family for the pastor when he is willing to hear. And many will walk through any fire with their pastor's family.

A Bump in the Road

Pastors need to see unacceptable conduct in their children as a warning of things that could lie ahead. Every alcoholic starts with a first drink; thieves begin by stealing petty items.

But not every undesirable act creates a negative domino effect on someone's entire future. Ted and Pat need to confront Josh's conduct, to be sure; and Ted must satisfy himself about what the incident means to Josh and the family. They need wisdom and discernment.

People often paint pastors' children into a corner over one mistake, and often the situation prevents the children from coming back. Such distrust can encourage the kids to do the same thing again. Their immature reasoning says, *If you think I'm bad, I guess I am. So I'll show you just how bad I am.* Such a downward spiral destroys relationships and faith—a result no one wants.

RISK FACTOR

35 percent of pastors report that their children's walks with God is the biggest concern about their families.

To bring Josh through, both the Abbotts and their congregation need to offer the opportunity for confession plus large doses of forgiveness and grace. This is a perfect opportunity for family and church to demonstrate what they believe and—like in the story of the prodigal son—welcome an offender home as if he'd never been away.

Parenting Adult Children

The elderly man from Ted's congregation was right when he pushed the pastor to face the fact that Josh would soon be leaving home for college, a colossal step on the road to adulthood.

What he didn't have time to discuss were the opportunities Ted now has to lay the groundwork for a coming adult relationship with his son. As long as they live, Josh and Ted can profoundly influence each other's faith, if they choose to. Parenting adult children works like that.

For all pastors, the clear message is: Get serious now about the spiritual influence you have on your children. This caution applies regardless of a child's age. The time is short.

Sincerity about Ministry

Josh questioned his father's sincerity concerning ministry. Though a child's suspicions may be inaccurate, parents need to evaluate every time a child hints at a question about their authenticity. The head man at home or church can easily fool himself without frequent reality tests.

At such a time, this self-diagnostic question may be helpful: What am I doing that makes my children question my commitments to ministry? Teens and children have an uncanny ability to spot a phony. This does not mean a parent caves in to a pouting child's remark: "I do not think you are much of a minister." Such a word uttered in a fit of anger is probably not reliable.

On the contrary, every challenge concerning authenticity should be tested against reality. A child's doctrine of God starts to form in the cradle as he or she interacts with parents.

Teens and children have an uncanny ability to spot a phony.

LETTERS ABOUT PARENTING
FROM CLERGY COUPLES

A good family requires more than money in the bank, an acceptable neighborhood or top-notch schools. Unconditional love is the cornerstone for a strong family unit. Parents must intentionally build this love into their family relationships.

Heart-wrenching letters from pastor-parents repeat a recurring theme. To them, many parenting problems seem to revolve around their fishbowl visibility in the church and community. Some letters suggest they might solve these issues by involving their children in the ministry team. Others idealize the life of the laity, thinking clergy families would avoid routine parenting frustrations if they weren't in the ministry. Consider the serious concerns clergy couples write about their families, as we try to offer a few practical solutions.

Uprooted Family and Church Politics—
God Uses Ambiguities

A pastor's wife in the Northwest writes:

> We serve a mission congregation that's five years old. In the last three years, things have become extremely political, and those who were the founding roots of this congregation have turned against us saying the church isn't growing fast enough. Our district leader took their side and listened to the political garbage.
>
> Through the process my husband, Gus, was voted out of the church. This will uproot our family from this lovely area and good schools simply because of politics in the church.
>
> We've been living in limbo for six months. We have no place to go. I've been "counseling" four sad children, not knowing what to tell them except, "Life isn't fair, but

God is good." Those are hard words for teenagers. It's difficult to explain to them that their dad has been diligently preaching God's Word, leading people to Christ, but then a few families have the right to tell us to leave. I'm trying not to lose heart.

"Living in limbo." Gus's family is shaken. They want to believe in God and church leaders. But they're confused, and waiting is hard. These children need ministry and time to find healing. Even more immediately, they need a place to live.

"It's difficult to explain to four sad children." Satisfying explanations for radical losses are difficult for anyone to find. However, the spiritual health of the children in this family is a significant and long-term issue. Their parents need to help them not to lose trust in the Church and all its people.

While they seem to be locked in waiting mode, if the parents in this family express confidence in God, that will eventually help heal this family's wounds. God often surprises us. He turns what others intended for our harm to be our good. Old Testament Joseph is a shining example (see Gen. 50:20).

Let's get it straight. A new assignment is one of God's specialties. However, this minister's family, like a trapeze artist, must let go before they can move on to the next stage of life together. An insightful devotional writer calls this the grace of relinquishment.

Though families in ministry may move from place to place, they must remember that they're never uprooted from God's generous provisions and amazing providence.

Many Sacrifices—God Remembers Them

A pastor's wife in New York writes:

> We serve an aging congregation in an inner city and minister to a welfare community. On Sundays, my three kids

are often the only ones in their Sunday School class. It's tough, but I try to communicate to them that God sees and remembers their sacrifices. After four years in this place, we pray for good Christian friends for our children, for a home larger than our present 800 square feet and for at least one or two solid leaders in our church.

"The only ones." This mom carries a heavy load. She's wise to bring her children into the commitment circle of ministry. In a practical way, these parents can deliberately help their kids find friends by putting them in touch with young people in a nearby church, putting them in contact with students in a Christian school or helping them get acquainted with another minister's family.

"800 square feet." Space for living is a common problem for urban dwellers, not just pastors. The family might lessen their frustration by using existing rooms imaginatively, making family use of the church facilities or exploring available public spaces, such as libraries, museums and parks. In one situation in which a family lives next door to the church, they use the church's fellowship hall as their family/game room and do all church-related hospitality there rather than in their home. Another family uses the church as their study hall two nights each week; the children study their school lessons, Dad studies for his sermons, and Mom studies for her adult education class.

"God sees and remembers their sacrifices." "Sacrifice" is a tricky word that we need to use with caution. One person's sacrifice is another's blessing. Consider, for example, a missionary who leaves family, receives low wages and needs to adjust to new cultures. While people at home speak of the missionary's sacrifice, the missionary talks of her privilege. Which is it?

Though ministry sometimes places restrictive constraints on families, it also offers benefits not always available to other children. The privilege list may include tight family bonds, opportunities to meet special speakers who come to the church, an extended family among the people of God and flexible time with their parents. Underscoring these benefits helps children realize that sacrifices like these will always be part of life.

Kids are sturdy people. They can endure more than most of us realize. One clergy couple tells each of their children every day, "You're privileged to be a pastor's kid."

A Family in Christian Leadership— Allow Children to Help

A minister from Montana writes:

> Many pastors work so hard helping other people's families that they neglect their own. My district leader asked me how I would resolve the conflict between ministry and family. My answer was to involve my family in ministry.

From a pastor in the Northeast:

> As a family involved in Christian leadership, we feel we must live our lives beyond reproach. How much involvement in the ministry is good for our children?

Children need to learn that the one who gives is often as fully blessed as the one who receives.

"Involve my family in the ministry." Many pastors' letters mention taking family into ministry. Some see it as a problem and others as a grand potential for growing sturdy Christians. Children need to learn that the one who gives is often as fully blessed as the one who receives.

Pastors' families want to avoid two extremes when it comes to involving their children in ministry. The first is intensity. Ideally, a child's growth potential should determine his or her level of participation. Make the good of the child a higher priority than the survival needs of the church.

The second extreme is no involvement. Some ministers' families view the church as nothing more than Dad's place of employment. This perspective creates problems in the children's development of faith. Regardless of age or family ties, all Christians—including members of a clergy family—miss out if they don't have a church home where they serve and grow spiritually.

"Good for our children." Pastors' kids will love and cherish the church if they're involved in its ministries. And ministers' families feel much less isolated from their pastor-father when they observe his work up close.

RISK FACTOR

66 percent of pastors and their families feel pressure to model the ideal family to their congregations and communities.

Family-operated farms of past generations offer a good example. Family bonds grew strong as children and parents worked side by side to harvest the crop and build up the farm. The same dynamics work in the church.

When pastors' families live long distances from their own extended families, they might try to view the church as a surrogate extended family. This happens when you welcome the people of God into your heart and home.

"Beyond reproach." Like all believers, the minister's family must model Christlikeness and live according to biblical standards. The quality life that results will be a joy to the individual and pleasing to Christ. It will cut down on a thousand efforts to

second-guess what others think or say. Living in a way that pleases Christ will please every serious follower of the Lord Jesus; the rest probably can't be satisfied anyway.

Bad Kids from Good Homes— Trust Them to God

A pastor's wife in the West writes:

> Unfortunately "bad kids" sometimes come from good homes. This bothers me because some of the elders in our church feel the pastor should step down if his children aren't believers or are disobedient. Is it fair to have a man's whole pastoral career jeopardized because his children have fallen away?

"Is it fair?" No. God gives human beings choice. Like everyone else, pastors' kids can choose their own way, and they do. Children from any kind of home can go bad, and they can also go good. Parenting comes with no guarantees. When asked about raising children, one veteran summarized, "Do your best and trust God with the rest."

During the children's brief years at home, train them, love them, lead them, believe in them and get ready to let go. Conscientious parents have a strong factor on their side—children never escape the shaping influence of good homes.

In the long term, the good or bad choices of a minister's children shouldn't determine his effectiveness. One of the most powerful witnesses a pastor can have to his family or surrounding society is to make a full-fledged commitment to modeling the biblical concepts of morality, fidelity and faith in his home.

Heavy Loads and Long Days—Cherish the Wonder Years

A pastor's wife near Indianapolis writes:

> Please excuse me for not taking out my typewriter for this letter. I have a five-year-old son, a three-year-old daughter and an eight-month-old baby girl. I'm sure they'd want to help me type, and I'd never finish this letter. And as a bookkeeper and part-time baker, if I wait to recopy this letter, you may not get it.

"They'd want to help." Parents need to cherish those precious first five years of a child's life as a special gift from God. Sometimes when loads get heavy and days seem long, parents of young children wonder if they'll ever grow up. The answer is yes and very soon. Treasure those early years and know that the frustrations are worth it. Make the most of your molding influence on the children at the same time that you enjoy the incredible richness they bring into your life. Bonding during the preschool years greatly influences a successful future for everyone in the family.

Little Time at Home—Be Present When You're There

A pastor from South Carolina writes:

> Yesterday my four-year-old daughter said, "Daddy, don't you love us anymore? You didn't eat with us once this week." I tried to explain, but my words didn't make much sense. I wonder if it's the meals I miss or something else she needs that I've failed to give her.

"Daddy, don't you love us anymore?" On the surface, the question sounds frightening. This dad may paint a self-portrait of being a bad parent if he dwells on the long-term implications

of her question. But he's not a bad parent. In fact, his concerns show he is probably a good or above-average parent.

At four years old, his daughter likely means she needs him and wishes he were home more often. In place of giving a long explanation that she won't understand, this pastor can correct her lonely feelings by building more family time into his calendar, especially at mealtimes. The idea is to spend energy correcting the issue. Action is usually more useful than worry.

"Something else she needs." Highly motivated, task-oriented career people often don't see the present-but-absent syndrome. Here's how it happens: A tired pastor comes home for dinner after a long day of counseling, sermon preparation and administrative duties. When he sits down to eat with his family, his mind dwells on the details of the day rather than on the relationships that need cultivating around the table.

The first step is recognizing the problem. Take a few quiet moments to refocus after getting home. Listening to your children will provide a pretty good gauge on how well you're doing at really being present.

SUGGESTIONS FOR STRENGTHENING STABILITY IN YOUR HOME

Strengthening clergy families requires an intentional dedication to abiding family values. Three assumptions are true:

1. Whatever the minister's family has—good or bad—is contagious in the church.
2. Families should be seen as bundles of potential, satisfaction and commitment.
3. Habit is the main enemy of family renewal.

Begin strengthening family stability by searching for ways to enrich your life together. You can find ideas for enriching your family in many places: bookstores, libraries and magazine stands. General recommendations for nonclergy families will also work well for you. As you read, research and think, start doing what your heart sanctions. You don't need to make the changes complicated, but they're essential because business-as-usual won't work. Put into practice what you already know. You'll be amazed at how satisfaction from your family increases as you start seeing them through eyes of enjoyment and potential. Fully accept and celebrate the fact that your lives are intertwined forever—that's a long time.

Living in a pastor's home, done well, allows a quality life that you and your family might not enjoy in any other profession. Fine-tune your family relationships to foster the emotional, spiritual and physical development of each individual.

Please the People Who Matter Most

View your family not as a sociology textbook to be analyzed, but as a living segment of society headed by you. Celebrate their uniqueness.

Pastors tend to talk like preachers, act like preachers and relate to their families like preachers.

Look at your family relationships through the eyes of your spouse and children. Ask them to talk to you about family and put their suggestions to work. In fact, children are sometimes more perceptive about family needs than their parents. Give them credit in public with simple words like "My children taught me to love" or "My family plans the most exciting vacations." These powerful affirmations will nourish affection.

Get Your Family in Tune with God

Pastors tend to talk like preachers, act like preachers and relate to their families like preachers. Drop your ministerial voice and religious explanations for a while so you can lead your family to discover the meaning found in Bible reading, prayer, praise and compassion for needy people. Allow your children to see you as a person who's hungry for God—something significantly different than being a mere religious professional. Ask your family to help you get to know God better. Expect pleasant surprises.

Feed Faith to Children

Pessimistic messages about life, church and the world regularly bombard children. They overhear much from their parents at home, friends at church and neighbors in the community. And all the bad news and ideas transmitted via the secular media make it even worse.

They need an antidote to this negativity overdose. Feed children faith to stabilize their spiritual growth. Offer explicit examples of how God is working in the Church. Remind them of miracles you've experienced in your family. Talk to them about amazing victories in the Bible. And create an environment of faith.

Refuse to Blame Problems on the Ministry

Without question, ministry has difficulties not common in other professions. But ministry doesn't cause all the problems in a pastor's life and home. Blaming consequences resulting from bad judgments on the ministry misleads children. Attributing the results of poor work habits to the church is a lie.

View Family as a Gift from God

Few things in the human pilgrimage bring more joy than a stable family. As a special gift from God, you must invest time, energy, imagination and money in your family. The more effort you devote, the more the family repays.

Open your heart to the rich possibilities built into your family connections. Nothing else, short of the grace of God, can gratify a pastor for as many years. Ask God for a vision of what your family can be and how He wants you to fulfill that dream. A family in ministry is a laboratory for living where love is the supreme ingredient. Amazing but true, family is a splendid miniature of what God wants His Church to be.

Focus on the Present

Years of schooling can condition clergy to dream of bright tomorrows after they finish coursework and become active as ministers. Sometimes this future focus lasts for a lifetime. As a result, some pastors spend their lives dreaming about what their next assignment will be, how many members they'll have in the next church and what they'll attain someday. But what if that someday never comes? Fluffy fantasies about the future can't fulfill anyone.

Rearview-mirror perspectives that control some pastors cause just as much damage. They remember a past that never was and long to go back to the romanticized old days. But they need to face a startling reality: The past is gone forever; all we have is today.

This present focus needs to be specific in family relationships. When a pastor heads home in the afternoon, he needs to leave problems in the car, concerns at the church and the future in God's hands. Children need undivided attention. Today is tomorrow's happy memory, and it's the only time you have to build a stable family.

Start a Family Support Group

Why not start a self-help parenting group for pastors? In the United States alone, more than 500,000 self-help groups exist, organized around every imaginable concern. Think of the advantages of such support for clergy families. Each self-help group supplies face-to-face interaction between people who share similar experiences, feelings and struggles. As a result, group members discover ways to make personal changes, mobilize support for a cause, strengthen each other and get personally involved in each other's lives. Then a sense of camaraderie develops between participants.

Pastors and their families need all these advantages. Remember the Abbotts from earlier in this chapter? They had no experience in dealing with their first child's eagerness to be an adult; a group with whom to discuss these matters would have helped immeasurably. The family living in small quarters in an urban setting could receive insight from discussing its frustrations with others in similar situations. And the mother who struggled with her three preschool-aged children might get help from other women who've successfully survived similar situations.

Receiving the benefit of a support group requires taking the first move. Why not get one started now? You could contact persons with similar situations in your denomination. Or you might test interest across denominational lines within your community. The main issue is to recognize that someone like you is already coping, and they can help you understand how God intends for you to move beyond family endurance to enjoyment.

Keep Yourself in Parental Training for Life

An effective parent never stops learning, regardless of the number of years in ministry or the age of children. When church or society presents a new problem, the parent in training seeks ways to master it with God's enabling. Like an athlete in training, this effort keeps you alert, energetic and in top mental condition—ready to win.

You don't need to feel locked in to whatever happens in your family. Instead dare to believe what can be. New problems and critical issues often lead to deeper understandings and renewed relationships. In the process, you can find answers you don't now have and enrich your family relationships.

ALLOW YOUR FAMILY TO NOURISH YOUR MINISTRY

Let's change the mood in clergy families from worry to support, from surviving to thriving and from self-pity to winsome satisfaction. Such an overcoming strategy calls you to love and be loved by family. Allow the most significant people in your life to nourish your inner spring.

Allow the quality of your family relationships to transform your home into a sanctuary where love, acceptance, affirmation and accountability recharge your spiritual and emotional batteries. Use family togetherness to renew your whole being and to enrich each other.

Resist competition between family and ministry. Make them complementary and mutually beneficial. God desires for them to supplement, enrich and nourish each other.

During overwhelming demands of ministry, turn your heart toward home where love, support, intimacy and friendship await you. Make your family members the most significant people in your life. Most churches want you to give your family a high place in your affections, priorities and values. Take them up on it.

Every pastor needs his family's love fully as much as he needs a strong church to strengthen his ministry. Remember that the miracle of family enriches your life and empowers your service for Christ.

R E N E W A L   S T R A T E G I E S

HELPING YOUR KIDS STAY WELL-ADJUSTED

✓ Please the people who matter most.
✓ Get your family in tune with God.
✓ Feed faith to children.
✓ Refuse to blame problems on the ministry.
✓ View family as a gift from God.
✓ Focus on the present.
✓ Start a family support group.
✓ Keep yourself in parental training for life.

OVERCOMING THE
RISKS IN YOUR
PERSONAL LIFE

A Personal Word from H. B. L.

Finding Joy in Ministry

This week, while reading the book of Hebrews, I saw again those words written to a group of people about their pastors: "Obey them so that their work will be a joy, not a burden" (Heb. 13:17).

I thought a bit about what the phrase "joy, not a burden" really means. I'm sure it doesn't mean that people are to be little robots to their pastors. Rather, they're being urged to honor the calling of their pastors and to conduct themselves in a way that brings joy to pastoring. Obedience grows out of mutual trust and love.

What would make ministry joyful for you?

- People who continue to show growth in their walk with the Lord.
- People who have a genuine concern for their brothers and sisters in the faith.
- People who don't turn a deaf ear to the lost.
- People who walk by faith and not by sight.
- People who pray rather than faint.
- People who are drawn to peace rather than contention.
- People whose self-image is based on who they are in Christ rather than on what they accomplish by themselves.
- People who pass the torch of righteousness to the next generation.
- People who love the church and give themselves to it.

I think each of us has a joy meter. No matter what happens around you, find your contentment in Christ and the job He's given you to do. Rejoice!

CHAPTER SEVEN

RECOVERY FROM STRESS AND BURNOUT

A CONVERSATION WITH ARCHIBALD HART

RISK FACTORS

- 45.5 percent of pastors say that they've experienced depression or burnout to the extent that they needed to take a leave of absence from ministry.[1]
- 70 percent say they have a lower self-esteem now than when they started out.[2]
- 57 percent of pastors do not have a regularly scheduled and implemented exercise routine.[3]
- 8 top areas of stress for pastors (in random order): time, boundaries, isolation, conflict, mobility, life in parsonage, concern for children and spouse and family dynamics.[4]
- 55 percent of pastors say evening and weekend work puts pressure on family.[5]
- 60 percent of pastors report that they've "never doubted their call"; 70 percent say they've never seriously considered leaving the ministry.[6]

While no pastor goes seeking stress or burnout, it often comes with the territory. A high rate of burnout and stress among pastors is why we're focusing a significant portion of this book on this problem and tackling it from different perspectives.

What a pastor does, the hours he keeps and the raw side of human nature constantly expose him to the possibilities of stress and burnout. He's at risk every day, and he must continually apply preventative measures to his inner world to keep himself spiritually and emotionally healthy. Should the malady strike, he must recognize and treat the first symptoms. If he suffers a full-blown attack, he must use all the remedies of faith and emotional health he so often prescribes for persons in his congregation.

Though a pastor may not be able to avoid his own tensions, pressures and anxieties, he can choose his responses. And though he needs in-depth relationships to minister to people who feel tortured by a hundred kinds of brokenness, he can learn from the experiences of others in their broken places how to expand his own soul.

AN INTERVIEW WITH ARCHIBALD HART

In the following conversation, Archibald Hart, former dean of the Graduate School of Psychology at Fuller Seminary, offers a unique take on helps for the prevention, diagnosis, prescription and restoration of stress and burnout among pastors. Known for his research on depression, anxiety, stress, sexuality and the hazards of ministry, Hart is uniquely qualified to address these issues.

London/Wiseman: You've been leading a crusade to help pastors understand, prevent and recover from burnout. Talk to us about the basic relationship between adrenaline and stress.

Hart: "Postadrenaline depression" seems to be the most descriptive term I've found. Nearly everyone has some firsthand experience of this physical condition following an unusually heavy demand on the human system. Most pastors should expect it on Monday, after a demanding Sunday when they have a long, continuous and heavy adrenaline drain.

London/Wiseman: Is that the same as Monday-morning gloom?

Hart: Yes, the same kind of drain happens to pastors, speakers, athletes, salesmen, politicians, doctors and many other professions after they charge themselves up for a big event. After doing their best and pushing hard, they have a significant letdown—a discomforting depression. That makes Monday tough for pastors.

London/Wiseman: What causes those depressed feelings?

Hart: It's a biological reaction in the aftermath of being revved up. Much of ministry requires a lot of adrenaline. With preaching, for example, if you're going to keep people awake, you'd better have a lot of energy going.

London/Wiseman: Then you think it's a physical problem rather than an emotional or spiritual problem?

Hart: It's an overuse of the system of energy that crashes suddenly on Monday morning and puts the body into short-term depression. It's the body saying, "I need to rest. I need to recover. I need time for rejuvenation."

London/Wiseman: If it's physical, why do so many pastors whip themselves like it's a spiritual problem?

Hart: I wish I knew. I guess that is the reason I'm on this soapbox to free pastors from guilt over what's often a natural situation. They mistakenly see it as spiritual—that "Satan is getting me, and my ministry wasn't good yesterday." But often, it's simply a lack of understanding of adrenaline management.

London/Wiseman: Or maybe a gift from God calling us to replenish, to slow down and to regroup.

Hart: That's it. I really think this system is designed as part of God's intelligent creation to facilitate the healing process within our bodies. If we scorn that process, it's to our own peril, because the consequences of ignoring those calls by the body for rejuvenation will invariably increase the likelihood of burnout and stress.

Monday—A Bad Day Off
London/Wiseman: Let's share a scenario from our own pastoral practice. We often didn't take Monday off. We worked through those Monday-morning glooms by about noon, and then we could have a positive week ahead—ready to go. Does that fit in with your idea?

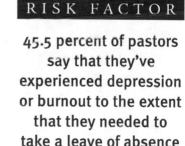

RISK FACTOR

45.5 percent of pastors say that they've experienced depression or burnout to the extent that they needed to take a leave of absence from ministry.

Hart: That works, providing you didn't go full speed on Monday.

I advise pastors to work on Mondays, but to use that day to do low-energy or routine activities. It's the time to tidy your desk, throw out the trash or do some filing. I worry about your term "ready to go." If you mean low-exertion activities, I am for it.

London/Wiseman: What should pastors avoid?

Hart: It's not a time to pick a fight, go hassle those who annoy you, make a critical decision or deal with difficult budget problems. If you get your adrenaline up again, you may feel all right, but you'll rob your body of rest and recuperation.

London/Wiseman: What does that say to thousands of pastors who traditionally take Monday off?

Hart: I recommend a day off later in the week—maybe Thursday or Friday—when energy is good, you feel alive and you can give your family quality time for bonding and recreation.

London/Wiseman: Many pastors faithfully take Monday off, thinking they're doing a good thing for themselves and their families. But too often pastors can't give their families all of themselves on Monday because they're too preoccupied with how the weekend went at church.

Hart: Many pastors' wives tell me they get out of the house on Monday. They say, "I split. I don't want to be around him."

London/Wiseman: What are the symptoms in this heavy adrenaline draw?

Hart: You're irritable. You have little patience. You want to be quiet. You don't want to talk. You don't want to be with anyone. You're not good at communication.

London/Wiseman: What a bad deal for the pastor's wife, who only gets time from her husband on Monday.

Hart: Exactly. That is exactly what scores of pastors give their spouses on Monday. If that's the only time they give their wives, it's not quality time, and it's not adequate to build a good marriage.

London/Wiseman: Do you think a clear correlation exists between Monday-morning doldrums and troubled pastors' marriages?

Hart: I am afraid so. And it seems worse among pastors who take ministry very seriously. It seems that our evangelical world is adrenaline dependent and driven. We're committed to the Great Commission, and that means lots of work for pastors. Yet somehow we've lost sight of the importance of being able to rest in Christ. Christ is our Sabbath rest, and we must learn not to usurp His work—only to be a servant to it.

Distinctions Between Stress and Burnout

London/Wiseman: That leads naturally to our next question. Is there a difference between stress and burnout?

Hart: Yes, they are two different conditions and experiences.

Stress is primarily a biological phenomenon: too much adrenaline and too much pressure. You're on high and using too much energy to perform certain functions. You have too many deadlines. And you're often overcommitted. Stress is the loss of fuel and energy that often produces panic, phobic and anxiety-type disorders.

In someone going through a stressful time, the body is in an emergency mode. So cholesterol goes up, blood pressure goes up, the heartbeat goes up, and hands get colder. This accelerated wear and tear on the body can lead to stomach ulcers or high blood pressure. It can clog your arteries and put you on the road to heart disease.

The stressed individual is characterized by overengagement, and his emotions become overreactive. Stress may kill you prematurely, and then you won't have enough time to finish what you started.

London/Wiseman: How is stress different from burnout?

Hart: Burnout is much more of an emotional response. In burnout, the victim becomes demoralized and knows things aren't going right. People aren't affirming him. He begins to lose the vision he had for his ministry. He loses hope. A burning out disengages from the main task. And a state of crushing discouragement—almost despair—sets in. Demoralization is a good way to summarize it.

London/Wiseman: Many pastors live with feelings of helplessness and hopelessness every day. Some live that way all their lives.

Hart: It's very difficult. Think of the misery for the sufferer: "I no longer care. I no longer feel like I once did. My horizons are closing in. My heart is numb. It's difficult to love anymore."

For pastors, this process often comes about when the victim has no adequate emotional support, no one to talk with. It happens when he's alone or even cut off from people who could help. Then he turns inward because he thinks he has to be strong and not share his problems with anyone else. That's burnout.

London/Wiseman: Where does it lead?

Hart: Stress and burnout both lead to the same place—depression. Stress and burnout just take you there by different routes.

Four *As*: Arrogance, Addiction, Aloneness, Adultery

London/Wiseman: Do stress and burnout lead a pastor to errat-
ic behavior?

Hart: Yes, they do. A Harvard Medical School specialist identi-
fies four *As* in the secular world that I think I see at work in the
Christian world.

The first is *arrogance*, where the pastor says "I can make it,
and I can do it myself; I don't need anyone else." And that person begins to make his own rules.

The second is an adventurous *addiction*, where the person
becomes taken up—excited and energized—by what he's doing.

The third is *aloneness.* That's the point where the pastor is at
risk for depression because he cuts himself off from other people.

And the fourth is *adultery*, where he begins to see sex as the
only thing that can give a real kick. He turns to sex to make up
for the sense of loss in his life.

London/Wiseman: What a devastating downward spiral! How
can it happen to pastors who live so close to holy things?

Hart: These are consequences of too much stress and burnout.
And ultimately, it *is* a spiritual problem. It has to do with not
keeping a balanced spiritual orientation in your ministry.

Warnings of Stress and Burnout

London/Wiseman: What are the red flags that lead to either
stress or burnout? What signals a pastor that he's on a collision
course with either one?

Hart: For stress, are you getting sick often? This may be a
sign that you're compromising your immune system. You need
to regard stomach problems, ulcers, headaches—any of the

classic stress symptoms that come regularly—as a sign that you're pushing yourself too fast, too hard, and that you're overstressed.

Burnout signs are more subtle. You slowly find yourself beginning to hate the telephone. You begin to avoid people. You go into a panic whenever there's a new problem. You lose confidence in yourself. And you often become narrowly focused on petty issues.

London/Wiseman: Can you illustrate that last one?

Hart: Yes, I have a graphic illustration. One pastor in advanced stages of burnout would go to his office on the second floor of the church building, overlooking a parking lot that's next to a supermarket. He'd sit there for hours looking out the window to see if he could catch people parking in the church lot and going to the supermarket. Keep in mind that the church wasn't having services and had no need for the parking spaces. When people dared to park on church property, he'd run down the stairs and angrily tell them to move their cars. We see how petty it is. We call it the fetishization of tasks.

London/Wiseman: So how do pastors deal with this?

Building a Support System

Hart: When facing stress or burnout, I think a pastor needs to resist overloading his family for a solution. Most marriages simply can't take these pressures. I think a pastor needs a support system outside his family. Then when he's with his family, he's not solely dependent on them to provide him with emotional sustenance, spiritual support and healing. The family needs to have some idea of what's going on, but they can't be the sole support of a husband-father in difficulty.

London/Wiseman: What do pastors' wives tell you about this issue?

Hart: They say, "He dumps on me. I dread the moment he comes through the door because I know what's going to happen. He doesn't want to listen to my problems. He doesn't want to hear about the kids—good or bad. He thinks it's all petty stuff. So I have to sit there and receive all that dumping."

London/Wiseman: Where can the pastor get the support he needs?

Hart: He needs to build an adequate support system—preferably with peers—where he can turn for nurture to share his hurt, to open his soul and to unburden himself. When pastors bear one another's burdens, they can find the healing that Christ can bring.

Suggestions for Learning to Live with Your Profession

Archibald Hart helps us see that pastors need pace and balance for spiritual and emotional health. Pastoral counselor John A. Sanford speaks of the advice his father-in-law physician gave him, "Every man must learn to live with his profession."[7] In his book *Ministry Burnout,* Sanford develops this idea when he advises a pastor to think of his work as that of a long-distance runner who can't overexpend himself by running the first part of the race at a pace he can't maintain.[8]

Ministry today certainly demands more from pastors than they've ever known before. But pastors must manage and balance these demands to lead their churches and to proclaim the power of the gospel to society. Maybe these are the best of times

Ministry today certainly demands more from pastors than they've ever known before.

and the worst of times—best because we have to rethink so much, and worst because the changing demands come so rapidly that we find them hard to respond to.

In protecting yourself against burnout and stress, seek to be your best self and to do your best work. But never live with the burden of an artificial persona. Being someone you're not takes way too much energy. This burden dramatically increases stress. It's far more healthy to try to live up to your absolutely best true self at all times. The people you lead will welcome such reality; surely God is pleased with the way He made you.

Why not embark on a lifelong pilgrimage of wholehearted adventure in the pastorate? It might make you good at avoiding stress and burnout. Here's a list of first steps to consider.

Rethink Your Day Off

Monday may not be the best day off. If you work Monday, get a slow start into your week and do light work. At least for one day per week, be half as good to yourself as you've been to your congregation. One of the mystics advised, "Remember, you hold your body and nervous system in trust from God, and you must treat His property well." God approves of your taking care of His servant, and it is a good investment in your future.

This simple adjustment might provide colossal improvements in your family in just a week or a month. Everyone gains—your spouse, your children, your church and yourself.

Welcome Your Spouse into Prevention

Your wife may see solutions to your trials, but she might not offer them because she thinks you'll ignore or scorn her suggestions. Listen to your wife and your children. Begin to view your marriage and family as an energy source that can enrich your whole life. Then you'll see the most important people in your life as something significantly different than another series of oppressive obligations.

Reach Across Isolation

You may be isolated from your peers by either geography or theology, so you have to reach across these boundaries intentionally for friendship and support. Or you may be a loner by disposition. Either way, your isolation is real, and it increases your chances of stress and burnout. Successful ministers can't be lone rangers. You need others and they need you. If you don't have some sort of ministerial association in your area for mutual support, get together with a few other pastors and start a group that meets regularly.

Take Charge of Your Prevention or Recovery

Just as no one else will get you to a doctor for pain in your side or a dentist for pain in your jaw, no one else is likely to take drastic steps in dealing with your burnout or stress. You alone control the action.

One pastor wrote of his bold remedial action for a less stressful future:

> I've been battling this emotional stress for eight years, and I've finally decided to make some changes in my lifestyle and deal with it. I'll be undergoing a complete physical checkup next week; I've begun a diet to lose some excess weight; and I've recently started to walk three days a week for exercise. I'm even trying to rotate my daily schedule. My next step is to seek counseling from a Christian agency as I contemplate a change in pastorates or maybe even a career change at 58 years of age.

Confront Your Addictions

An addiction is any fixation of your mind or body that commands so much attention that normal functioning isn't possible and you neglect your spiritual development. Don't allow yourself to use ministry as a narcotic to keep from developing personal relationships, especially in your marriage or your family.

Limit the Number of Clinging Vines

Every church has at least one person—many have several—that therapists describe as needing maintenance counseling. These are people who don't have the emotional or spiritual energy to live life on their own. Some of them might be able to exist on their own strength, but for their own reasons they want to cling to you, the pastor. While many of these clinging individuals may never be strong or able to walk alone, emotionally you simply can't carry too many of them at one time. The greatest danger is that you could become like them. If you allow the load to get too heavy, you'll become stressed or burned out instead of a needy person becoming whole.

Get Back to Doing What You Want to Do

Could it be that your stress comes from dreading or even resisting some phase of your ministry? Most pastors could use more satisfaction and less obligation. It sounds strange to say that you should do what you want to do when there's so much that has to be done. But the categories "urgent" and "essential" are difficult dimensions to sort out in ministry. You need to understand the difference. By doing the essentials like preaching, teaching and giving pastoral care, you can get past the urgent pressing demands to the more satisfying achievements of influencing people in life-changing ways.

YOUR   CHALLENGE

SEEK GOD'S GUIDANCE FOR BALANCE

Though it sounds mystical, it's still true that God guides surrendered wills and Christ-centered thinking. By close association with Him, with your peers and with spiritually aware laypeople, you can find your way through the thicket of overloads. While you may not be able to do a whole lot less, you can ask God to help you balance your life. No datebook, time management seminar or pastoral strategy book can do the work for you. And it's doubtful that you can do it for yourself, or you already would have.

Finding balance is the key to avoiding stress and burnout. As United States Senate Chaplain Lloyd J. Ogilvie says,

> I've never known a person to have a nervous breakdown doing what the Lord wills. He never asks us to do more than He is willing to provide strength for us to do. He does not guide us into burnout.[9]

R E N E W A L   S T R A T E G I E S

LEARN TO LIVE WITH YOUR PROFESSION

✓ Rethink your day off.
✓ Welcome your spouse into prevention.
✓ Reach across isolation.
✓ Take charge of your prevention or recovery.
✓ Confront your addictions.
✓ Limit the number of clinging vines.
✓ Get back to doing what you want to do.

A Personal Word from H. B. L.

TAKE A VACATION AND ENJOY IT!

What are you doing for vacation this year?

The last time I returned from a week away, it occurred to me that when I was a pastor for three decades, I didn't really vacation much. This vacation was wonderful. I swam, ate, shopped, read, ate, spent time with family, fellowshipped, ate, did some introspection, planned, ate and determined I would do more of this in days to come.

I regret those years of not truly getting away. Instead of taking a real vacation, I kind of popped in and out of time off. I'd interrupt our family times to perform a wedding or funeral. Or I'd use my allotted days to preach at a youth camp or another church. When the summer ended, I was often more weary than when it began. In short, I robbed my family of valuable time together.

I still find it difficult to let down totally. I call the office a lot, bug the staff too often and find myself very restless during the first few days away. But when this recent vacation came to an end, I was ready to do some heavy relaxing. One day I'll get it right.

My heartfelt encouragement to you: Do as I say and not as I did. Treat yourself and your family fairly. Make the most of those opportunities to get away for refreshment, retooling and renewal. You'll be a better servant-shepherd if you do. If you don't, you will pay a price. Guaranteed.

Remember that the Lord "gives strength to the weary and increases the power of the weak" (Isa. 40:29).

CHAPTER EIGHT

HELP AND HEALING FOR WOUNDED HEALERS

A CONVERSATION WITH BOB AND SANDY SEWELL

- 56 percent of pastors regularly take off one day each week; 21 percent say that they do not get any days off.[1]
- 63 percent of pastors indicate that they do not receive sufficient vacation time each year.[2]
- 92 percent of parishioners say that their pastor took a vacation in the past year.[3]
- 49 percent of pastors say that their favorite means of relaxing, escaping and releasing—taking care of themselves—is doing leisure activities such as reading, watching TV, seeing movies or listening to music; 21 percent get active with exercise or sports to escape.[4]
- 91 percent of pastors feel very satisfied about being in ministry; 75 percent say they want to stay in ministry.[5]

A church we know well wanted to become as effective now as it was 25 years ago. So they asked us to serve as consultants for a few months. They called a loving, capable pastor—a second-career graduate of a Bible college. They seemed willing to try everything we suggested to improve pastoral relationships.

This consultation started where it should—with a challenge to lay leaders to take full responsibility for implementing 1 Thessalonians 5:12-13 *(THE MESSAGE)*:

> We ask you to honor those leaders who work so hard for you, who have been given the responsibility of urging and guiding you along in your obedience. Overwhelm them with appreciation and love!

That's what this church did—and did well. They upgraded their parsonage, increased the financial package and committed to fund every self-care effort the pastor requested. They refurbished the pastor's office, added a generous increase in the budget for continuing education and promised to support an annual one-week study retreat. They even planned a year ahead for appropriate celebrations for pastor appreciation day, the minister's anniversary for coming to this church and for the pastor's family's birthdays and anniversaries.

As we thanked the lay leaders of this church for their loving effort, one thoughtful man with a troubled expression on his countenance asked if he could speak. With tears running down his cheeks, he asked, "Does anyone speak to pastors about their part of the honoring instruction from Scripture?"

That was a new idea we'd never thought to consider.

He continued, "Sometimes our church reminds me of a dysfunctional extended family. I think we're eager to avoid past mistakes and establish healthy relationships with our new minister.

From our interviews with him, I believe we have convincing evidence that our new spiritual leader is a great match for our congregation. And I think we all want to do better in pastoral relationships. He's already restored a hope for the future of this church in us and he hasn't even moved here yet."

Then a Mount Vesuvius erupted with tears and sighs of anguish as he continued, "Does anyone ever say to pastoral leaders that in order to qualify to receive the honor the apostle Paul describes in 1 Thessalonians 5:12-13, it requires hard work and taking spiritual responsibility for ordering and guiding the people of God in obedience?"

As the dialogue went on, it was evident that this church found it hard to honor former pastors. And some of their reasons were legitimate.

In 20 years, the church had had several pastors. Some didn't know how to work. Worse yet, some didn't provide spiritual leadership. One pastor, who had no previous experience, had a wife who was ready to make war on any issue—and did. She blamed her outrageous conduct on her nationality and her high-strung mother.

Another pastor brought four family members into paid staff positions and wondered why people in the church considered such nepotism a problem.

Yet another pastor was so enamored by computers that he never had time to provide even the most basic kinds of pastoral care.

Still another excused himself from supervising the staff he hired by saying he wanted to be a spiritual adviser rather than a supervisor. He turned supervision over to three lay leaders who didn't know how to do it. Chaos prevailed. The pastor soon left, the staff members were bruised for life, and the lay leaders faced the no-win situation in the congregation as gossip and misunderstanding spread like wildfire.

One pastor frequently called the flock of God apathetic because individuals wouldn't volunteer for assignments recruited from the pulpit on Sunday mornings during the worship service. Meanwhile, one staff member didn't put in a full day's work in four years; the mood "why should we work if he won't" prevailed. One lay leader observed, "Since our pastor believed we were apathetic, we came to believe it ourselves." Little did the pastor realize that many apparently apathetic people will become enthusiastic participants when challenged with a great cause.

If you think these lay leaders were exaggerating, discount what they said by 50 percent. After that math, doesn't it seem they had a point that needs the attention of pastors everywhere? It's grossly unfair to claim that our source of stress comes from the church and built-in pressures of ministry when sometimes it's a case of unusually bad judgment on our part.

ON THE VERGE OF BURNOUT

So much of a church's effectiveness hinges on the soul burden and hard work of the pastor. Both ability and effort are as important in ministry as in any other vocational field. But the soul burden comes from really seeing God's vision for the congregation He entrusts us to lead, listening for His voice and looking squarely at the opportunities of this particular congregation.

Pastoring also requires a realistic view of your assignment. No congregation in the world is ideal in an ultimate sense. Feeling overworked, misassigned, overwhelmed or underappreciated takes energy—a lot of energy—that you instead should be using to achieve the main task.

Pastoring requires a realistic view of your assignment.

If your inner response to an assignment is less than what it needs to be, you need to do something to get spiritually healthy to serve this congregation. Try a reality check. Are your feelings of fatigue and depression based on the actual situation? If so, reducing your load, sleeping well for a few nights or taking time away may revive your tired soul. If the feelings don't change after these attempts at rest and recuperation, you probably have the start-up virus of burnout. That calls for outside help. Get it promptly.

RISK FACTOR

63 percent of pastors indicate that they do not receive sufficient vacation time each year.

Though few ministers are lazy, sometimes a sort of ministry mesmerism takes place when we don't know what to do next. So we don't do anything next. A kind of ministry paralysis happens.

HELP, HOPE AND HEALING FROM TWO WOUNDED HEALERS

All these questions about healthy relationships of honor, affection, hard work and realistic expectations are the raw materials that can make for a well-rounded, satisfying ministry—or that can create more debilitating stress and painful dysfunction.

In the following conversation, Bob and Sandy Sewell offer many suggestions on how to creatively overcome some of the stresses that can lead to burnout. The Sewells themselves are wounded healers who established SonScape Ministries in Woodland Park, Colorado, to share their own discoveries of healing, grace and restoration. Their ministry has become a sanctuary and beginning-again place for weary, worn-out pastors.

The Sewells' Personal Experience

London/Wiseman: You started your ministry—SonScape Re-Creation Ministries, as a result of your own burnout. How did the burnout process start for you?

Sandy: We actually began to see burnout signs in ourselves like withdrawal, depression, boredom with ministry and spiritual emptiness. We realized something had to happen to change our way of life or we'd become much like the casualties we'd seen around us.

Bob: It felt like we were traveling on a fast freeway with no off-ramps. It seemed that the only way was to keep going in our frenzy or crash.

London/Wiseman: What happened next?

Bob: We were desperate and looking for help. About that time we came across Dr. Louis McBurney's book *Every Pastor Needs a Pastor,* which spoke to our needs. We checked out his ministry and realized we needed to spend time with him. So we registered for a two-week, intensive therapy retreat at his center at Marble, Colorado. Our experience there started our healing process.

Sandy: McBurney asked questions like, "If you knew you could do anything for God that you wanted and knew you wouldn't fail, what would you do?" He opened doors for us to think in new ways about ourselves in ministry. Soon we realized that our deepest desire was to help pastors and their spouses find renewal and adventure in their work for God. That's how SonScape started.

London/Wiseman: To use Henri Nouwen's powerful term, you are "wounded healers" with a heart to help pastors and their spouses find restoration and new focus for ministry.

Bob: That's it. Sandy and I know the stress and the struggles from firsthand experience. So we wanted to help others in the ways we'd been helped.

London/Wiseman: Talk more about the events leading up to your burnout.

Bob: When my burnout was taking place, Howard Hendricks looked over his desk at me one day and said, "If you don't do what you're professing and teaching others to do, you're a spiritual con artist." I think that as we continually give out when our inner reservoir is dry and empty, we become spiritual con artists, as we call people to spiritual exercises that no longer matter much to us.

London/Wiseman: Con artists—that's pretty strong language.

Bob: It's strong language, but that's exactly what I was becoming as I talked to others about a full life in God while I was empty—dangerously empty.

London/Wiseman: While we recommend your ministry to pastors, many will never have opportunity to participate in a week-long retreat. Would you share some practical ways to prevent ministerial burnout or what to do for recovery of a full-blown case of burnout? What self-help prevention strategy can you offer a stressed pastor? What commonly causes burnout?

Symptoms of Burnout

Bob: Spiritual dryness or emptiness is probably the most common—we see it over and over. Many victims live in a state of denial. Many spend their days doing irrelevant tasks because they can't see anything to do that will make a difference. Some wait until too late to get help and face the consequences this burnout behavior causes for the rest of their lives.

London/Wiseman: So, that's the symptom of burnout. Tell us what you think the root causes of burnout are among pastors.

Bob: There are almost as many causes as there are people. Veteran warriors tire of fighting the same old battles year after year. New recruits become disenchanted when they realize they're expected to baby-sit stagnant churches. Some pastors try to do too much without sufficient resources. Some discover that ministry isn't a cushy profession where people do whatever the pastor wants.

Others get to the place where they can't stand the intense emotional demands that come from representing Christ at the bedside of a dying leukemia patient at 3:00 P.M. and then the same day officiating at the wedding of a wonderful young couple at 6:30 P.M.; or when they have to referee conflict between two or three outspoken board members in a discussion group and be forced to serve the same people Communion on the next Sunday.

While recent surveys of pastoral satisfaction seem to be up, 4 in 10 pastors across the country say they doubt their call; 3 in 10 say they think about leaving the ministry; 10 percent say they're depressed some or all of the time; 40 percent report being depressed or worn out some of the time; and 76 percent say they're either overweight or obese.[6]

Obviously pastors have a lot of problems. And every pain is a potential reason for severe burnout.

London/Wiseman: This must break your heart.

Bob: Yes. People admire some pastors who fall as stalwart spiritual giants. But other failing pastors take up adolescent behavior. Some do stupid, destructive, sinful things like having affairs.

Others divorce loyal, loving spouses. Meanwhile we lose many of their children from the kingdom of God because of the strange behavior of their parents. What started out so grand and lofty turns to brokenness.

London/Wiseman: So, burnout to the spiritual and emotional part of life is like cancer—it can start anywhere—and no one's sure why some pastors can cope with more stress than others.

Bob: That's right. We've had clergy couples come to SonScape who had significantly less trauma in their lives and churches than many pastors have all their lives, but they came burned out and in need of a lot of help. Other pastors never think of seeking help. They seem to be getting along well in their ministries— they're happy, can deal with stress and can't see what the problem is with others.

London/Wiseman: Does that mean that the apparently weaker pastor isn't having real problems and doesn't need the best help he can get?

Bob: No, his problems are real and must be treated. And we're ready to help the stronger pastor should he call for help. I guess we have to admit that some people have a higher stress threshold than others.

London/Wiseman: Strength, stamina and stress thresholds are as different from person to person as blood pressure readings and weight are different.

Bob: Right. We need to treat and heal burnout regardless of the source. And no one except the person involved can evaluate how intense the pain really is.

London/Wiseman: We've talked in this book about what causes pastors to be overstressed. While we don't need to review those reasons here, it would be helpful if you'd briefly give your perspective on the causes of stress and burnout. For example, do you think congregations are responsible for pastoral burnout, or is it something inside the pastor?

Bob: It can start from either source.

Sandy: I'm afraid some congregations think they can treat spiritual leaders shabbily and then go out and "hire us another preacher." I'm sure that attitude displeases Christ, creates suspicion among those they try to hire and ultimately makes for a very flawed church.

London/Wiseman: It's sad and wrong, but many churches see themselves as the pastor's employer.

Some pastors pride themselves in never taking time off—a kind of self-destructive superman approach.

Sandy: I don't know where that employer-employee notion comes from. Maybe all of us, including pastors, are confused about whether the minister is a professional, like a physician, and essentially his own boss, or the head of a religious organization that provides benefits like secular corporations.

London/Wiseman: Neither concept is really satisfactory, is it? The pastor is essentially the spiritual leader of a congregation and should have whatever time away he needs to fulfill that ministry to the people of God.

Bob: I wonder if the employer idea isn't encouraged when pastors make a big deal of how many days of vacation they haven't taken. That's kind of a "I've given up my own needs and my rights so I can suffer for Jesus with you" mentality. I know pastors who pride themselves in never taking time off—a kind of self-destructive superman approach.

London/Wiseman: We wonder if church leaders know that 1 Thessalonians 5:12-13 *(THE MESSAGE)* says, "We ask you to honor those leaders who work so hard for you, who have been given the responsibility of urging and guiding you along in your obedience. Overwhelm them with appreciation and love!"

What a privilege and an awesome responsibility. I don't think I've ever heard of a pastor who has been overwhelmed by love and appreciation from his congregation—have you?

Sandy: Part of the problem also comes from pastors who've never thought about fulfilling their part of that verse: "leaders who work so hard for you." Some don't take seriously "the responsibility of urging and guiding you along in your obedience."

London/Wiseman: Do you think some pastors actually neglect their God-given responsibility to care for people's souls?

Bob: Misunderstandings occur on both sides—pastors and laypeople alike. Even many pastors who give their energies to the wrong things eventually suffer burnout from spinning their wheels to get nowhere.

Victims of Burnout
London/Wiseman: Who does a burned-out pastor hurt more—his family or the church he leaves?

Bob: Clergy burnout hurts everybody.

London/Wiseman: That's important to realize—that since everyone gets hurt, we need to avoid or heal burnout at any cost. What about the need for friends? Do burned-out pastors have friends in their church setting?

Bob: Often those who suffer most appear to be friendless. I often compare their situation to that of a tree that's been cut down, which doesn't seem to matter to anyone. In the congregation or in the denomination, the idea is to clean up the fallen branches and then move on. Usually that means finding another pastor and getting past this weakling.

London/Wiseman: Everyone needs someone to hold him accountable. Every pastor needs someone to come alongside him and say, "Have you thought about this? Have you questioned yourself about why you did what you did? Let me make a suggestion or two."

Scripture is clear: "Refuse good advice and watch your plans fail; take good counsel and watch them succeed" (Prov. 15:22, *THE MESSAGE*).

Burnout Issues

Bob: Some pastors think every aspect of ministry should always have the same priority. The truth is that sometimes ministry needs to be 90 percent pastoral care and other times 90 percent pulpit preparation.

London/Wiseman: We talk about that shifting-priority issue all the time in pastors' conferences. Apparently most pastors work hard, but some work at the wrong things.

Bob: That's one of the burnout issues. How can a pastor refocus to be more productive and by doing so find more satisfaction in his work for Christ?

London/Wiseman: What about change? Some pastors seem locked in to a time capsule.

Sandy: Attitude about change is one of the key burnout issues. Most of us like change we propose and hate change others suggest.

Bob: This statement on change from some unknown source helps me keep sane:

> Our great grandfathers rode horse-drawn carriages—afraid
> to ride trains.
> Our grandfathers rode trains—afraid to ride automo-
> biles.
> Our fathers rode automobiles—afraid to ride airplanes.
> Our generation flies in airplanes—afraid to ride horses.

Changes that result from transitions and losses produce a whole truckload of stress. Transitions include many things; but the most obvious are moves to new assignments, changes at home, care for an aging parent and tragedies like the death of a child, divorce, death of a spouse or death of a parent.

London/Wiseman: That kind of stress happened to me when my father died. Two days after he died, we flew to Oklahoma City for the funeral and burial. Then I jumped on a plane and went on about my work at another pastors' conference. I told myself I was strong and could handle it. But I couldn't. One night after the lights were out and I was trying to get to sleep, a wave of emotions came over me. This man I loved more than anyone in the world and who loved me dearly was gone. I was his only child. I hadn't even given him enough of my attention to stop my world for a few days to mourn his passing and celebrate his life. I'd never faced a transition like this one, and I didn't know how to react, not only concerning his memory, but how to ensure my own well-being and healing. I sure needed something like SonScape that week—maybe even now.

Bob: A lot of burnout gets intense during those transitions—we suffer loss and realize life will never be the same again.

London/Wiseman: How can a pastor help his congregation understand and accept his need for time away? How can he tell his key leaders, "I need to have more time and help to keep my soul healthy and well so I can serve better and longer." It's really an investment a congregation can make—right?

Bob: I think wellness and wholeness should be part of the initial interview process so it becomes an established priority before the pastor arrives in a new assignment. I don't think laypeople understand what a pastor needs because they've never been responsible for the spiritual care of an entire congregation. Most laypeople don't have a clue because they've never experienced it.

Prevention of Burnout: Self-Care
London/Wiseman: So let's explore some possible solutions for pastoral burnout.

Bob: Two concepts can make a world of difference—self-care and teaching churches to do ministry care.

Self-care starts with an awareness that effective ministry requires wellness of spirit, soul and body. Nearly every pastor needs some improvement in at least one of these categories.

London/Wiseman: The term "self-care" sounds a little self-serving for the pastor who believes he's called to provide selfless care for others.

Bob: Self-care isn't useless talk about pastors working harder than anyone else. Nearly every congregation has someone who works longer hours than the pastor—so that argument gets us nowhere. Rather, congregations need to recognize that the minis-

ter's work is unique and that the pastor must learn to recharge when he's depleted emotionally or spiritually.

London/Wiseman: Give us an example or two.

Self-care is an investment in the future of ministry.

Bob: The executive of a corporation might quickly recover from his stress by playing a few rounds of golf that get him out of the office for a few hours. But the pastor may need a round of quiet solitude to clear his head, examine his soul or refocus his perspective.

The construction worker may need a vacation to rest his tired muscles and get over the stress his boss causes him. But the pastor may need three days of hard physical labor to move him away from the world of relationships and study to help him understand the worlds of his congregation.

London/Wiseman: So self-care is an investment in the future of ministry, isn't it?

Bob: Yes, both for the minister and for the church. Here's its rationale and how it works: Self-care is a wonderful gift a minister gives to the church, because it results in the minister's becoming a whole person. It replenishes the deepest reservoirs of the pastor's spirit so that he can better serve the people of God.

The best model we have for this is Jesus. As busy as He was and as short as His earthly ministry was, He still gave us a self-care model. Think about how many times He invited His disciples to go to a quiet place for rest and recuperation. He took time to withdraw from the crowd, to pray, to even get away from the inner circle of disciples. How often did He leave the crowd to be with friends at Lazarus's home?

No one can prescribe specific self-care for someone else. It will be unique for each person: for one, fishing at the creek; for another, getting lost in a quiet library; for another, a course in computers or oil painting at a nearby college; and for another, staring into space in absolute solitude. The trick is making sure that it's being done.

London/Wiseman: How else can a pastor keep himself or herself spiritually healthy?

Bob: We think a pastor should establish a practice of getting away for a whole day once a month to a quiet place where he does nothing but read the Bible and think about personal spiritual growth. This isn't time away from ministry but time that feeds ministry. Without feeding our faith, we become church managers rather than spiritual leaders.

London/Wiseman: We'd add writing, reading, praying, waiting, listening and letting ideas germinate to your list.

Bob: I also recommend that every pastor make a serious commitment to a weekly Sabbath for himself. I believe God made the human body and mind to work on seven-day cycles.

Keeping the Sabbath might be hard to do, but it's incredibly beneficial. It's stepping into God's plan as a response to how He made us. Scripture's Sabbath commandment isn't an arbitrary requirement but a call to worship, to rest, to change the pace and to refocus. It's a call to be alone with God one day a week so we can make sense of all the other needs. A pastor can choose another day besides Sunday.

London/Wiseman: The Sabbath renewal idea needs much more attention than it is presently receiving among pastors and congregations. A serious commitment to return to the Sabbath might be part of the answer we've all been seeking for lowering stress levels among pastors. Philip Yancey raises this issue: "I wonder how much more effective our spiritual leaders would be if we encouraged them to take one day a week as a time for reflection, meditation and personal study. I wonder how much more effective our churches would be if we made the pastor's spiritual health— not the pastor's efficiency—our number one priority."[7]

RISK FACTOR

91 percent of pastors feel very satisfied about being in ministry; 75 percent say they want to stay in ministry.

Bob: Vacation time is also important. I wish every congregation could see their pastor's time away as an investment they give themselves. They need to view the pastor's vacation as a time when the minister gets reenergized and senses a new challenge.

I'd like to suggest that a congregation even help with the costs of a vacation when they're able to do so. Maybe a member of the congregation with a cabin or summer home would make that available to the pastor.

Pastors should work on their own sense of balance and rhythms for times away. Then they can explain what they need as a way to educate a decision group, a pastoral relations committee or the congregation.

Sandy: Another important way to encourage a pastor is to fund at least one annual ministry-enrichment experience. Everyone gains from this effort: The pastor feels honored that his congregation wants him to go; the pastor's new insights and skills bless his church; and working on ministry issues with peers often increases his spiritual stamina and energy when he returns.

London/Wiseman: Are there less complicated ways to accomplish this same thing?

Bob: Yes, a pastor can spend a day at a spiritual retreat center or even the sanctuary of his own church or the church of a colleague. One pastor told about a life-changing day when he waited before God for most of a day before the altar of his own church. He said, "Listening in a space where I usually did the talking was a great time of getting closer to the Lord and refocusing my priorities and assumptions."

Prevention of Burnout: Congregational Care
London/Wiseman: What about the ways a congregation can take care of the pastor?

Bob: Congregational care of the pastor is more likely to happen if key laypeople are trained to know the unique strains, as well as the blessings, of being a pastor. For example, most laypeople don't understand how many pastors have a Monday adrenaline loss after a busy Sunday. They have no experience with the constant demands, the frequent role changes, the willingness of parishioners to drop everything emotionally on the pastor. The "ain't it awful" syndrome we hear so often in the church; the peripheral issues that people bring to the pastor; the accumulative load from a thousand tiny parasites, like self-centeredness, control, pride and intolerance—these seem multiplied on Sundays, and they take their toll on many pastors the following day.

London/Wiseman: So it is not just workload that causes burnout?

Bob: More often, it's the combined demand, the accumulation of positive and negative emotions, the rapid transition from weddings to funerals and from hospital emergencies to social contacts. It's the stretch of being an introvert and having to do extrovert things, the stretch of spending time studying when one prefers being with people or vice versa.

London/Wiseman: How can a pastor educate his congregation about these dangers if he's afraid it might seem self-serving?

Bob: If the denominational group or fellowship of independent churches has a district superintendent, a bishop, an area coordinator, an overseer or whatever, the pastor can ask that person to help the local congregation understand that the pastor and the professional staff of a church are more than just employees. They are God-called ministers on a mission in a local congregation. And the more the church meets their needs, the more they'll function inspirationally, lovingly and wholeheartedly.

Sandy: Yes, and that's a big change for some congregations. It's moving from the attitude of "Meet our needs or we're out of here" to "How can we enable you to serve the Lord more effectively?"

London/Wiseman: Pastors who are weary need to hear these comforting words from Scripture as an affirming promise:

> Are you tired? Worn out? Burned out on religion? Come to me. Get away with me and you'll recover your life. I'll show you how to take a real rest. Walk with me and work with me—watch how I do it. Learn the unforced rhythms of grace. I won't lay anything heavy or ill-fitting on you. Keep company with me and you'll learn to live freely and lightly (Matt. 11:28-30, *THE MESSAGE*).

SUGGESTIONS FOR PREVENTING BURNOUT

What can you do if you feel dangerously close to burnout? Here are several ideas:

Check Your Potential for Burnout

Keep track of the symptoms and causes just like you follow your blood pressure readings with your physician. In most occupations burnout usually centers around physical health, overwork, poor organization and/or emotional overload.

If your need is truly emotional, seek help from a counselor, a psychologist or a psychiatrist.

If the problem is physical, seek and follow competent medical help.

However, the issue may be spiritual rather than occupational. One helper of pastors believes clergy burnout is more often than not a crisis of faith because the minister gives too much for too long without continual replenishment. If this describes you, your soul needs tending.

Try Viewing Your Situation from God's Perspective

French author Georges Bernanos says it well:

I've always had a secret kind of a notion that if we could take a God's-eye view of human societies [including family and church], we'd have the key to a good many things we can't understand.[8]

Your problem might look very different if you ask yourself how the situation looks to God.

Model How to Reject the World's Value System

Do yourself and your church a favor by rejecting the values of materialism, consumerism, secularism, cynicism and commercialization of the Church. When the people see the benefits from your example, they're more likely to believe your preaching against the spirit of the world. In the process, everyone gains.

Status quo leads to dry rot and dry rot leads to ceremonial Christianity.

Always Have Something New in Process

Status quo leads to dry rot and dry rot leads to ceremonial Christianity—a frightening reality in too many congregations these days. This kind of situation leads to cancerous boredom that seeps into your call, self-concept and marriage. Soon you'll feel like the eagle that was raised with chickens. Though he was meant to soar, he sees the barnyard as the limits of his life. God needs thousands of pastors who are bored with the chicken coop to fly and soar like eagles.

Refuse to Live at the Lowest Common Spiritual Level

Many longtime churchgoers suffer from a self-chosen spiritual infantilism. They may not have grown a single inch as Christians since five minutes after their conversion. They're spiritually alive, but just barely. If you allow yourself to live at their level or allow them to dominate the life of the church, you'll find the church becoming weaker and weaker.

Commit to Improving Ministry Skills

When you begin your ministry, your minimum skills will probably serve you well. But as the years pass, your abilities need to grow. Update your skills, concepts and the way you do ministry. We all know pastors who live in a time warp—everything about them is nearly what it always was, with the exception of increased weight and age.

Don't Expect Love from Everyone

A few pastors delight in controversy and even encourage an adversarial climate in their churches. Scripture calls the people of God to love, faith, hope and good works. So you want to cultivate a positive atmosphere of acceptance and good will in your church. However, you may be called upon to bear the offense of the gospel. During those times, you may not sense as much love as before because you're being called to discipline, to set things right, to restore order, to confront sin and to defend the weak. The salt Christ wants you to be sometimes stings as it preserves faith in a world covered with ulcers, sores and sinfulness.

Be Realistic About Your Use of Time

Most pastors have no experience in how to plan their workdays, weeks, months or years. Some work too long without adequate breaks for families and rest. Some think they can keep the most leisurely schedule of any person in town but wonder why their preaching and pastoral care never get done. Some have never had experience working without a boss to tell them what needs to be done. And nearly everyone in American culture thinks he's overworked—an idea that sometimes creeps into the thinking of ministers. Often, people who think they're overworked or too busy are simply unorganized.

To avoid burnout, develop a realistic strategy for use of time that works for you. Read books on organization. Visit with veteran pastors who seem to be productive. Find your own pace and work it. Above all, don't expect lay leaders to know how to advise you on the use of your time—not one of them has a job with as many different facets as yours.

Anticipate Consequences of Decisions and Actions

Every decision, every proposal and every activity you undertake will produce a result or response, positive or negative. One big cause of burnout among pastors is the difficult consequences of actions that they could have anticipated earlier.

Don't Be Surprised by Evil and Sin or Their Consequences

Evil and sin are both real and subtle—in high places, low places and in-between places. Evil often shows up at church disguised in Sunday clothes and shows itself at the most inconvenient times. While God forgives sinners, consequences remain after the sinful acts or evil attitudes have been forgiven, forsaken and forgotten. A church may be hindered for years by the consequences of someone's earlier sin. Sin in a church is a lot like malaria: It tends to break out again and again when the conditions are right—or sometimes when the conditions are all wrong.

Consider a Sabbatical or Extended Time Away

Getting your church to consider such an idea needs to start with an attitude change by a decision group, the congregation and you. Changing attitudes may be more a matter of educating than convincing.

The decision group needs specifics about your workload—be factual and show them how you spend your time. Show in detail how the work you usually do will get done while you're away.

List in writing the advantages of an extended period away from your work. Show the benefits to you, your spouse, your children and the church itself.

To avoid misunderstandings, propose a written agreement that you won't look for another pastorate during your sabbatical. Likewise, state in writing that the church won't look for someone else. Agree to stay in your current position at least two years after you return.

Make good pulpit arrangements so the quality of your church doesn't go down while you're away. Keep careful records of what you do on your sabbatical, and share them with the congregation so they understand that this isn't simply a vacation, but a gift of renewal they give themselves.

YOUR CHALLENGE

GOLDEN OPPORTUNITY FOR GREATNESS

Opportunities for true greatness come continually to every pastor in the *being* and *doing* rhythms of service to God, church and humankind.

Scripps Howard newspaper columnist Terry Mattingly clearly understands the connection between who a pastor is (being) and what a pastor does (doing). In an affectionate tribute written at the death of his pastor-father, Mattingly said,

> I'm convinced the main reason stress levels are so high is that so many people—in pews and pulpit—have forgotten that pastors are defined by who they are and what they stand for, not what skills they possess and what tasks they perform.

Later in the same column, he said,

Truth is, I rarely saw my father move mountains. But
I did see him preach, teach, pray and embrace sinners. I
am proud that he was a pastor. I still am.[9]

Your opportunities for *being* come from intimacy with Christ
as He draws people to Himself—sometimes through you. Then
your ministry provides the best seat in the house for what God's
doing through His Church. Other being opportunities come
when your soul encounters truth in Scripture as you prepare for
preaching. And even on those occasional bad days when mistreatment comes, the sweet spirit of Jesus will flow through you
and make you noble and spiritually strong.

More than anything else, your task—no, your life's work—is to
be a person of God. Our churches and our culture place high value
on efficiency and competency. We need both in greater supply. But
unless you know God and help others know Him better, your
attempts at being efficient and competent are worthless. Somehow,
that reality, that need, that value, that priority must become opera-
tional in deep and moving ways in the lives of thousands of pastors
if we're to make a difference in the spiritual future of the world.

Doing can enrich your life, too, as the gospel challenges you—
sometimes requires you—to lofty action. Your assignment as
shepherd of the flock of God gives you the right to ask hard
questions that the Spirit will use as stepping stones to the
human heart. Looking into the eyes of those you love with the
love of the Lord as you serve them Communion is an example of
doing that makes you rich in a way money never could. Another
way is seeing people transformed as a result of your preaching.

Not all in ministry are broken or ready to give up. Like
preferring wellness over surgery in the physical realm, churches
prefer healthy and whole pastors over those who are burning

out. But for those with parched souls and empty reservoirs, hope and help is available. And for those who enjoy good health right now but may face crises in the future, prevention is key.

Self-care, congregational care of the pastor, accountability, honor and time away are all good exercises for building strong ministries and increasing spiritual stamina. Not all ministry is dreary duty—some of it is the most fulfilling work a human being could ever accomplish.

Go for God's best with gusto. He will meet you at the point of your greatest challenge—just like He always does.

R E N E W A L   S T R A T E G I E S

HOW TO PREVENT BURNOUT

✓ Check your potential for burnout.
✓ Try viewing your situation from God's perspective.
✓ Model how to reject the world's value system.
✓ Always have something new in process.
✓ Refuse to live at the lowest common spiritual level.
✓ Commit to improving ministry skills.
✓ Don't expect love from everyone.
✓ Be realistic about your use of time.
✓ Anticipate consequences of decisions and actions.
✓ Don't be surprised by evil and sin or their consequences.
✓ Consider a sabbatical or extended time away.

A Personal Word from H. B. L.

I Pray for You

Each year in September and October I'm active on behalf of pastors to help congregations prepare for Pastor Appreciation Month. I tell the media—radio, print, Internet and television—how extraordinary you are. I do my best to paint an accurate picture of your importance and the pressure you face from a world in moral free fall. I attempt to make the point that the local church—your church—is the instrument God will use to turn our nation around. I will remind the media how blessed we were as a country to have you in your pulpit week after week.

I also pray for you and your family during these unprecedented days:

- That the demands on your time won't threaten your intimacy with God.
- That you'll give adequate attention to your family as you seek to guide people within your congregation.
- That you'll find a colleague to join you in prayer for your community.
- That your preaching and teaching will be courageous and purposeful.
- That the people you lead will respond to your passion and follow you with great enthusiasm.
- That America will wake up and realize that God's call on your life and the message you speak can't be ignored.

CHAPTER NINE

MARGINS: NEW WAYS TO MANAGE YOUR PRIORITIES

A CONVERSATION WITH DR. RICHARD A. SWENSON

- 32 percent of pastors say the first thing they put on their schedule each week is appointments, and nearly 28 percent say meetings; only 13 percent say the first thing they schedule is family time.[1]
- How pastors divide their time on the job: 14 hours planning and attending meeting and services; 13 hours eaching and preaching study and preparation; 9 hours pastoral care, counseling and conflict mediation; 6 hours in personal spiritual development; and 9 hours doing miscellaneous tasks. That leaves only 4 hours for long-range planning, developing leaders and evangelizing.[2]
- Pastors typically start their workdays at 8 A.M. and end them at 6:30 P.M., six days a week.[3]
- 40 percent of pastors say they work more hours each week than they did five years ago.[4]

We asked pastors at a retreat to write one phrase on an index card that describes weariness in ministry—either their own phrase or a phrase about someone they know. The replies came like a big break in a dam:

- cobwebs around my call
- leprosy of boredom
- death of hope
- trivial complaints
- growing gloomy and old before my time
- cynical, sarcastic Christians
- corroded idealism
- silly quarrels about control
- caring too much
- nagging feeling that I was missing something
- destructive self-pity
- no time for what really matters

Others wrote sentences like:

- My fascination for the gospel dried up, so ministry is now all duty and dread.
- My stamina for spiritual issues grew weak, and I'm afraid of the future.
- My feeling about ministry oscillates between disappointment and despair.
- I have an invitation to a new assignment that offers lots of promise and potential, but I chose not to go because I'd be forced to take myself along.
- I have professionalized my ministry so much that I feel dangerous to the people of God.

The discussion that followed lasted for a long time—well into the night—and with such intensity that everyone in the room realized many ministers feel overloaded and believe they're overworked. They're tired. They believe that they're underpaid and unappreciated. They're frustrated by not seeing results.

CAN YOU TURN STRESS POINTS INTO OPPORTUNITIES?

The real question—the biggest question—is if pastors can avoid or eliminate any of the pitfalls. Can we be overcomers? Can we work through our dilemmas back to the heart and soul of our task? Can we turn at least some of what seem to be weariness-producing difficulties into opportunities?

Dr. Richard A. Swenson—author, medical doctor and former professor—answers that final question with a resounding yes.

Margins Defined and Explained

London/Wiseman: Let's start with a definition of "margin." What do you mean when you use that word?

Swenson: That's a good place to start. Margin is something held in reserve for contingencies or unanticipated situations. Margin is the gap between rest and exhaustion, the space between breathing freely and suffocating. It is the leeway we once had between ourselves and our limits.[5]

London/Wiseman: You've also talked about the contrast between margin and marginlessness. Tell us what that means.

Swenson: Marginlessness is not having time to finish the book you are reading on stress; margin is having the time to read it

twice. Marginlessness is the disease; margin is its cure. Marginlessness is fatigue; margin is energy. Marginlessness is hurry;
margin is calm. Marginlessness is culture; margin is countercul-
ture.

London/Wiseman: You must have many people from many different vocational fields ask about these two ideas. How do they
relate to the world in which pastors live and work?

The Universality of Marginlessness

Swenson: Marginlessness is a near universal condition in our
society. So I talk about the need for margins to a lot of occupational groups—teachers, engineers, dentists, lawyers, housewives,
physicians and pastors.

London/Wiseman: So many pastors don't have margins, and
those they serve don't have margins either. Is that an accurate
statement of your conclusion after
these years of research and writing?

Swenson: Yes, exactly. And the no-
margins problem makes pastors'
work much more complex than ever
before. The pastor not only has to
live the details of his life with no
elbow room, but he has to serve with
people who have no margins, who are
seeking to lead others with no margins to come to Christ.

London/Wiseman: Do you have to
make major changes to adapt your
presentation from group to group?

RISK FACTOR

**32 percent of pastors
say the first thing
they put on their
schedule each week is
appointments, and
nearly 28 percent say
meetings; only
13 percent say the first
thing they schedule
is family time.**

Swenson: No, the problem is universal and common. I often have people ask me, "How did you get my calendar, my datebook, my journal or my Palm Pilot?" Being overextended—or "having my plate too full"—is so common in our culture that it's scary. I really don't see how most people could add any more commitments than they already have.

London/Wiseman: How do you account for this new burden?

Swenson: Progress works by giving us more and more of everything faster and faster. As a result, life has become more complex, more overcommitted, more overloaded and more stressful. And Christians aren't exempt. I have deep concerns for the Church because the culture needs the Church to be the Church now more than ever. But sadly, the Church is becoming more like the culture.

Margins and Pastors

London/Wiseman: Why do you think this margin question is so significant to pastors as an occupational subgroup in our society?

Swenson: There are two or three pressing reasons.

The first is the pastor himself.

Another closely related issue is that church members are so busy they don't volunteer as much as they once did. Since someone has to do the work, and because of the lack of volunteers, the tasks usually end up on the pastor's desk. And in frustration and confusion, the pastor starts preaching about apathy and low levels of commitment. Sadly, because the pastor is so convinced of the apathy conclusion, he offers no pastoral care to those who are overwhelmed with the busyness of their lives. The apathetic, overloaded people are true to their cultural frame of reference;

and when a pastor refuses to offer them pastoral care, it's like ignoring someone who has ruined his life with alcohol.

London/Wiseman: What about dysfunctional people with all the problems they bring to pastors? Aren't there more of those kinds of needy people in our time than ever before?

Swenson: Yes, there are many more dysfunctional people. And because not enough helpers exist in secular society, these troubled people often show up at church wanting to discuss their problems with a pastor.

Another issue is the pastor's lofty—but sometimes frighteningly overcommitted—God complex. Often, pastors think they're being godly by overextending themselves, when in fact they're compulsive and driven by something in their background that has little to do with godly qualities. That can keep a minister from saying no to anything anyone asks him to do in church or in the community. That problem of saying no means it is hard for a pastor to set boundaries or limits. As a result, the pastor gets overloaded.

In many minds, the pastor's role—what his job is—has changed since the terrorist attacks on September 11, 2001. The impact of that day could be the start of a great awakening if we do our part to make it happen. Remember, awakenings always start with individuals before they become movements.

London/Wiseman: How do people in supervision, like overseers, bishops and superintendents, view margin? Have you tried any of these ideas on people in those kinds of positions?

Swenson: Some church leaders think this overload argument is just a figment of pastors' imaginations. Others think pastors just aren't able to cut it anymore. One told me off the record,

"Pastors should stop groaning, suck it up and present a better face to the world." Others, however, clearly see the problem and are motivated to help in any way possible.

London/Wiseman: How does a call for margins fit into a pastor's preaching and teaching?

Swenson: It's often a tough, tight fit. While the work of ministry has always been complicated, its demands have increased, change occurs more rapidly, and fewer laypeople are able to help. At the same time, the pastor is often slow to give up ownership of any part of his calendar to anyone. But God won't give any of us more than 24 hours a day. If the demands exceed the day, the pastor needs to guard some activities, but he also needs to let some activities go.

If you lose joy and peace, examine your schedule and see if overload is the cause.

If preaching and teaching are important, the pastor must carve out appropriate space for these activities. If meditation, prayer and rest are important, he must budget space for them.

I've found that joy and peace are fairly good markers. If you lose joy and peace, examine your schedule and see if overload is the cause.

Two Kinds of Stress

London/Wiseman: Whenever we talk to pastors about their use of time, two almost contradictory ideas develop. First is the good kind of time demand, where a pastor is so immersed in ministry that he almost forgets to get tired. Even if there's a pressing deadline to a project and a lot of pressure with it, it's still more enjoyable if it fits his reason for being in ministry.

But the second is the dreaded task—the things he hates to do. Or maybe it's something that frightens or threatens him, that produces an almost crippling stress. This kind of stress seems to go deeper than a good night's sleep or a day off will help.

The first kind of stress is satisfying. The second kind of stress is a thousand times more debilitating.

Swenson: The difference between these two kinds of stress is related to decision control—that's a term we use in stress medicine. That's the idea that if you have a say or some control over what you're doing, it produces a kind of enhanced productivity stress. That's the kind that makes you do better work.

But if you don't have a say, then you feel others are loading your plate with their problems. This is called no-escape stress; and it often leads to damage—physical, emotional, relational, spiritual. You don't want this kind of stress.

London/Wiseman: A lot of the no-escape stress has to do with response to a crisis, doesn't it? The September 11 crisis provides an example where bewildering emotional, spiritual and life-and-death questions were on everyone's minds as the whole nation tried to make sense of the terrorist attack.

The pastor has no control over when someone will die, when a rebellious teen will go to jail or when his own child will act out some destructive behavior. Maybe it's an issue like not having control over a personal financial situation or the need to appear to have a perfect marriage. Things just keep stacking up.

Swenson: That leads us back to why I think margins are so important.

London/Wiseman: How does that work?

Room for God's Teaching Moments

Swenson: Pastors tell me that crises are often highly charged God moments that can provide effective spiritual teaching moments. Issues that could take years to deal with come out in the open in minutes. Then significant changes can take place in a short period of time.

However, if the pastor has his whole life scheduled, then he has no margin for dealing with this kind of crisis. If he's already scheduled at 120 percent of his capacity, he can't care for someone in crisis. Or if he does, he'll rush through it, and in the process, he'll let time rule the situation when, instead, the individual with the need should be the focus.

RISK FACTOR

Pastors typically start their workdays at 8 A.M. and end them at 6:30 P.M., six days a week.

London/Wiseman: Tell us more about how you see your margins concept working in a pastor's life and service to Christ.

Swenson: The idea is simple. A pastor needs to keep his schedule flexible enough so that he can make room for a crisis.

London/Wiseman: Do you mean setting aside a small portion of each day, week or month in reserve for the unexpected—which probably shows up more often than we think?

Swenson: That's one approach. Personally, I like an orderly, well-planned schedule and life just like the next person. I want to be effective and productive in my use of time. But I have to be flexible so that I'm ready to serve in a crisis if God calls.

London/Wiseman: Can you think of an example from Scripture or history?

Jesus' Model of Margins for Ministry

Swenson: The life of Jesus provides a wonderful pattern. He modeled spontaneity of service. Wherever He went, He had time for the person in front of Him. I can't remember one time in Scripture where He told a needy person to take a number or make an appointment.

When we don't make room for margins, the person in front of us is an obstacle we have to get around to get to our next appointment. But what if the person in front of us is the exact expression of ministry God has planned for us next?

Jesus provided a model of caring for the need of the person in front of you.

Inextinguishable Discontent and Comparison

London/Wiseman: You also relate this to the idea of contentment and discontentment.

Swenson: Discontentment has become normalized in our society. Just as soon as we get something we thought we had to have, we're discontent with it. We want something more or bigger or newer or more costly. We live out of the idea that the grass is always greener on the other side of the fence.

In fact, the grass isn't greener. The enemy of our soul has just spray-painted the grass with an attractive green to fool us. We think that when we've reached the threshold where enough is enough, it will be enough. But it's never enough.

London/Wiseman: That happens with pastors in their work. There is too much "bigger than theirs," "more than them" or "more seats in the sanctuary than they have." That comparison/

competition drives a pastor to want more. Then the motivation for ministry gets out of sync with Kingdom values, and contentment becomes nearly impossible.

Swenson: This comparison thing in the Church is really fed by the consumerism of our culture. I doubt that God uses the performance criteria we use.

It's time to say loud and clear that God is pleased with pastors who serve smaller churches in ways God loves and honors.

The Gift of Contentment

London/Wiseman: What message about contentment do pastors—and their people—need to hear?

Swenson: I believe the concept of contentment is key to the future well-being of the Church and to its effectiveness. Three pretty significant scriptural passages inform my thinking about the contentment issue.

The first is Philippians 4:12-13,19:

> I know what it is to be in need, and I know what it is to have plenty. I have learned the secret of being content in any and every situation, whether well fed or hungry, whether living in plenty or in want. I can do everything through him who gives me strength. And my God will meet all your needs according to his glorious riches in Christ Jesus.

Let's consider this idea carefully. The apostle Paul wasn't in some rosy situation from a human or even a cultural point of view. When he wrote these words, he was old, sick, lonely and imprisoned, but he was content because he found himself in God's will. In the will of God he could do anything that God wanted and he could take anything others did to him.

Also, it's my understanding that Paul's choice of the word "secret" means exactly that -a secret from God. So what Paul was saying about contentment wasn't something he just stumbled upon or something his years of experience taught. It wasn't something an old saint shared with him. It wasn't something the culture taught him.

No. His secret was a gift from God—something transcendent.

Paul sought contentment, and God gave him a tremendously valuable secret to carry him through the good times and the not-so-good times. I think there's a great antidote for weariness among pastors here.

The second passage about contentment is Hebrews 13:5:

Keep your lives free from the love of money and be content with what you have, because God has said, "Never will I leave you; never will I forsake you."

The third is 1 Timothy 6:6-9:

But godliness with contentment is great gain. For we brought nothing into the world, and we can take nothing out of it. But if we have food and clothing, we will be content with that. People who want to get rich fall into temptation and a trap and into many foolish and harmful desires that plunge men into ruin and destruction.

These passages are messages for pastors, for the Church and for the culture. If taught clearly and consistently, the biblical message of contentment could revitalize marriages and many pastor-people relationships. It will revolutionize churches. In the process, pastors and people will slow down their pace and have time to cherish their situations in life. They'll find time for family, fellow church members and neighbors.

London/Wiseman: So sum up what this secret is. Help us understand a good working definition of contentment. Pastors need that if they're going to practice and share the secret that Paul found so transforming.

Swenson: It's a great question. I like what a missionary friend wrote to me: "Contentment is wanting what you already have."

Contentment is a freedom from being controlled by the things we would like to change. It is not pretending things are right when they aren't. Rather, contentment is an inner peace that comes from God. It's an awareness that God is bigger than any problems.

Contentment for the Swensons

London/Wiseman: What forced you to deal with all of this in your own life?

Swenson: I'd always been successful in everything I tried. I thought I had the formula for the perfect life. I had a prestigious profession as a physician, practicing medicine with a group of well-recognized doctors in a great clinic located across the street from a brand-new hospital. I had a wonderful family, and I was making plenty of money. Our faith was strong and we worshiped in a wonderful church. My patients were all grateful for what I did for them, and I was never sued by anyone.

London/Wiseman: Sounds like a good life.

Swenson: So it seemed. But I was getting many migraine headaches. And one evening I found my wife, Linda, crying in front of the house. Diagnosis: we were marginless. I was so busy that I resented my patients getting sick because I had no additional time for them. It was 1982. We finally had to stop and ask some serious questions—what's going on here? We were living in Utopia, but it wasn't Utopia—it just looked that way.

So we decided to make serious adjustments in the direction of simplicity and contentment. I went into academic medicine, which took less time than private practice. Life came alive again. Our family had more time for each other. I accepted the reality that I had limits, and I even came to believe God is the author of my limits as well as my abilities.

To this day, I have to keep space—margins—in my schedule so that I have time available for what really counts for this life and for eternity. I work hard at saying no to things that don't matter, so I don't get overwhelmed by the details of life—especially the details that others try to impose on me.

Contentment for Pastors
London/Wiseman: How can these ideas translate into the lives and work of pastors?

Swenson: Pastors' lives are filled with details and schedules and programs. Many of them are so busy they resent people with problems, just like I did in medicine, because they have no time to fit them in.

One pastor told me he found it hard to listen to people who had new cutting-edge ideas for church ministry because his plate was so full with what was already taking place.

London/Wiseman: So what can pastors do about this situation in their lives?

Swenson: I think it's important to be good diagnosticians of our lives. We need to do self-diagnosis in order to understand accurately the forces that shape our busy lives. We have to realize that the comparison values in our culture are making all of life more complex, more overloaded and faster than ever before in history.

London/Wiseman: How do we do self-diagnosis?

Swenson: It starts by making a checklist like the medical history a doctor takes. We ask ourselves questions about the basics of prayer, solitude, Bible reading, service, fellowship and expressions of compassion. In addition, what drives us? Why are we hyperliving? What role does guilt play in our overwhelmed lives? Which of our inappropriate expectations are cultural rather than biblical?

Then we need to go back to those three Scriptures about contentment. Study them. Put your name in the middle of them. Apply them. Check your life against them. Repeat over and over to anyone and everyone throughout the Church: "Don't listen to the cultural effort to stir up your discontent with what you have or don't have."

If we're going to do what God wants us to do with our lives and in our churches, we have to make space for what He values. It means we stop running at the speed of light down the road that goes in the opposite direction from the kingdom of God.

We need to trust God. We need to realize that He controls His Church and His people. The Church belongs to God and He can care for it. For God, life and the condition of the Church are never out of control. Before the pastor arrived at his present community and before he preached his first sermon, God was there. Before we were born into this generation of hurry and stress, God was already there. And He providentially placed us here to use us for His glory in His Church.

SUGGESTIONS FOR PUTTING MARGIN INTO PRACTICE

Dr. Swenson offers pastors a lot to think about when it comes to margins, boundaries and contentment. What are some practical ways you can apply all of these concepts to your ministry?

Fine-Tune Your Own Shaping Influences

Seek to understand the influences that cause discontentment in your life. Perhaps you're living too close to the culture where people get their satisfaction from new cars, bigger houses, more prestige and commanding power. If you know what feeds your discontent, you can begin to question yourself on those issues— sometimes a bit of self-conversation opens up brand new ways of thinking and reacting.

Continually Commit to the Main Thing

From the loftiest cathedrals in Europe to the tiniest house church in the United States and everywhere in between, every spiritual leader and every congregation has the tendency to give energy to survival rather than to try to rediscover the main reason for existence. It happens to spiritual leaders who get caught up in side issues rather than the main thing. When we lose focus on the Church's reason for being, we often become boring leaders who are more given to keeping the store than building the faith.

Live the Three Scriptures About Contentment

Read and study Philippians 4:12-13,19; Hebrews 13:5; and 1 Timothy 6:6-9. Put those three Scriptures side by side every day for a month, and you'll be delivered from competition and comparison forever. Read the context of each passage. The promises are magnificent and the demands are so great that no one can keep them without the help of God.

Live in the Present

You can ruin today by groveling over all you'd like to change about yesterday. It's gone and the record has been written. Tomorrow hasn't arrived, so what you think about that is pure hope. But you do have today. What can you do with it that will bring glory to the Lord, satisfaction to you and helpfulness to those you serve?

You can ruin today by groveling over all you'd like to change about yesterday.

Keep Check on Three Words

The words are "cynicism," "callousness" and "criticism." Any one of them will bite when uttered about you. But many pastors allow those three words to shape their thinking and affect their ministry to others. Avoid them like the plague—they always hinder, sometimes sting and frequently tear tender relationships.

Serve Someone Worse Off Than You Are

Intentionally serve someone whose problems are so great that you utter praise for your own situation while you're helping. Competition and lack of contentment can't thrive well in this kind of environment. Someone nearby is poorer than you are, sicker than you are and serves a smaller church than you do. Any one of these people would gladly trade their problems for yours.

USE MARGINS TO KILL THE TIME MONSTER

Can you count on the promise of Jesus for your toughest times?

> Are you tired? Worn out? Burned out on religion? Come to me. Get away with me and you'll recover your life. I'll show you how to take a real rest (Matt. 11:28, *THE MESSAGE*).

Can you depend on the apostle Paul's words at your lowest points?

> So let's not allow ourselves to get fatigued doing good. At the right time we will harvest a good crop if we don't give up, or quit (Gal. 6:9, *THE MESSAGE*).

To raise the question another way, can you find inspiration in these words?

> When you find yourselves flagging in your faith, go over that story again, item by item, that long litany of hostility he [Jesus] plowed through. *That* will shoot adrenaline into your souls (Heb. 12:3, *THE MESSAGE*).

Reread the list pastors gave about weariness at the beginning of this chapter. As you review their words, is it possible that the list contains ideas that are both discouraging and affirming? Could you use the phrases as a supporting argument for staying as well as quitting?

Like few other occupations, most pastors have enough troubles to make them want to quit every week. But you have to answer the question, Why do some leave and others thrive on the same difficulties and use them as stepping-stones to victory?

As long as you see ministry as a kind of holy chaplaincy to serve existing church members and their ailing friends, you'll find it easy to give in and give up when some event or person threatens you. But if you can instead see your congregation as a living cell of the eternal Church of Jesus Christ, you can find hope for staying at your post, guarding the territory and investing your life—not only for the people you serve, but for Him.

An old veteran pastor, scarred from many battles and overworked from heavy labors, was asked how long he had served his present church. With humble pride, he answered, "30 years." Then the person who asked the question remarked, "Most pastors have a maximum of 45 years to serve, so this church has consumed two-thirds of your ministerial lifetime."

The old man, with a flowing mane of white hair, an intensity in his eyes and a ring to his voice, replied, "I gave my life to this little group of people. No one *took* it. I gave it willingly, and I'd gladly give them another lifetime if I had it to give."

Do you have room in your ministry to answer the same way?

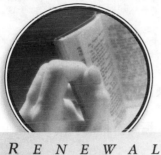

R E N E W A L   S T R A T E G I E S

Putting Margin into Practice

✓ Fine-tune your own shaping influences.
✓ Continually commit to the main thing.
✓ Live the three Scriptures about contentment.
✓ Live in the present.
✓ Keep check on three words.
✓ Serve someone worse off than you are.

A Personal Word from H. B. L.

A Pure Gift for the Church

Once each year we celebrate another birthday of the living Church of our Lord—Pentecost Sunday. The question is, What gift do you get a Bride who has everything?

Think about it. The American Church has money. It has talent and exposure. It has massive buildings and gifted leadership. It knows how to get its message out better than ever before. It has variety and acceptance. It speaks nearly every language and its story is in print virtually around the world. Men and women attend to every need of the Church. It would seem that on this birthday the Church would say, "Oh, don't bother, I have everything I need." But not so.

Instead, the Church needs a cleansing. It's not as radiant as it should be. It's stained, wrinkled and blemished. It desires to be holy and blameless (see Eph. 5:27). It calls for pastors to be faithful and bold and to proclaim the gospel with clarity and passion. The Church cries for its members to love one another and cast aside things that divide. The Church weeps over the multitudes around the world who know about Christ but don't really know Him. It longs for a revival of the apathetic and a stirring of the comfortable. Why? Because time is short and, whether they know it or not, the people of the world desperately need the Church.

What can you give to the Church—the Bride of Christ? *Yourself*—in a renewed commitment to its cause and message.

CHAPTER TEN

ONLINE SEX OR OFF: FINDING FREEDOM FROM SEXUAL ADDICTION

A CONVERSATION WITH TED ROBERTS

- 20 percent of pastors say they view pornography at least once a month.[1]
- 49 percent of pastors say they spend less than 5 hours a week on the Internet. Nearly 30 percent spend 5 to 10 hours a week.[2]
- 20 percent of pastors admit to having had an affair while in the ministry.[3]
- 12 percent of pastors say that since they've been in ministry, they've had sexual intercourse with someone other than their spouse.[4]
- 51 percent of pastors say that Internet pornography is a possible temptation for them; 37 percent admit that it's a current struggle.[5]
- 33 percent of the clergy and 36 percent of the laity have visited a sexually explicit website; of that number, 53 percent of the clergy and 44 percent of the laity say they have visited the sites a few times in the past year. A total of 18 percent of clergy respondents say they visit such websites between a couple of times a month and more than once a week.[6]
- According to Focus on the Family's Pastoral Ministries Division, approximately 20 percent of the monthly calls to their pastoral care line deal with sexual misconduct and pornography.

Pastor Sam Brooks found himself tangled in a frightening web—an Internet web of cybersexual addiction. It all started innocently enough, and he certainly never planned to go where it eventually took him.

It started when Sam was asked to become a member of a community moral action committee to fight easy Internet access to sexually explicit materials for children and teens. He decided it was his duty to visit his first sex website—to see firsthand what he was fighting.

Though he felt shocked by what he found, he was also curious—almost mesmerized. So he stayed online for about 30 minutes that first time. Erotic images from that initial visit seemed imprinted on his memory for days and weeks. Those explicit sex scenes showed up at unguarded moments—sometimes when he was preparing a sermon and even once while he was serving Communion.

His problem became even more snarled when Tom, a lay leader in the church, asked Sam to be his accountability partner. Tom told Pastor Sam he needed a dependable, pure man to help him resist his temptation to view Internet pornography.

Tom had confessed his compulsion to his wife earlier. She'd insisted that they see a Christian counselor together. One of the first steps the counselor recommended was for Tom to find a trusted friend to hold him accountable for his actions and thoughts. Tom chose Sam. He respected him, more than anyone he knew, for his apparent integrity.

Of course, Tom had no way of knowing Sam was himself engaged in a losing battle with sexual temptation on the computer monitor. It was always just a few computer clicks away.

Now Sam deepened his growing addiction by convincing himself he had to check out what Tom was fighting. In the process, he became more and more trapped. To help keep his own growing problems secret, Sam felt obligated to accept Tom's request. Of course, that required that he lead a kind of double life. While playing the role of accountability friend to Tom, his own unquenchable thirst for Internet pornography kept increasing. His seductive secrecy ate at his conscience day and night. He frequently felt depressed, irritable and miserable. Family, ministry and marriage suffered.

Even before Sam's first visit to a pornographic website, his marriage was shaky from years of overcommitment to his work, isolation, poor communication, decreasing attempts to build more satisfying intimacy with his wife and gross neglect of self-care. As an easy alternative to working to improve his marriage, pornography was always accessible, affordable and anonymous. He turned his meetings with his computer into an alluring, always-available substitute for working on his marriage.

While the details are different for each person, something is out of sync, sinful and even destructive among many men in our society. Some are leaders in our churches; obviously, even pastors aren't exempt. The facts are staggering and the enslavement real.

SEXUAL ADDICTION—A DESTRUCTIVE MORAL CRISIS

Pastors have a lot of work to do concerning these issues. At least four concerns need immediate and continued attention.

1. Some men in every church are likely to be pornography addicts.
2. The Church must find ways to help people build stronger marriages.
3. Every pastor is subject to temptation. Pastor and author Bill Perkins says, "If you think you can't fall into sexual sin, then you're godlier than David, stronger than Samson, and wiser than Solomon."[7]

4. Every pastor must maintain the highest levels of pure thought and appropriate action toward his people, especially toward the young and members of the opposite gender.

We need to follow Paul's admonition scrupulously: "Among you there must not be even a hint of sexual immorality, or of any kind of impurity, or of greed, because these are improper for God's holy people" (Eph. 5:3).

CHARACTERISTICS OF SEXUAL ADDICTION

Beyond the statistics and risk factors, we need definitions and descriptions to understand the full impact of this problem. In their book *Every Man's Battle*, Steve Arterburn and Fred Stoeker list the following characteristics of addictive sexual behavior:

- Addictive sex is done in isolation.
- Addictive sex is secretive.
- Addictive sex is self-focused.
- Addictive sex is victimizing.
- Addictive sex ends in despair.
- Addictive sex is used to escape pain and problems.[8]

WHAT CAN WE DO TO RESTORE SEXUAL PURITY?

The following conversation with Pastor Ted Roberts offers help, hope and healing for overcoming sexual addiction. Roberts serves as senior pastor of the Foursquare Church in Gresham, Oregon. His church has experienced phenomenal growth through small-group ministries to those who suffer from sexual addiction, drugs, alcohol, divorce and dysfunctional families.

The Snare of Sexual Addiction

London/Wiseman: What motivated you to start your ministry to men caught in the snare of sexual addiction?

Roberts: Two reasons—big ones. A large percentage of men in our church were involved in Internet pornography. At the same time, the problem had reached epidemic proportions among men outside the Church. So we decided it was our duty to mount a counterattack.

London/Wiseman: Many pastors may never have had sexual sin touch their lives. They've been sheltered, so they find it hard to realize the devastation it brings to a family. How do you talk about this problem with those who've never had experience with it?

Roberts: I point to King David in Scripture. His life is a classic example of someone who became hopelessly tangled in sexual addiction. It was more than his sin with Bathsheba. Remember the devastation in his family all the way back to Absalom. Sexual addiction always turns into a family issue that shreds relationships within the family.

Or sometimes I explain how four elements of sexual addiction turn into a noose around a believer's soul. If the addicted person isn't helped to healing, he'll end up drowning spiritually in his own guilt and shame.

Sexual addiction always turns into an issue that shreds relationships within the family.

London/Wiseman: What are those four issues?

Roberts: The four elements in that ever-tightening noose are addictive roots, an addictive mind-set, an addictive lifestyle and an addictive cloak. The addictive roots are closely tied to family dysfunction, personal trauma and an addictive society. The mind-set is shaped by destructive concepts including sexual highs, feeling worthless or feeling unlovable and alone. The lifestyle issues are fantasy, ritual, keeping a lid on the sin, plus further shame and guilt. The addictive cloak builds on denial, delusion and blame.

London/Wiseman: What do we know about causes?

Roberts: In almost every scientific study, the sequence starts between ages 10 and 12. With the Internet so available, the age is dropping to even younger children. So by the time an individual reaches his 30s or 40s, he's developed a deeply rooted sin that goes to the core of his being. When offering ministry for sexual addictions, we need to remember that we're dealing with some of the most profound, visceral issues that go to the depths of creativity, of relationship with God and of relationship with one's spouse.

London/Wiseman: Is it necessary for someone to reach bottom before he can get help with sexual addiction?

Roberts: It seems that way, because the starting point for healing is to stop denial. This is important, yet so many people aren't willing to tell the truth. We've even started giving lie detector tests to people in our program.

London/Wiseman: Is that true of pastors, too?

Roberts: Yes—it is particularly hard to find the truth with pastors because ministry can be so seductive. Pastors want to hold on to their position, so they lie to counselors. Some have lied so long that they actually believe their own stories.

London/Wiseman: We've heard that sexual addiction isn't all about sex—is that right?

Roberts: Right. It's almost never exclusively about sex. It's frequently about family background. The way a person thinks and processes life is a big part of the problem.

London/Wiseman: What is it that lulls people into complacency so that they think sexual sin isn't so bad?

Roberts: They go through a stop-and-start self-deceptive con game—promising themselves, "This is the last time." They stop their behavior because they get caught or almost get caught. Or maybe they hear a sermon that inspires them to resolve to do better. But when the conditions are right and they feel alone, they go back to the sin. We have to realize that this is a master strategy from hell that has culture on its side, and readily available technology provides the resource.

London/Wiseman: Explain what you mean. What's the importance of all this for the church's ministry?

Roberts: I believe this never-ending struggle is caused by the enemy of our souls. The devil uses sexual sin as a primary tool of destruction and devastation against individuals, families, churches and society.

The Church's Role in Recovery
London/Wiseman: How can the Church work to stem the tide?

Roberts: The issue is bigger than most churches have ever imagined. If the Church doesn't become a place of healing and sexual wholeness, I believe sexual sin will break our society. I think it's the single most pressing issue in the world today. The Church is the only place where people can find the answer.

London/Wiseman: But in many places, the Church is afraid to even mention it.

Roberts: That's the brutal paradox. We have the answer but either don't know how or don't have the will to use it.

I speak as one who feels called to this issue. I think the Church has to change the way it relates to the problem. We have to see ourselves as holding the answer, which makes us responsible to give the answer. At our church, we have people coming to Christ so they can find the answer to their sexual addictions. We even have secular counseling agencies sending people to us. That tells us they don't know what to do.

When someone comes to us for help, we insist on full disclosure—no denials. Then we deal with the addictive lifestyle—what the person is doing. They need accountability and help with the way they relate to others, especially their wives.

RISK FACTOR

20 percent of pastors say they view pornography at least once a month.

As we deal with full disclosure and lifestyle surrounding the addiction, we have to help them identify and work through the roots of their addiction. We have to get to what drives them—family issues, various kinds of trauma, child abuse, sexual molestation or any number of serious background problems.

London/Wiseman: What do you know about those roots?

Roberts: We know that 81 percent of the people who are out of control sexually were sexually abused themselves. Seventy-two percent were physically abused, and 97 percent were emotionally abused.[9] So we try to get at the core issues. Our effort isn't to pray that a spirit of lust will be taken from a man. Instead, we work by God's grace to help him reprogram the computer between his ears.

London/Wiseman: Is it possible to be freed from childhood wounds like abuse?

Roberts: Yes. Many men have a deep father-wound issue. It really seems to trigger a lot of these problems. What we say is, "So you're messed up because your father let you down in some way." But then we teach them how to work with that woundedness, so they can say, "I'm not blaming my father for my problems, but the enemy uses that weakness against me."

London/Wiseman: How does healing from sexual addiction affect wives?

Roberts: When we first started the ministry, the men started getting well and their wives were going crazy. In many marriages, wives have either accepted or supported their husband's behavior for years. Many wives make excuses for their husband's behavior.

Even when a wife doesn't understand or even hates her husband's interest in pornography or cybersex, she may have concluded that that's the way men are—a kind of "men will be men" attitude. Or she may have been in denial about his addiction for years.

Add to that the fact that most women don't understand pornography. It just doesn't make sense to them. So when a man starts confessing, he throws his wife into a comparison mode where she can't win because she's competing against a fantasy person that doesn't exist. You have to provide a support structure so that the wife isn't forced to play sheriff or live up to her husband's fantasies.

Another problem is when the guy comes clean and dumps all this stuff on his wife. He feels great because his guilt is gone, but she has to face the fact that he's been living a lie with her all these years. She's likely to feel hurt, confused, angry, betrayed—maybe all of those emotions.

Another step the couple has to work through is how to replace what they've had with the great sex life God wants them to have. We have to help this couple come to a healthy understanding of sexuality.

London/Wiseman: It provides opportunities to get started or expand authentic intimacy in the marriage, doesn't it?

Roberts: Yes. But it's important to remember the time factor. Most addicts don't get into all these problems in a day. So I tell the men, "Okay, this is a two- to five-year process—it's going to take a miracle every day to get there, but God wants to help you with that miracle."

The effort is a war to fight. I tell the men, "Don't give me this word, 'I'm going to pray once and it will be over.'" This thing is war, and either the guy will win or this sexual addiction will take him out. I advise them, "This is absolute war, and you'd better draw a line in the sand about where the battle line will be."

London/Wiseman: Do you have licensed counselors?

Roberts: When we have severe mental problems or serious legal issues, we refer people to specialists. But our most effective way is to put those who want help in touch with those who've been through it. Transformed people can really help the most. It's God's way, you know—set sinners free and use them to free other sinners.

The psalmist explains how God gets people ready for this work:

> God, make a fresh start in me, shape a Genesis week from the chaos of my life. Don't throw me out with the trash, or fail to breathe holiness in me. Give me a job teaching rebels your ways so the lost can find their way home." (Ps. 51:10-11,13, *THE MESSAGE*).

That's where the Church's power really is—God helping transformed people show needy addicts the way home.

London/Wiseman: Like in Alcoholics Anonymous, men in your ministry receive the help of a fellow struggler rather than a counselor or professional psychologist or psychiatrist. Your people have lived through the problems and are overcomers.

Roberts: I'm not opposed to trained professional counselors; but I know that when we take the light of Acts 1:8, "You will be my witnesses," into a sick world of the dark, secret closets of people's lives, the gospel works. It lights the darkness and heals the wounds.

London/Wiseman: So the emphasis isn't let's blame our past, but how can we get free from the past?

Roberts: That's exactly right. But there's also the present situation where the man has come to Christ, but try as he will, he can't get past his addiction. He tries to live free from his past enslavement but can't. When I speak away from my own congregation, I find that 50 to 60 percent of men in other churches are struggling, too. Sadly, pastors often aren't even aware of what they're feeling. What rips your heart is that these guys honestly want to pursue God passionately. They want to be able to sing honestly "Let's lift up holy hands," but they know their hands aren't holy.

London/Wiseman: They feel forced to live with disillusionment. Someone told them that everything would be okay if they would give their hearts to Christ. So they did. But they know it's still not all right. So they either pretend that everything is fine or they leave the church.

Roberts: Either action—leaving or pretending—leads nowhere. We have to offer people more than lifelong frustration, because Christ offers so much more.

Guilt and Shame

London/Wiseman: Let's go back a moment and talk about the difference between guilt and shame.

Roberts: That's a good idea because it fits here. *Guilt* is what you feel when you do something wrong; it's about your behavior. *Shame* is the belief that something is wrong with you; it's about the essence of who you are.

Shame communicates that you're flawed in some way. Shame means you're defective.

People who come to Christ know they're forgiven. But sadly, many continue to feel shame. They feel worthless. They believe, *No one would love me if he or she truly knew who I am.*

So people with addictions feel shame because of the way they are. But they return again and again to sexual addiction activity to diminish the pain their shame causes.

Shame can't be counseled away. As Scripture says, the Cross is the only answer:

> Let us fix our eyes on Jesus, the author and perfecter of our faith, who for the joy set before him endured the cross, scorning its shame, and sat down at the right hand of the throne of God (Heb. 12:2).

What a passage! And what a strength the passage communicates.

On the Cross, Christ took both our guilt and our shame on Himself. So the person recovering from sexual addiction must give his shame to Christ. The message must be clear—Christ came both to take away the shame of who we are and to forgive us of the guilt for what we did.

Christ came both to take away the shame of who we are and to forgive us of the guilt for what we did.

Ted Roberts's Story

London/Wiseman: That's so helpful. We understand that your own journey brought you to your present ministry. Can you tell us a little more of your own story?

Roberts: Sure, I openly talk about my addiction. I've learned that vulnerability is one of the most powerful ways to share the gospel. People need to witness the reality of what God has done in our lives to understand what He can do in theirs.

I made a commitment to Christ in a bunker in Vietnam in the middle of a rocket attack. My wife had sent me a letter expressing her love and reminding me of God's love. I responded to Christ largely because of her life and testimony. I describe myself as a total pagan up to that point—all I wanted to do was fly airplanes and fight.

When I came back from Vietnam, God revealed to me that I was a rageaholic. I was an alcoholic and a sex addict into pornography. I was doing such crazy stuff that I would have been arrested if my superiors knew what I was doing. I was out of control. I went to places that were off limits for Marines. Like all addicts, my life was unmanageable. My behavior was destructive, and the problems were increasing in intensity.

God freed me in a moment from alcohol. But it took four years of a knock-down, drag-out fight to finally break the grip of pornography. It was a battle. Every day it was like my head was going crazy.

Since then, God has used that weakness and turned it into a great strength for His purposes. I feel that it's my calling and passion in ministry to help free people from addictions. But I also believe that any pastor who'll listen to the heart of his men will hear the same agony I felt firsthand. If a pastor has a heart for God and a desire to win people, God will ignite the opportunities his church has to help people.

Pastoral Ministry to Sexual Addicts

London/Wiseman: Given the sensitivity of the issues, how can a pastor begin?

Roberts: My prayer is that when a pastor reads these words, he'll feel God starting a burden in his heart. Many are already aware of the problems but are afraid to start a ministry like I have suggested.

The next thing a pastor can do is to begin teaching on the meaning of healthy human sexuality. I just started a series on God's gifts for a great sex life. We've already had several hundred people come to know Christ during this series. Such biblical teaching will have a powerful impact on our society. We need to become much more aggressive in a positive way on this issue.

The reason for preaching and teaching on this subject is to give people accurate information about their sexuality. Teach them that sex is God's good gift to them. We need to help people begin to think and talk about the spiritual dynamics of their own sexuality.

Then churches can provide groups that will help the pastor facilitate the ministry and provide materials that we know will work.

Advice for Wives

London/Wiseman: Do you have any advice for wives?

Roberts: Yes, I have two things to say to wives: Don't justify his behavior, and don't blame yourself. His addiction isn't your problem. It's his, and he must own it and solve it.

Let me read a few sentences concerning wives from my book *Pure Desire*: "One of the first things we do is try to help the wife understand that in most cases this is not just his problem. It is usually a family problem. . . . The wife has to face the fact that God is the only One who can change her husband. But there are things she can do to create an environment for change: learning to let go, setting healthy boundaries, working on her self-esteem and learning to trust again."[10]

SUGGESTIONS FOR COUNTERATTACKING THE VIRUS OF SEXUAL SIN

At a time when technology has made pornography accessible with just a few clicks of a mouse, pastors and faithful lay leaders must shout "Stop!" At a time when sexual allegations, charges of abuse and accusations of cover-up are leveled daily at the Roman Catholic Church, pastors like you must take preventative steps to be sure that this never happens in your congregation. At a time when millions of men—probably some in your church or maybe even yourself—have allowed flickering sexual images to dig fantasy-filled ditches in their minds, the Church must plead for repentance from every pulpit and warn every believer not to swallow deadly poison.

Every pastor must accept the challenge to keep clean and be true to his marriage and ordination vows. Simultaneously, pastors must teach, challenge and show the men they serve how to keep themselves free from the emotionally crippling clutches of pornography.

The following exercises are meant to help you do both—keep yourself pure and help the men in your sphere of influence to saturate their minds with Christ so completely that they will be able to live in this world without being of it.

Celebrate Marriage

Marriage has fallen on hard times, so people marry and divorce as they would buy a house or choose a suit to wear. Teach men in your spiritual care to live their marriages according to these insights from C. S. Lewis:

> The Christian idea of marriage is based on Christ's words that a man and wife are to be regarded as a single organism—for that is what the words "one flesh" would be in modern English. And the Christians believe that when He said this He was not expressing a sentiment but stating a fact—just as one is stating a fact when one says that a lock and its key are one mechanism, or that a violin and a bow are one musical instrument. The inventor

of the human machine was telling us that its two halves, the male and the female, were meant to be combined together in pairs, not simply on the sexual level, but totally combined.[11]

Check What Scripture Teaches About Sexual Purity

Gather the following Scriptures into a list that you can print out often for your own use and for those you teach and lead. Read these Scriptures often, at least once a week. You can even mark these readings on your calendar to be sure you do it. Carry the list in your Bible or personal organizer when you travel or when you're alone—anywhere you might feel tempted.

Duplicate the list and circulate it among the men in your church. The message of the combined passages is clear and victorious—God wants men to be pure and blameless before Him. Check out God's expectations as well as His promises to empower you:

> There's more to sex than mere skin on skin. Sex is as much spiritual mystery as physical fact. As written in Scripture, "The two become one." Since we want to become spiritually one with the Master, we must not pursue the kind of sex that avoids commitment and intimacy, leaving us more lonely than ever—the kind of sex that can never "become one" (1 Cor. 6:16-17, *THE MESSAGE*).

> But don't think you've preserved your virtue simply by staying out of bed. Your *heart* can be corrupted by lust even quicker than your *body*. Those leering looks you think nobody notices—they also corrupt (Matt. 5:28, *THE MESSAGE*).

God wants you to be holy and pure, and to keep clear of all sexual sin. For God has not called us to be dirty-minded and full of lust, but to be holy and clean (1 Thess. 4:3,7, *TLB*).

Turn your back on the turbulent desires of youth and give your positive attention to goodness, integrity, love and peace (2 Tim. 2:22, *Phillips*).

So be careful. If you are thinking, "Oh, I would never behave like that"—let this be a warning to you. For you too may fall into sin (1 Cor. 10:12, *TLB*).

RISK FACTOR

20 percent of pastors admit to having had an affair while in the ministry.

I made a covenant with my eyes not to look lustfully at a girl (Job 31:1).

How can a young person stay pure? By obeying your word and following its rules (Ps. 119:9, *NLT*).

Commit to Absolute Personal Sexual Purity

As we've researched, pondered and written about these issues, a very old conviction has deepened in us. Like any other profession or occupation, the ministry requires a high level of dedication, hard work and competency. But as pastors, we need something more—something higher and more basic and more noble—in our personhood and character. To be an authentic shepherd of souls requires that your whole being—including your sexuality—be pure. That means thought, intention, speech and action.

If you're one of the statistics about sexual sin and addiction, you need moral cleansing. Why not seek God's purifying Spirit so that you can live by the satisfying standard of Jesus: "You have heard that it was said, 'Do not commit adultery.' But I tell you that anyone who looks at a woman lustfully has already committed adultery with her in his heart" (Matt. 5:27-28).

Or the apostle Paul's standard, "Don't allow love to turn into lust, setting off a downhill slide into sexual promiscuity, filthy practices, or bullying greed. Though some tongues just love the taste of gossip, Christians have better uses for language than that. Don't talk dirty or silly. That kind of talk doesn't fit our style. Thanksgiving is our dialect" (Eph. 5:3-4, *THE MESSAGE*).

Choose Maleness or Redeemed Manhood

Discuss the ideas on this subject found in the Your Challenge section at the end of this chapter with three or four other men whom you trust. Discuss them with your wife and enough men so that the concepts become clear in your thinking. Share it with men in your church's men's group. Discuss these ideas with an accountability partner. If you don't have such a relationship established, start one today.

Training the will starts by deliberately going against our natural desires.

Develop Small Accountability Groups

Start by making yourself accountable and then stick to it. Ted Roberts's book *Pure Desire* offers helps for starting a ministry to sexual addicts. But to make it work, you must see the need and also accept the resistance you'll encounter. This is a fight against the forces of evil, so it doesn't need official approval from any committee. But before you start, make sure you understand how big the problem may be and then go for ways to heal it in your fellowship.

Help Other Men Live Pure Lives

Training the will starts by deliberately going against our natural desires—in this case, what we sometimes call our natural maleness.

Encourage the men in your church—those for whom you bear spiritual responsibility—to keep their marriage vows because it is their duty and it is right. Teach them to keep their eye on the goal of sexual purity all day long. Challenge them to pursue joy that comes from pure roots in the marriage. Teach them to express gratitude to their wives.

You might want to tell them about the parable of the couple who decided to break their engagement. They agreed, "We should return each other's letters." Then she suggested, "Since we are returning treasures, shouldn't we give each other all our kisses back?" They did. And in a short time, they renewed their engagement and were soon married.

As this process of setting our wills to do God's will develops, watch marriage satisfaction soar in your church.

Commit to Two-Dimension Purity

In this war, the pastor himself must be pure, and he must do everything possible to call the men of his church and of the culture to purity. Bring the problem of sexual addiction out into the open.

Ask men in every contact you have with them, "What can our church do to help you and other men resist sexual temptations and live a life without guilt before your wife and before God?" The conversations may lead your church to creative solutions no one else has thought about. The dialogue will encourage everyone to be alert to his own temptations. And a high standard of sexual purity will pervade the whole church.

Help Couples Nourish Marriages

Disappointment with the intimate side of marriage is one of the most popular excuses people use for sexual sin. Overcoming sexual temptation and developing lifelong sexual satisfaction with your wife starts and grows in a commitment to Christ and in a healthy desire to satisfy your spouse. No flickering computer image can do that. Sometimes, years of quiet desperation can be solved with the smallest amounts of how-to information. Revisit your own marriage vows often to add new joy and deepen your commitment. Encourage the people of your church to do the same. Make your church a place where you help good marriages become great marriages and where sick marriages find healing.

In an essay titled "Bold Next Steps," Steven Fetrow of Stone Gate Ministries advises:

> Sexual fulfillment is a part of the intimate relationship of marriage for which God designed us. It is a PART of God's plan and NOT the WHOLE of God's plan. A marriage that fails to provide sexual satisfaction and fulfillment is a marriage that has yet to discover selfless surrender, tender vulnerability, loving and sacrificial need-meeting, and open, honest communication.

He continues,

> My advice to anyone who claims to have a poor sexual relationship with a spouse is to make the effort to work on the marriage instead of running to a quick fix that does not last, is not real, and shatters the marriage vows. Working on the marriage may require a lot of painful examination and intensive emotional effort, but the end result is worth it. Turning to pornography is the lazy way out. Instead of facing the real desires within us and risking the potential pain and disappointment of a real relationship, we take CONTROL and we dive into a fantasy

world that is merely a shadow of what God created us to experience.[12]

Find as many ways as possible to help your people build great marriages. Fill your church schedule with seminars, sermons, accountability groups, books, videos and testimonies of the sheer satisfaction of building great marriages and strong homes. Honor marriage. Enrich marriage. Great marriages help make churches relevant and attractive—sometimes even magnetic.

NATURAL MALENESS, REDEEMED MANHOOD AND PURE PASTOR

As you deal with sexual addiction issues both as a person and as a pastor, you need to consider what's naturally male against what's sinful. Stephen Arterburn and Fred Stoeker help us by making a distinction between maleness and manhood—perhaps the ideal should be called redeemed manhood.

To be male is to have a natural desire for sexual release on a regular cycle of 24 to 72 hours. This periodic growing intensity tempts the male's mind and body to ignore God's standards. Arterburn and Stoeker explain,

> We have a visual ignition switch when it comes to viewing the female anatomy. . . . As males, we draw sexual gratification and chemical highs through our eyes.[13]

That's reality—and in a great marriage, it's fun, pleasurable, miraculous, exciting, passionate and enjoyable. The question here is the identical question of our entire quest for God: How do we use this gift in ways that are pleasing to God and satisfying to us? In terms of our sexuality, a great marriage seems to be a great gift we give ourselves.

Of course, no man can eliminate his maleness—what man would if he could? Again Arterburn and Stoeker put the issues in clear-as-day, earthy-but-true language:

> We want to look at our wives and desire them. They're beautiful to us, and we're sexually gratified when we gaze at them, often daydreaming about the night ahead and what bedtime will bring. In its proper place maleness is wonderful.[14]

But if our maleness is also the root of our sexual sins, what can we do? Are men slaves to their sexual urges? The answer is to choose to live as a male who's been redeemed by Christ. This means that with the help of Jesus, you rise above the male tendencies of wandering eyes, fantasizing minds and flirting adventures. It means you choose sexual integrity. It means you apply God's grace to sexuality. And then, though maleness is strong and an important part of you, you choose to be a pure male and to use your sexuality joyously in the ways God intended within your marriage. Our Father's standard of measuring up to sexual purity doesn't come naturally, but it is possible with His enabling.

Here's His promise for victory in all phases of your life, including sexual purity: "His divine power has given us everything we need for life and godliness through our knowledge of him who called us by his own glory and goodness. Through these he has given us his very great and precious promises, so that through them you may participate in the divine nature and escape the corruption in the world caused by evil desires" (2 Pet. 1:3-4).

Your purity will make your ministry powerful and inspiring to your congregation. At the same time, it will bless and reassure your wife. As she shares your life and lies in your arms, cherish her as a precious gift from God.

RENEWAL STRATEGIES

COUNTERATTACK THE VIRUS OF SEXUAL SIN

✓ Celebrate marriage.

✓ Check what Scripture teaches about sexual purity.

✓ Commit to absolute personal sexual purity.

✓ Choose maleness or redeemed manhood.

✓ Develop small accountability groups.

✓ Help other men live pure lives.

✓ Commit to two-dimension purity.

✓ Help couples nourish marriages.

A Personal Word from H. B. L.

Be an Example

Example: One who serves as a pattern to be imitated or not to be imitated; one who is worthy of imitation or duplication.

The apostle Paul wrote to a young pastor, "Set an example for the believers in speech, in life, in love, in faith and in purity" (1 Tim. 4:12). That's pretty straightforward. Peter said that Jesus left us "an example, that you should follow in his steps" (1 Pet. 2:21).

With all the scrutiny that political and religious figures are under these days, it would seem that we'd all be wise to do everything possible to set an example for our families and for all of those who watch us. We are examples, whether positive or negative.

I pray that you'll be an example of a faithful life. What a way to live—not because you have to but because you love God and you love doing it. It's a great way to live—a believer in speech, in life, in love, in faith and in purity. Your people will be attracted to that kind of pastor.

CHAPTER ELEVEN

PURSUING AND PRACTICING PERSONAL HOLINESS

A CONVERSATION WITH JERRY BRIDGES

- 86 percent of pastors say their top priority is personal relationship with God.
- 12 percent report that their number one priority is family.[1]
- 55 percent of pastors indicate that they're a member of a small group that provides support and holds them accountable.[2]
- 32 percent of pastors say that reading is the activity that provides sustained renewal in their spirit; 31 percent say that renewal comes from being alone.[3]
- 50 percent of pastors say they'd see another pastor if they felt the need for personal counseling.
- 20.5 percent indicate that they'd go to *no one*.[4]
- 70 percent do not have someone they consider a close friend.[5]

By now you're realizing that much of ministry has become an endless grind of crippling crises—both personal and in your congregation. Maybe you've even questioned why God didn't stop you at the blooming of your call or why a seasoned pastoral veteran didn't slow you down on your hurried path to ordination.

Anglican priest Leonard Griffith's imaginary but true-to-life words from Jesus say it well:

So you feel beaten, bullied, and whipped by the demands that people make on you, inconsiderate people who are so troubled that they can think of no one but themselves. Well, that's what you bargained for when you entered *my* ministry. And it is *my* ministry.

Griffith continues his digging around the roots of ministerial motivation:

Read about it in the Gospels. They tell you about a typical day in *my* earthly career, a day that begins, continues and ends with crises, a day of involvement in human need, battling with human hypocrisy, a day that leaves *me* depleted, exhausted, and ready to quit—except that I find renewal in prayer.[6]

When we feel whipped, we respond with a high-sounding excuse, "I don't have the resources for ministry that He had." But we do have them.

These possibilities pull at our motives as we experience the dual challenges of the world and the persistent inner call to be holy. We need both. We know that we want an effective exemplary life resourced by a holy inner life. But how can we have both?

God "resources" us even when ministry depletes us. God enables us when ministry baffles us. God makes us sufficient for every situation we encounter for Him. What exhilarating news—this inward pursuit of Christlikeness rejuvenates mission, renews stamina, rekindles passion and refocuses vision.

The holy life pays off in quality living as it shapes us into people who are more and more like Christ—even in our frustrations and at the close of demanding days. The supernatural reality that pastors so often forget is that in ministry our whole self is being molded into the image of God's Son even as we labor for Him.

THE PURSUIT OF PERSONAL HOLINESS

When a pastor experiences intimacy with Christ, it nourishes his ministry. As he pursues holiness, it keeps his soul in shape. But when a pastor feels perplexed, strained or fearful, his life tends to become shallow and his ministry perfunctory. While many ministry frustrations are external and environmental—even out of our own control—our only sure way to revitalize the Church is to renew our own inner world in fresh old ways. That's the exciting journey Jerry Bridges helps us start.

London/Wiseman: Let's discuss personal holiness and its impact on ministry. The title of your book *The Pursuit of Holiness* suggests a personal pilgrimage. It has had an amazing and widespread influence. Thousands have been inspired by your call to Christlikeness in that book and the others that followed.

Bridges: Yes, *The Practice of Godliness* is a sequel to *The Pursuit of Holiness,* which started when the lights went on for me that

Ephesians tells us to put on the new man as well as put off the old man. *The Pursuit of Holiness* focuses largely on dealing with sin or putting off the old man. But we need to place equal emphasis on putting on the new man—those godly traits that Paul calls the fruit of the Spirit in Galatians 5.

London/Wiseman: That progression is so significant for pastors. It was a life-changing day in pastoral ministry when we realized that personal holiness was the most important thing we could bring to our congregations and to our families. A miraculous new chapter of ministry opened when we understood that pursuing personal holiness was the essential underpinning of ministry. Would you agree?

Our pursuit of holiness is amazingly attractive to the people we lead.

Bridges: Absolutely. I believe ministry flows out of our lives—out of who we really are. Therefore, we can't adequately convey spiritual reality to others if we're not pursuing holiness. People will always pick up on our weakness and follow us into spiritual shallowness if we're not pursuing a holy character and a pure lifestyle.

London/Wiseman: We often hear people describe a pastor as being godly. What that really means is that he's a spiritually authentic person who causes others to believe he lives close to God. Our pursuit of holiness is amazingly attractive to the people we lead.

We do believe a pastor can be holy and successful at the same time. But if a pastor has to choose, we encourage him to be a godly man.

Bridges: I agree, but a pastor can be both holy and effective. You could make a strong case that a pastor can't truly be effective if he's not holy.

Confidence in God's Unfailing Love

London/Wiseman: The message about holy living is clear in your book *Transforming Grace*; and the subtitle—*Living Confidently in God's Unfailing Love*—amplifies the grace issue.

What's the main thesis of the book and where did it start in your own journey of faith?

Bridges: This book started while I was writing *The Pursuit of Holiness*. The earlier book caused me to sharpen the focus on holiness in my own life so that I was forced to question myself, *Am I really practicing what I'm writing in this book?* In that process, I always came back to an awareness that anyone who seriously pursues holiness must come to grips with God's grace. Without an emphasis on grace, we lapse into a performance relationship with God. Then our relationship with Him is gauged on how well we've been doing in pursuing holiness rather than depending on the provisions of Christ. This interdependence of grace and holiness made me consider titling the book *Saved by Grace but Living by Sweat*.

London/Wiseman: Thousands of pastors can relate to that concept.

Bridges: There is a fascinating reality in this relationship between grace and works. We all know we are saved by grace. We happily agree with the biblical teaching and preach it. But for some strange reason we lapse into living by the sweat of our performance in our day-to-day relationship with God. Then we think, *I've been good today, so I expect God to bless me. But the days I fall on my face, I don't expect much from God.*

London/Wiseman: In that vein, we assume we must be in tune with God if our church is succeeding, if our ministry is well-received, if attendance is growing and if people are coming to Christ and being filled with the Spirit. It seems we think we're more personally spiritual when the pews are packed and everyone is saying nice things about us. We think the success couldn't happen if we weren't holy.

RISK FACTOR

86 percent of pastors say their top priority is personal relationship with God.

Bridges: It's easy to forget that visible success isn't the issue. Genuine relationship with Christ and absolute dependence on Him is. It's possible to be successful without being holy, and it's feasible to be a miserable failure without being holy.

London/Wiseman: That's exactly right. Tell us more about your discoveries about transforming grace and what it means to live confidently in God's unfailing love.

Bridges: The reality is that many believers don't fully enjoy living in God's grace so that it can have a transforming effect on their character. In 2 Corinthians 3:18, Paul says we are being transformed into His likeness from one degree of glory to another. In the context of 2 Corinthians 3, Paul contrasts the glory of the Law, which came through Moses, with the exceedingly greater glory of the gospel. So when Paul talks in this passage about the glory of Christ, he is really discussing the glory of Christ as we see it in the gospel.

I believe we need to put ourselves up against the gospel every day. By this frequent and intentional application of the gospel, we build continual realization of God's grace and its transforming effect on our character. We need a review every day to see if we're living it. And when we do such a daily reassessment, we get excited about the gospel at work in us. We become so aware of the grace of God that we want to live an effective Christian life, and it continually transforms us.

Holiness is hating sin and loving righteousness in the details of our lives.

Holiness Defined

London/Wiseman: In *Transforming Grace*, you devote a whole chapter to describing holiness. In brief capsule form, what do you mean when you speak about holiness?

Bridges: Holiness is conformity to the likeness of Christ. Paul says in Romans 8:29 that we have been "predestined to be conformed to the likeness of [God's] Son." The likeness of Christ is the bottom line of holiness for me.

That means we must deal with sin in our lives. But we also put on godly character by continually dealing with the question, How can I be like Christ, and how would He live in my circumstances?

Jesus hates sin and loves holiness. Hebrews 1:9 says that our Lord loved righteousness and He hated wickedness. That's what He wants us to do. We should hate wickedness; we should hate sin; we should resist sin; and we should put sin to death.

But there is much more—Jesus also loved righteousness. Consequently, we should love righteousness. Righteousness is living a godly character. Holiness is hating sin and loving righteousness in the details of our lives.

London/Wiseman: How can pastors make personal holiness practical? As pastors, it seemed that when we were on a successful fast track—receiving accolades and commendations from congregation and peers—that we were less holy than at any other time. Were we different from others?

Bridges: Success or lack of it is never a reliable way to measure personal holiness.

One way to gauge ministry is to ask yourself, *If the Holy Spirit were to back out of this effort, would it collapse?* Many ministries would continue because they are humanly produced programs.

Let me illustrate from my previous ministry assignment. I worked in an administrative capacity with The Navigators in which I dealt with business and legal issues. But I was just as dependent on the Holy Spirit to enable me to function in that work as a pastor is in preaching or building a church. No matter what I do, in my time alone with God I keep reminding myself of my dependence on Him.

God honors dependence on Him. Every morning in my quiet time, I read the Bible and pray, but I also take time to sit back and evaluate whether I'm depending on the Holy Spirit or on my own talents and the fine staff around me.

London/Wiseman: Personal holiness requires time with God, doesn't it? Pastors, busy with their ministries, often overlook that point.

We think of highly visible pastors and Christian leaders whose lives are filled to the brim. They travel, speak, write, administrate and still allow adequate time for the Lord to do for them and to them what you have just been discussing. Though details differ in every ministry, the pressures to bypass daily renewing are real for every pastor regardless of the size of his church.

Many pastors write, "My life is out of balance. I don't have time to pray. I don't have time for my family. I don't have time to fulfill the expectations of my church. I'm going crazy."

That adds up to the strong possibility that they're probably not spending much time with the Lord either.

Bridges: Personal time with God is usually the first thing that goes in our busyness.

The Traps of Performance and Self-Discipline

London/Wiseman: Do you think clergy are more prone to performance mentality than the people in their churches?

Bridges: I think more. Most of the correspondence I receive about *Transforming Grace* comes from pastors or full-time Christian workers who say, "You've hit me right where I've been functioning. I've been basing my relationship with God on the success of my ministry or my performance."

I think this happens because the more committed a person is, the more tempted he is to feel self-righteous about his religious activity. Then defective reasoning sets in and he thinks, *I'm more committed than these people and I work harder than they do.*

It often happens subtly because a deeply committed pastor is kind of pulling his congregation along in many situations. Then it's easy for him to feel self-righteous. I find that the more committed Christians become, the more they tend to live by performance and to judge others harshly.

London/Wiseman: How can that be?

Bridges: Before I make our readers anxious, I am all for discipline and commitment. But many disciplined and committed people are not even born-again. An example—Olympic athletes need to be disciplined and committed or they wouldn't be finalists.

Since discipline and commitment aren't exclusively Christian virtues, a lot of people who are disciplined by temperament are wholeheartedly committed to different causes. When those kind of people accept Christ and learn about holiness and Christian growth, they begin to pursue these character traits with every fiber of their being. Unfortunately, they may depend unconsciously upon the natural discipline in their genes. Then it's easy to judge other people who don't have that natural discipline. These people mistake natural discipline for genuine godliness.

London/Wiseman: So, let's propose a scenario from a pastor who enjoys study, loves books and finds satisfaction in going to his office at 5:30 A.M. where he insists nobody phones him or knocks on his door for the next six hours. Every day he gives himself to that lofty-sounding schedule. Is it possible that there may not be much real devotion to the Lord in that effort but that he's only meeting the needs of his natural discipline?

Bridges: That's an excellent example of performance that's likely motivated by natural discipline. As a result, his preaching may be flawless but sterile and academic or prepared but not powerful.

The Transformation of Discipline to Devotion

London/Wiseman: Say you had a relationship with that pastor and were trying to help him transform discipline to devotion. How could he change? Or should he?

Bridges: That's a great choice of words: "transform discipline to devotion." A good place to start would be to talk about 1 Corinthians 13; the first three verses teach that we can have knowledge, gifts of speaking and language, faith, zeal and commitment. But it amounts to precisely nothing—absolute zero—without love.

Then I'd suggest to him that his sermons are terrific—well-organized and well-constructed. I would tell him that he does thorough research. But then I'd ask him to consider 1 Corinthians 13:4, which says that love is patient and kind.

Then he'd realize that he shouldn't totally abandon his zealous study habits, but he needs to begin to work on love—an absolutely essential element of personal holiness. And then he questions himself, *How am I going to build love into my ministry?*

London/Wiseman: We often ask ourselves how pastors—with their busy schedules—can make time to love people.

Some pastors work 60, 70, 80, 90 hours a week and serve a congregation that's clamoring for attention. Few people realize that an effective pastor creates an increased demand for his time, so he's at it early in the morning and late at night.

The problem: He doesn't have time to fit aloneness with God into this equation. What do you say to him?

When we stand before God to account for what we've done, all ministry without Him is going to be sounding brass and tinkling cymbals.

Bridges: I'd say, "You do not have time *not* to fit God into your equation." It's as essential as food and water and oxygen for his personal spiritual well-being and for his congregation. All his success is going to come tumbling down, either in this life or at the judgment, if he doesn't build personal holiness into his ministry.

When we stand before God to account for what we've done, all ministry without Him is going to be sounding brass and tinkling cymbals. It may have looked good statistically in this life, but how will it really look for eternity?

I'm convinced that we can't build into our people what we don't have in our lives—personal holy character.

The Real Source for Ministry

London/Wiseman: Are you saying there's no way to give the people the spiritual realities of God unless we possess them ourselves?

Bridges: Yes. The real resourcing for ministry is personal holiness. So I strongly urge overly busy pastors to cut down other ministry activities by an hour every day; then spend that first hour with God during which the pastor forgets sermons and people, and prays, "Lord, here I am. What do You have to say to me today?" Effective ministry to people grows out of intimate experiences with God. Consequently, relationship with Him energizes and informs all phases of ministry.

London/Wiseman: This conversation generates life-giving hope for pastors who have fatigue in their voices, their handwriting, their conversations and on their faces. This reminder can be revolutionary. In place of performance, they can live in transforming grace.

As we discuss rekindling love for God and the pursuit of personal holiness, we discover a spiritual stamina and supernatural toughness available to pastors, pastors' wives and pastors' families. A strength from beyond flows from and through those who are genuinely holy. It provides a significant supernatural strength and insight in the intricacy of their calling and complexities of their pastorates.

All of this means that when a pastor gives first priority to personal holiness, he'll be astounded at what he's able to accomplish in his ministry.

The thought of the Holy Spirit's enabling power flowing through a holy pastor into the agonies and ecstasies of ministry is a powerful image. Let's try to be specific and practical. How can pastors do this?

Bridges: I think we need to spend about an hour with the Lord each day to feed our souls and to provide energy for ministry.

London/Wiseman: You believe it takes an hour a day?

Bridges: No question in my mind. I spend 5:45 to 6:45 with God every morning. Approximately half of that time is spent reading Scripture to allow it to minister to me and to ask the Holy Spirit to speak to me. I read with the question, Lord, what do You want to say to me this morning?

Then the second half hour is for praying. I pray for the Church and the nation. I pray about the assault on the family. Issues that are larger than my own needs.

I think that one of the most important things I can do is ask God to keep me on a short leash. I want a tender conscience to keep me from straying in my thought life or to prevent me from rationalizing about little things.

RISK FACTOR

50 percent of pastors say they'd see another pastor if they felt the need for personal counseling.

For an example of a short leash— let's say I lead in a church where I have an expense account. Like any businessperson, I face the temptation to fudge on my expenditures when I'm away from home. No one intends to be crooked, but it's easy to rationalize that you deserve something.

Maybe you've noticed how extravagant some Christian leaders become when the church or organization is paying the bills—the kinds of restaurants they patronize and prices of meals they order compared with what they do when it comes out of their own pockets. It is slippery business and easy to dupe ourselves.

So I simply ask God to give me a tender conscience because, as the Song of Solomon 2:15 says, it's the little foxes that spoil. I believe the battle is won or lost in the little things. If we let little things go, the big things will devour us, maybe even wreck our witness and destroy our relationship with God.

London/Wiseman: Is it fair to say that the pastor who becomes mired down in a fault, a moral indiscretion, sexual infidelity or tax cheating is likely to be one who has not been pursuing personal holiness?

Bridges: Yes. And I don't think it's judging to say that, but merely diagnosing a preventable catastrophe.

London/Wiseman: So you think these problems can't be blamed on childhood, heredity or environment, but on the simple fact that the person didn't keep a tight and intimate relationship with God?

Bridges: That's right, and it doesn't have to happen.

London/Wiseman: How can pastors guard against these destructive downfalls?

Bridges: Jesus taught us in the Lord's Prayer to pray to be delivered from temptation. So we should pray every day, "Lord, keep me from temptation. Keep me from the assaults of Satan. And keep me from being blindsided by my own unworthy desires."

Jesus also advised us to watch and pray so that we don't enter into temptation. I believe this watching is our own vigilant scrutiny of our lives, which includes being brutally scrupulous with ourselves. The praying part expresses dependence upon God. We need both to rely on God and keep a prudent watch on ourselves.

London/Wiseman: So you consider a pastor's personal holiness to be his first responsibility both to his church and to himself, no matter how many hours he works or what pressures he experiences?

Bridges: Yes. It's his first obligation but also his extraordinary source of spiritual vitality.

The Negotiation of Priorities with Church Leaders

Bridges: Let me add a word to pastors who may be frustrated by what I've said. Share your concern about time for pursuing personal holiness with your governing group—those leaders who could ultimately say you have 30 days to get out of town.

Help them see that your walk with God is your greatest duty to your own soul and your most pressing obligation to the church. Help them understand that you have a limited number of hours and that you have to give first priority to this connection with God. Ask them to help you set priorities in your ministry. Seek their evaluation with the question, What's most important for the church? And then share what you think is most essential.

Negotiate priorities with them. You may think sermon preparation is tops, and they may consider discipling six men as lay leaders to be first. In this evolutionary effort, you will soon run out of time with an unfinished list of things that still need doing. But it's important and enlightening for everyone on your leadership team to have a part in the decision. As a result, some tasks may not get done or else someone else in the church will have to do them.

Pastors often mistakenly underestimate laypeople's understanding of spiritual realities. Any spiritually alert lay leader wants his pastor to be a developing disciple of Jesus who's growing in Christlikeness. Trust them with the fact that you want to pursue personal holiness. In most instances they will be supportive of or even generous with helping you find ways to do it. And the discussion creates a commitment to follow through on your part.

Advice to Pastors

London/Wiseman: That's a great way to take responsibility for your personal holiness and at the same time to share the ministry of the church. How would you apply pursuing personal holiness to the pastor who wrote this letter: "I'm preacher, counselor, secretary and sometimes maintenance man at our small church. I carry a heavy burden for the spiritual and emotional well-being of my flock. Satan is always attacking in one way or another. Sometimes I don't have energy to fight the battle anymore." How can he find help?

Bridges: I think he needs a vacation with God where he repairs his relationship with the Lord—a time to recharge his spiritual and emotional batteries. A family tour of Disneyland won't cure this fatigue in his soul.

This pastor needs to view his problem like a serious physical illness where he backs off from some commitments for a period of time or maybe forever. If he had serious surgery, he would be out of work for six weeks. That's just the way it is when the doctor says, "No, you can't go back to work yet." Why should it be different for a fatigued pastor?

Without proper care his spiritual exhaustion will only get worse. And his weariness won't be repaired by one hour per day; the hour a day is maintenance for a spiritually healthy pastor. This man needs intensive care for his soul.

London/Wiseman: You think this pastor could get well by continuing his regular routine at a slower pace?

Bridges: It seems that he's on an endless treadmill. So he'd probably get much worse without resolute intervention. His condition can become chronic or spiritually life threatening. Either way, he's in trouble and needs prompt assistance.

London/Wiseman: Another letter from a devoted pastor: "My greatest worry is to set a consistent Christlike example—first before my wife and children, and then before the congregation. I truly long to be a spiritual leader, to be someone who, by virtue of his intimate relationship with Christ, greatly influences others to be like Him."

That sounds like a laudable goal, but is he taking too much obligation on himself?

Bridges: I think his goal is worthy and achievable. But I suggest to every pastor that he be honest about his own weaknesses and failures. I've been a Christian for more than 50 years, and the pastors who ministered most effectively to me sometimes came to the pulpit and said, "Hey, folks, I don't have anything to say today."

The goal of the pastor-parishioner pilgrimage is to pursue holiness together. I remember one Sunday our pastor said, "I was ready to come to church this morning, and my wife wasn't ready. I got upset with her because she was going to make me late getting to church." By telling us that from the pulpit, he helped us see that he was one of us and that we must pursue holiness together. Now he was a godly man, and he didn't tell us every time something went wrong in his life; but by being open on occasion, he came across as a person who's eager to be like Christ. He conveyed both spiritual eagerness and day-by-day realities.

London/Wiseman: So you think being transparent is useful for a pastor?

Bridges: Transparent—that's the idea exactly.

London/Wiseman: It's really preaching confessionally when a pastor is willing to stand before his people and say, "My feet of clay sure showed this week."

Bridges: Transparent and confessional—those are liberating acts for the pastor and for believers under his care.

London/Wiseman: Let's consider one more letter: "My greatest challenge isn't to become so involved in administration, visitation and other phases of the work of the Lord that I don't have quality time for getting to know the Lord of the work."

It is easy to forget that it is the Lord's work, and we let it become our work. How can pastors keep themselves reminded that it's God's work they're doing?

Bridges: I use visual reminders. I have a pen with a pedestal on my desk, so I write a Scripture reference on a small slip of paper, like John 15:5: "Apart from me you can do nothing." Then I tape that Bible reference across the pedestal of that pen so that I see John 15:5 every time I look at the pen.

Another especially useful Scripture is the well-known story in Luke 10 where Martha was distracted over her business while

Mary was sitting at the feet of Jesus. On that occasion, Jesus said to Martha, "One thing is needed" (v. 42). Only one thing.

As an overworked pastor, I might tape that phrase—"one thing"—to the dashboard of my car or on the pedestal of my desk pen.

Another passage is Psalm 27:4: "One thing I ask of the LORD . . . that I may dwell in the house of the LORD all the days of my life, to gaze upon the beauty of the LORD and to seek him in his temple." Psalm 27:4 is my number one prayer request for myself.

London/Wiseman: If you could only say one thing to the average pastor, what would it be? What advice do you have to help a pastor become a better pastor, husband, father and Christian?

Bridges: I would go to Enoch, who is mentioned only a few times in the Bible. Genesis 5 says that Enoch walked with God, and Hebrews 11 tells us that he pleased God.

Enoch is one of my favorite Bible characters because he clearly stands for those two things—walking with God and pleasing God. Every pastor can do both; no one can stop him. And every pastor needs the resources that come through such an intimate relationship with God.

Suggestions for Pursuing Personal Holiness

Pastors need to hear Jerry Bridges's energizing message. For too long pastors have shortchanged themselves by separating personal holiness from the practice of ministry, competency from character and service from spirituality. To work on ways to bring these inner and outer worlds together, meet Michael Messner.

Michael Messner was a typical minister in the making. He earned good grades, married well the day after college graduation and was voted by classmates as the most likely to succeed. When church leaders came to recruit pastors during his last semester in seminary, he had his choice of several strong entry-level churches.

Michael and his wife, Suzanne, moved to their first church and did well for two years. But he soon missed the academic stimulus of the seminary and felt trapped by the repetition of ministry. He hit an invisible wall like a high-spirited jogger and didn't know how to get around it.

Changing environments seemed to be his only answer. With his charisma and outstanding academic achievements, it was easy to move to another church in another state. But unfortunately, he had to take himself with him. So the same pattern developed again: great start, boredom, frustration, loneliness and an eagerness for new challenges and scenery. Soon the fast-tracker fizzled again and moved on to become a counselor in a mental health clinic. Now he grieves over what happened to his dreams for parish ministry.

Recently, Michael and Suzanne met a lovely retired couple, Tom and Sarah Kratz, who shared satisfying pastoral ministry for 40 years in three churches. As the two couples developed a strong friendship in spite of their age differences, Sarah asked Suzanne, "What did Michael do in his ministry to feed his soul?" She continued, "Tom and I found joy for the journey because we discovered early on that he had to keep his soul fat, or he had nothing that mattered much to give to others. So he committed time and effort to developing a holy character, and I encouraged him to do so because he was more fun to live with when he was spiritually strong and fulfilled."

Sarah's right. Ultimately, nothing is more powerful or influential in a church than a fulfilled pastor who does his work with an inner zest, rooted in a pursuit of personal holiness with God. The following suggestions help to answer the question *how*.

Use Devotion as a Catalyst for Discipline

While duty, obligation and accountability are part of ministry, deep-seated devotion to Christ is what gives discipline meaning.

Pleasing the Father is easier when you're inspired by devotion, rather than required by responsibility.

A foundational principle of effective ministry is that devotion fuels discipline fully as much as love sends us out to earn a living for our families. Love energizes discipline—that's the secret that makes Christian obligations satisfying. Pleasing the Father is always easier when you're inspired by devotion, rather than required by responsibility. For example, a meaningful ministry requires you to have quiet times. But those will have much more meaning when you think of them as warm, caring conversations with a trusted Friend. And Bible reading will always be more rewarding when you view it as reading a love letter from God.

Refurbish Your Original Vision

As the years roll on, you can easily forget about the magnet of meaning that first attracted you to ministry. Without continuous miraculous enabling by God, your work can turn into trifling do-goodism. But if you can have a supernatural vision for your work, it will enliven your ministry and make it fruitful. This supernatural "something beyond" renews your vision and causes your ministry to influence people in life-changing ways as nothing else can. And it will make your work seem worthwhile even on dark days. Like Enoch, cultivating God's friendship gives importance to everything else.

To refocus your vision, keep close to the basics of faith. Return often to the vision God gave you when you started your present assignment. Polish the original vision. Preach it. Write about it. Be controlled by it. Celebrate the satisfaction that ministry brings into your life. Relish ministry as a marvelous way of life and make it true. Remember what God promised when He called you.

Drop All Pretense

Because pastors are public figures, they live much of their lives on platforms and before the watchful eye of crowds. It becomes easy for them to believe their own press releases or the compliments people shower upon them. As a result, their entire ministry can become a subterfuge, maybe even a lie. They work to create an impression of lofty service to God and people, when actually the pastors' egos are seeking their own satisfaction.

In such situations, pastors live in fantasy, sham and hype—all make-believe illusions. They delude themselves by overestimating their worth to the church, overestimate commitment to individual prayer and overestimate faithfulness in applying the Bible to their own lives. All rubbish. Such self-deception produces spiritual rigor mortis and destroys the spiritual vigor of a congregation.

Face the facts: Pretending to be holy takes more effort than the real thing. Pretending to be generous costs almost as much as the genuine article. Pretending to be loving is harder than really loving others. It takes much more effort to look back over your shoulder to be sure of a good impression than it does to do the right thing for the right reason.

Jesus honors honesty, but hates pretense. He challenges you to make your speech, attitudes and actions match.

Seek Clarifying Solitude

Solitude may be hard to find and harder still to face because we may not like what we discover about ourselves during our quietest moments. Withdrawal from our public life tends to bring buried issues and toxic relationships into candid focus.

An hour of solitude where you "take captive every thought to make it obedient to Christ" (2 Cor. 10:5) can clear spiritual, emotional and relational cobwebs out of the corners of your life. In some quiet corner of life, you need to practice what the Quakers call centering down on Christ. Seasons of solitude with God will help you see life and ministry accurately.

Take God into Your Realities

Ministry is tougher now than ever before. But that's also the reason it has to be done well. Since your ministry is linked to the omnipotent God, look beyond the problems to His power, beyond the scarcity to His abundance and beyond the hurt to His healing.

If you try to do ministry in your own strength, you'll be swamped by minutia or stressed to the breaking point. The load, however, will lighten significantly when all the resources of God focus like a laser beam on your best efforts.

Taking God into the realities of ministry also helps identify things that you're distorting that can so easily wreck ministry. Such a God-closeness enables you to see if you're putting the complex pieces of ministry together accurately. Who among us has not come to a false conclusion that slowed or squelched ministry? Perhaps pastors need to consider an additional beatitude: Blessed are those who allow God to help them see things as they are.

This process isn't meant to deny difficulties, play down problems or use empty words to pacify crises. Rather, it's meant to bring the Lord of the universe into your everyday ministry—to bring Him into the midst of your misunderstandings, overly tight budgets, feelings of despair and sense of isolation. It makes real the promises "I am with you always" (Matt. 28:20) and "Never will I leave you; never will I forsake you" (Heb. 13:5). It often starts with a powerful five-second prayer break in difficult situations: "God, please see me through this difficulty to victory." And indeed He does.

Review Patterns of Ministry

The direction you go in ministry will determine its outcomes, and the patterns you use to conduct your ministry will govern its effectiveness. So you must intentionally invest energy and effort in what you want the years of your ministry to do for God. You need to commit to the impact you want to make on believers under your spiritual care. You must know what you want your work to accomplish.

To review and refocus the direction of your ministry, ask yourself these questions: Where do you want your ministry to go? Is your preaching happy or judgmental? Does your counseling help people to Christlike wholeness, or is it rigidly restrictive? Is your leadership liberating or enslaving? Do people come to redeeming friendship with the heavenly Father because of your ministry, or are their fears about God reinforced? What's the direction of your ministry, and is it going where you want it to go?

Recognize Your Need to Control as a Power Drain

Maybe what is attributed to Dostoyevsky is right, "Without God we are too strong for each other." Controlling an organization can be enticing and destructive, even to spiritually minded people. People don't stop following a leader because he's spiritually strong or persevering. Rather, they quit or quietly turn to apathy and mediocrity because they believe their leader is controlling or ego driven.

Though the Bible calls for a pastor to be an overseer, it never permits manipulation, conniving or dictatorship. In the work of

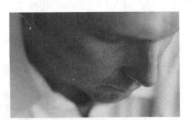

God, pastors must hold leadership privilege or position loosely, while they take the work seriously. The Bible trusts the pastor with authority for achievement, but this authority was never intended for ego gratification.

Though the Bible calls for a pastor to be an overseer, it never permits manipulation, conniving or dictatorship.

Power seduces pastors in situations of every size. A little organizational authority turns some mild-mannered ministers into controlling tyrants. Positional power hopelessly locks others into trivia where they do everything because their egos want to be in charge. Either way, the controller suffers spiritual heart damage, and it stifles the congregation's creativity.

Four lies about power will sabotage a pastor's efforts to be like Christ, if he believes them:

- I'm special and not subject to entanglements others face.
- I don't need to play by the rules—not even God's.
- I deserve my position in the will of God.
- I'm brighter and holier than those I lead.

Ask for help and share success. Follow this pattern of Jesus and you'll get more work done, and in the process, it frees your time and emotions to develop your inner world. Make sure to give both your ministry and yourself continually to the trusted control of God.

Resist the Too-Busy Syndrome

Obligations and expectations will keep your calendar loaded. Since you can't escape the calendar, why not use it for something that really matters? Schedule time with God just as intentionally as you schedule the Sunday-morning worship service. Remember that the busy pastor is the one who most needs time alone with God.

YOUR CHALLENGE

GET YOUR SOUL INTO SHAPE

As a favor to yourself and your ministry, pursue personal holiness at any cost. Such an intimate connection with Christ will revitalize your motivation for service and provide the raw materials of tenacity and fulfillment in ministry. It's the cornerstone of productivity and the underpinning for satisfaction. Personal holiness will keep your soul in shape.

Compelling demands of ministry will easily deplete your spiritual stamina. You'll feel dry, empty and exhausted. But you have a life-saving alternative: it's an intimacy with Christ that will invigorate you so you can victoriously meet the rigors of your task with restored focus and vigor.

Even if you know something about personal holiness in a theoretical, idealistic way, you may not know how to initiate intimacy with Christ effectively. The first step to discover growth in personal holiness is to move from vagueness to specifics. If you're overworked physically and undernourished spiritually, intimacy with Christ can start to flow from many faith-formation tributaries. Henri Nouwen, the Catholic encourager of Christian leaders, offers a starting list of three: "contemplative reading of the word of God, a silent listening to the voice of God, and trusting obedience to a spiritual guide."[7] What a faith-building list.

In the midst of the frightening hazards you face as a pastor, the pursuit of personal holiness is God's wake-up call to move you from professional religion to personal faith. Such a pursuit will revitalize your sense of direction, stimulate your confidence in society's need for righteousness and intensify your passion for doing God's work in this kind of world.

Unleashed in your inner world, who knows where personal holiness might take you in your outer world.

The world and the Church will follow spiritual leaders who demonstrate and enjoy personal intimacy with Christ in the tiniest particulars of their lives and ministry. A reactivated faith that laughs at risks and overpowers the hazards pastors face starts with renewed intimacy with Christ.

RENEWAL STRATEGIES

DEEPENING YOUR INTIMACY WITH CHRIST

✓ Use devotion as a catalyst for discipline.
✓ Refurbish your original vision.
✓ Drop all pretense.
✓ Seek clarifying solitude.

✓ Take God into your realities.
✓ Review patterns of ministry.
✓ Recognize your need to control as a power drain.
✓ Resist the too-busy syndrome.

A Personal Word from H. B. L.

You Can Because He Can

One of the most dramatic moments of the 2000 Summer Olympics occurred when American Laura Wilkinson came from far behind to win the gold medal in the 10-meter platform dive. No one had given her a chance. When the network commentator asked her to put the emotion she was feeling into words, Laura said, "I can do all things through Christ who strengthens me."

Remember when the apostle Paul first uttered those words? He was in prison—cold, sick and lonely. He wrote about his circumstances in the midst of a so-called impossible situation. Most would have looked at the overwhelming odds and given up—but not Paul, and not Laura Wilkinson. Paul would exclaim, "I can do everything through him who gives me strength" (Phil. 4:13).

You may find yourself in an impossible, hopeless situation. You're tempted to say, "What's the use?" But it's never hopeless. Never forget you serve an awesome God who loves you and who knows your needs.

You too can be a come-from-behind winner.

You can because He can.

CHAPTER TWELVE

TWELVE STEPS TO MORE EFFECTIVE MINISTRY

For pastors who do their work continually in a world of half-hearted commitments, moral bankruptcies, devastating sins and dysfunctional people, spiritual dryness and emotional starvation are occupational land mines.

Their situation can easily become hypnotic so that they see only problems with no hope. Blaming others or suffering in stoic silence wastes emotional energy they could use more constructively. These foes—dryness and starvation—are hard to recognize, and it's difficult to imagine what havoc they'll trigger tomorrow, next week and deeper into the new century.

We need strong corrective action immediately. But diagnosing accomplishes nothing without a remedy. What can be done? Who will do it? Who should do it? And after we start the medication, surgery or rehabilitation, what's the prognosis?

Where will solutions come from? Help won't come from church structures—they frequently cause monstrous complications for pastors without intending to. Theological educators can't do it because nothing in their experience or training provides a frame of reference for teaching students how to deal with times like these. Culture and society, grossly misinformed about ministry, assume most pastors are counterfeits and charlatans. And laypeople in the churches simply aren't fully aware of the risks pastors experience.

Where can pastors find help? Perhaps the best hope is themselves.

Apparently, pastors are the only change agents who are aware enough to correct the problem. And no other group is likely to feel the problem so keenly or have more interest in finding a solution.

The present predicament could be alleviated quickly by the positive resources they already possess, if properly used: a Bible in their hands, God's love in their hearts, a passionate will to do right in their souls and an energized commitment to win their world in their plans.

Examine the other choices: Curse the darkness and live in passive acquiescence. Accept festering inner rage for the predicament. Carry protest placards. Raise a new generation in their own homes who resent what their fathers' calling does to their lives.

None of these possibilities sound useful or attractive. Doesn't it follow that pastors themselves must initiate improvements? While such an effort could be difficult, awkward, discomforting and self-serving, a frontline attack will shape the whole future of ministry and contour what the Church becomes in the new century

Doesn't it make sense for pastors to band together to overpower the risks? And if the answer is yes, what kind of person, leader and Christian will the pastor for this new day have to be? What attributes and actions

Doesn't it make sense for pastors to band together to overpower the risks?

will encourage this necessary and satisfying bond between personal piety and professional competence? Consider these 12 steps that pastors—you and your ministerial teammates—can take to overcome the greater risks you face today.

STEP 1: RESIST PERSONAL SPIRITUAL POWER LEAKAGE

Just as oxygen is necessary for human life or gasoline is necessary for an automobile, so your intimacy with Christ is the irreducible minimum for useful ministry. Without personal faith shining through all expressions of your ministry, you're simply an empty echo of what God intends you to be. Everything in ministry depends on your personal faith.

No spiritual leader who is not holy can be productive. Jesus Himself is the inner vitality for ministry. Our Lord was absolutely correct when He warned that we could do nothing without Him.

Admittedly, it's easy almost unknowingly to blur the differences between personal faith and professional performance. But merely standing close to spiritual fires every minute of every day won't make you a vibrant believer. Without clear personal faith, you'll soon become shallow, your vision superficial, your influence minimal and your satisfaction near zero. You'll be a pathetic imitation of the real thing.

But perpetual demands militate against personal piety. Obligations for public prayers make it easy to bypass wholehearted engagement in your private praying. No ministry will have less power than that of a pastor who seldom prays personally.

You can render the care of souls in your office with trifling compassion and little Scripture or prayer. Of course, such an empty effort is often a poor simulation of secular counseling and a shoddy excuse for pastoral care. Instead, your personal relationship with Jesus should make your counseling uniquely different from the work of all other helping professionals.

You can routinely call on hospital patients without getting too involved in their pain. Sure, a pleasant bedside manner with a professional flair and a ready smile produces a pleasing public image. But without your personal faith, the hospital visit is merely social with no physical or spiritual healing.

Or consider your preaching ministry. If your Sunday sermon is worth hearing, it must be a distinctive connection of biblical research, systematized doctrine, skilled speaking and accurate exegesis of the world in which your people live. Like a lawyer in the courtroom or a surgeon in the operating room, as the pastor in the pulpit you must hone your skills for maximum effectiveness. But no matter how skilled or experienced you may be, your effort will be only egotistical rhetoric if your personal faith is missing.

To be genuinely productive, all of your ministry must integrate personal piety and painstaking competence. The techniques for feeding your soul aren't as important as the sources. Author and pastor Eugene Peterson argues that ministry can't be shaped by God without three connecting angles— Scripture, prayer and accountability to a soul friend.[1]

Such an alive intimacy with God will make you different from all other professionals. It will prompt people to listen actively to your preaching. And it will inspire them to

The temptation of professional performance is one of the most deadly perils you face.

call on you in their crises. Nothing you do has lasting value unless you nourish it with your own closeness to God.

No one can force you to feed your own faith, and no one can keep you from it. The temptation of professional performance is one of the most deadly perils you face. But when these inner resources energize your soul, pastoring is one of the most gratifying works in the world.

STEP 2: COMMIT TO CONTENTMENT AND CHANGE

Contentment and change—how can these words be "shoehorned" into the same sentence? By their essence, contentment seems to encourage a "don't rock the boat" mentality, and change seems to signal discontentment. But the two ideas can be on friendly terms in the pastorate.

Contentment—gratitude for what you have—will keep you from chafing about what you don't have. A lay leader provides a refreshing perspective: "We're embarrassed by what little we are able to do for our pastor, but when he expresses thanks for what we do, it makes most of us try harder to improve his lot in life." Discontentment, conversely, slows change to a snail's pace or stops it dead.

Discontentment for some people is a perpetual habit in marriage, family or ministry; it's a costly attitude that robs them of the joy of living. The apostle Paul shares the secret of a satisfying life: "I have learned to be content whatever the circumstances. I know what it is to be in need, and I know what it is to have plenty. I have learned the secret of being content in any and every situation, whether well fed or hungry, whether living in plenty or in want" (Phil. 4:11-12). When you're stressed by a truckload of limitations and hindrances, existing opportunities and privileges will be hard to see.

Contentment and change are also tied together in another way: When you show contentment with what you have, you gain credibility for asking people to do better. Subsequently, you'll ask for and get change that benefits the church rather than yourself. That surprises even the most annoying skeptics who find it hard to fuss about improvements that benefit the congregation. Contentment boosts credibility.

The formula, then, for achievement goes like this: Contentment plus thought-out, proposed change equals a willingness to change. Commitment to contentment is a prerequisite for change.

STEP 3: REENVISION YOUR MISSION

Why does your church exist, and why are you in the ministry? Those are probing questions that help reenvision ministry for yourself and your church. Serious answers to these questions unleash the power of purpose. If the church is to thrive rather than merely survive, your practices and priorities must be consistent with your vision. A worthwhile, clearly understood purpose frees a church from paralytic passivity.

A church's reason for being—an understandable purpose that links mind, motivation and muscle—is easily lost in the hubbub of ministry. Perhaps the declining involvement of laypeople is rooted in unclear purpose; maybe they just don't see the point in much of the church's efforts. Or an unclear mission may be why some congregations tenaciously clutch traditional methods as the only way to do ministry. Stubborn allegiance to conventional methodology and decreasing interest in church activity may be deadly symptoms forcing churches to rethink the way they articulate purpose and mission. The pressing question in implementing vision is, Why does the church exist?

Mission and vision belong together and greatly influence each other. Anglican priest Leonard Griffith warns:

> If the church ever drops the word mission from its vocabulary, it will have written its own obituary, and its buildings will be like war memorial museums, related to the past but not to the present or the future.[2]

An uncomplicated process for reenvisioning ministry according to purpose is to begin with the end in mind. Think how charged up your ministry could become if you could plan it in light of what you want to accomplish for God with your life. Consider how this end-in-view concept could help you keep all ministry centered on mission. It would bring God into the smallest details of church life as you intentionally seek to understand what God wants done in this particular situation at this specific time.

Stephen R. Covey, the secular management guru, more thoroughly explains the value of a crystallized purpose:

People from every walk of life—doctors, academicians, actors, politicians, business professionals, athletes, and plumbers—often struggle to achieve a higher income, more recognition, or a certain degree of professional competence, only to find that their drive to achieve their goal blinded them to the things that really mattered most and now are gone.[3]

Could it be that feelings of futility among Christian workers come from giving too much of themselves for too long to things that don't really matter? Perhaps some pastoral stress is rooted in being too active to be really effective. If your vision for the task is obscure, out of focus or mistaken, it's easy to consume enormous energy on useless struggles and unproductive actions.

To return to what really matters, try to reenvision your task. Write a purpose statement that incorporates your most compelling reasons for ministry, your goals and timetable for them, and to which causes you're willing to commit vast amounts of personal energy. Then use this purpose statement to control your ministry and life. Lead your church to be mission driven, too.

STEP 4: CHOOSE AN ABUNDANCE MENTALITY

The term "abundance mentality" comes from Covey.[4] But its application in the Church is as old as the New Testament. Jesus taught over and over again that His little band of weak, spiritually blinded followers could transform the world because of His profuse provisions for them. The Lord intended their scarcity to remind them of His abundance.

Abundance mentality simply means that everyone possesses sufficient grace, faith, victory, provision, good results, creativity, imagination and accomplishment. None of these provisions has a limited supply. This idea isn't meant to support a name-it-and-claim-it theology. But it does insist that God's provision is bigger and more abundant than we usually allow ourselves to believe.

An example in secular society is the retail developer who builds three fast-food restaurants in the same block. All three flourish, much to an outsider's amazement. One marketing expert explains, "They feed off each other's success." That's abundance mentality.

Abundance mentality believes that God wants to bless His people in every situation and that He can enable every congregation to succeed. It believes there are more successes in ministry for those who move forward with initiative and dependence on God than for those who are afraid to risk living on the cutting edge.

> **Abundance mentality believes that God can enable every congregation to succeed.**

One missionary's experience illustrates abundance mentality. During the years of the Great Depression, a young woman went as a missionary to Africa to open a specialized ministry to teenage girls. This mission effort became so effective that they needed additional facilities, but no money seemed to be available. The young missionary wrote to her mission superior stationed in another country complaining about her deplorable working conditions. In a few days the superior wrote back, "Daughter of the King, if you don't like your conditions, change them. Your Father is rich."

Your ministry setting may have severe limitations that could cause you to think that abundance mentality is a myth. But take another look. If conditions seem limiting, you can change them with your Father's help.

The issue isn't how little you have, but how much your Father has to give. The potential for a fulfilled ministry may be right at your fingertips, but you'll miss it if you don't live by abundance mentality.

STEP 5: CULTIVATE A BREAK-OUT SPIRIT

Imagination and innovation seem to be in short supply in the Church. For some unknown reason, many church members want things to remain like they've always been—as if that were possible. Such a hold-the-line posture just doesn't square with reality because the essential nature of both people and the Church is to change, adapt and grow.

Christian history, particularly near the dawn of the Early Church, offers many examples of people who took the gospel to their times in maverick ways. They weren't afraid to change methods or patterns of action. But they didn't try fresh approaches for the sake of newness; they discarded archaic ways because they no longer worked. Circumstances and failures often forced them to break out of old ways of thinking and doing.

We can see this break-out spirit in the long pilgrimage of faith. For example, the decision to choose the first group of lay leaders in the Early Church came about because the disciples couldn't meet the increasing demands of an assistance program for needy widows. They solved the problem in a new way, which became the foundation of all shared leadership between clergy and laypeople. That decision provided a partnership in ministry that was completely new to their way of thinking.

National prejudice was the order of the day in the Early Church until Peter found himself declaring, "God does not show favoritism" (Acts 10:34). From that day until now, the Church has been struggling to tear down walls of separation between people groups. Even old stick-in-the-mud Peter broke out of his traditional patterns of thinking to open the Church doors to people of all ethnic origins.

Luther forever changed the heart of Christianity when, after drawing close to God, he saw things in a whole new light. Luther's break-out spirit first sought the mind of God and then asked persistent questions of his environment. He sought demanding cures and applied them to himself, his church and his world. As a result of his break-out spirit, he became a Christian revolutionary that renewed the Church, taking it back—or was it forward?—to the authority of the Bible.

Wesley sharpened his break-out spirit when he applied the gospel to problems in his society and started the Methodist movement, which continues to affect the world to this day. Like all break-out leaders in the history of Christianity, Wesley intersected personal faith, needs of the times and the power of the gospel.

Ministering with this kind of break-out spirit requires you to be proactive in ministry, a trait few have observed firsthand. From the world of business, Robert J. Kriegel and Louis Patler offer an observation about being proactive that applies to churches:

> Research shows that the overwhelming majority of Americans (85 percent) are reactive and static, not action- or dynamic- or instinct-oriented. They wait and meet, meet and wait. With a ready arsenal of conservative, conventional wisdom at their disposal, they try to control outcomes in an out-of-control world.[5]

Being proactive means taking initiative to find solutions, to make things happen and to make the church more influential in the lives of the people it serves. Initiative is the key ingredient. That should not be too hard to accomplish because human beings were created to be active rather than reactive and to solve problems rather than be overwhelmed by them.

A useful way to start is to try to think like a beginner again, like you did before you were burdened by experience, expertise, success or the necessity to defend your position. The challenge, then, is to live out your imagination, vision and conscience and to resist the effects of your conditioning, failure and disappointments. Your stress will go down and your hope increase when you realize that you don't have to be at the mercy of your setting or history.

Don't be afraid of having a break-out spirit, and don't wait for others to correct situations and improve environments. The people you're waiting for might not even see the problem. Then an achieve-nothing gridlock results.

Remember the Serenity Prayer? It can help you boldly respond to your own break-out spirit: God, grant me the serenity to accept the things I cannot change; courage to change the things I can; and wisdom to know the difference. Give that second phrase—"courage to change the things I can"—substantially more attention than you're used to giving it. Let the break-out spirit in you replace nonchalant compliance with resolute competence. Then instead of allowing situations to victimize you, you can transform them into golden opportunities for the gospel.

Secular management specialist John Akers's advice to business leaders speaks loud and clear to pastors:

> The people who are playing it totally safe are never going to have either the fun or the reward of the people who decide to take risks, stick out from the crowd, do it differently.[6]

STEP 6: QUESTION THE QUALITY-VERSUS-QUANTITY MYTH

We need to stop making false choices between quality and quantity in ministry, because the two are inexorably tied together. Ministry usually gets bigger when it gets better.

Think how the two are linked in the business world. Quality determines how many cars General Motors sells, on what timetable and at what cost. Quality of service, on-time arrivals and departures and safety of aircraft determine how many passengers fly with Southwest Airlines. Construction quality affects how many houses a local building contractor will sell in a year.

Since quality affects quantity on many levels of human existence, we shouldn't be surprised that a pastor's stress increases when outside forces expect him to increase attendance and improve the church's influence. Quality and quantity are simply professional expectations that people in many vocations have for themselves; in fact, they'd be surprised if anyone thought it should be any other way.

It's always possible to take simple steps toward improved quality. Nearly every church, regardless of size or location, can immediately improve quality in some way. As a result, improvement in one area creates an awareness and a commitment to improvement in other areas. In this process, the next step of quality becomes easier than the first. In some astounding, almost imperceptible way, every attempt at quality encourages, or perhaps empowers, a church to move up the spiral of improvement and growth.

A subtle crunch in this reasoning occurs when a pastor and a church offer quality ministry, yet attendance drops. Perhaps the answer is like a blue-chip stock's value, which doesn't grow every day; quality may not always produce immediate increases, but growth usually comes over the long haul. If there is no quantity result from quality ministry, the leader should evaluate the quality.

A pastor's frustration only increases if he thinks someone is chasing him with a demand for increased numbers; a glance over his shoulder might reveal that this is often a self-imposed expectation. Who makes the demands? The problem may be in his head.

We often overlook another dimension of the quality issue. Leading people to Christ invigorates ministry. Pastors who effectively introduce people to Christ are among the most fulfilled people on Earth. They know from experience that, like love and marriage and food and fullness, quality and quantity cannot be separated.

The Lord Jesus, our flawless model for all ministry, practiced both quality and quantity. He counted 12 disciples, 120 at Pentecost and 5,000 men (not counting women and children) as being present at the miraculous breaking of bread and fish. In all these situations, He offered quality ministry, but at the same time He counted the people.

You can rid yourself of this draining inner menace if you come to terms with the reality that you don't need to choose between quality and quantity. Bona fide quality in ministry means more people become interested in what the Church has to offer them—Christ.

Why not be free from the numbers game by recommitting to the basic motivation that initially drew you into ministry?

STEP 7: TRANSFORM AMBIGUITIES INTO AUTHENTICITIES

The Church's prominent ministries of words—preaching and teaching—presuppose that language determines attitudes, actions and achievements in the speaker as well as the hearer. Therefore, disheartened pastors need to listen to what they say to those they love and lead. They need to practice what they preach.

In many situations, preaching has conditioned laypeople to believe that deep thoughts and doctrines about God are too complicated for ordinary people to comprehend. And if they hear that reasoning often enough, it makes them believe that Scripture is also too difficult for them to understand.

Because of their training or the way they've always preached, pastors often impede their communication in at least one of the following four ways:

1. By using professional language—technical vocabulary that speaks clearly to theologians, Bible scholars and fellow pastors.
2. By using insider language, sometimes known as King James speech—it is wonderfully familiar and generally understood by believers but sounds like a foreign tongue to those outside the Church.
3. By using pop psychological language—jargon that describes phobias, aggression, obsessions, compulsions, codependence and anxieties in place of clearly articulated demands and Christ-provided solutions found in Scripture.
4. By using empty speech—words calculated to sound impressive but that say nothing.

The ministry, like other occupations, has *professional language* that may communicate rich meaning to the profession but is meaningless to amateurs. Medicine is a striking example of a technical vocabulary, where diseases have long names, body parts have strange-sounding designations and prescription drugs have impossible-to-pronounce names. The pastor's technical list includes such terms as orthodoxy, incarnation, predestination, revelation and theism. Then, without meaning to, the scholarly Bible preacher complicates communication when he mentions his research in Greek, his thorough exegesis and his studies in the history of Christian thought. Why be astonished then, when a junior high physical education teacher, mechanic or policewoman says he or she doesn't understand preaching?

Insider language—like "being saved"—might be precious to saints, but it has no meaning to people outside the Church. Hymns and worship choruses often contain insider language like "wonderful grace of Jesus," "break Thou the bread of life," "He hideth my soul in the cleft of the rock" and "Sun of my soul."

No one inside the Church wants to give up on these beloved phrases, and we shouldn't. But if the purpose of language is to produce understanding, then the man and woman on the street need someone to interpret religious language when they go to church. Otherwise, they consider the Church to be an irrelevant relic.

Pop psychological jargon rolls like the mighty Jordan from pulpits today. Much of it is neither good psychology nor accurate theology. In a mistaken attempt to be relevant, pastors use self-help terms without judging them against Scripture. Meanwhile, the gospel says that our only real help is in God alone.

Anglican pastor Alan Jones notes,

> One of the things I dread is finding myself terminally ill and being trapped by an eager, young, therapeutically orientated, and humorless clergyman, who will walk all over my psyche by insisting on my sharing my feelings when all I want are the traditional ministrations of prayer and Scripture.[7]

Good psychology and good theology have much common ground. But fads that focus the proclamation of the Church on popular psychology rather than biblical truth leave listeners emotionally confused and spiritually lean.

Empty speech, thin verbal communication, presents still another problem. Maybe you've heard the story of the hard-of-hearing woman who was escorted to the front row of a church to hear a famous preacher. After about five minutes of high-sounding chatter, the woman said in what she thought was a whisper, "He hasn't said anything yet, has he?" Too many pastors preach a bushel of niceties mixed with a bit of technical theological jargon and then send people out to face another week of struggle.

By using plain speech, eternal truth and logic on fire you can release the gospel's authentic life-changing power. Remember the words of another old saint when she shouted from the congregation to her pastor, "Make it plain, brother; make it plain." Your listeners don't need more religious double-talk. Instead, give them your best shot at a life-changing word from the Lord that they can truly understand.

STEP 8: CHERISH PEOPLE

A veteran pastor lectured beginners:

> You can't learn ministry in commentaries, classrooms or cloisters. All three help, but flesh-and-blood human beings are the raw material of ministry, just as the human body is the basic element of medicine. You only learn ministry among people.

There's no way around it. God intends ministry for people—not for pastors, denominations, theological systems or social action. The genuinely fulfilled pastor authentically loves people even though they often surprise him. They're the reason Christ came. Their heart for ministry is what provides millions of hours of volunteer service every week for the cause of Christ. People make life both fulfilling and frustrating for pastors.

God's strategy is for a very human vessel called the pastor to take the good news into the fabric of people's lives. In the process of nurturing people, the pastor must remember that regardless of age, appearance or gender, people are tender, sensitive and often lonely. In spite of their callused exteriors, inside they hold gentle feelings and nervous concerns.

Ministry, therefore, needs the Common Harry Test. Common Harry is a tenth-grade high school dropout who runs a plumbing shop in everyone's town; he knows ordinary life well but has almost no interest in theoretical reasoning. He needs ministry and he knows it. In the losses and uncertainties of his life, he can't get along without the good news of the gospel. And if he can understand ministry, so can everyone else in the typical congregation.

Much of your frustration with ministry will be rooted in being physically or emotionally isolated from people.

Everything the pastor proposes and plans should pass the Common Harry Test. Will it help Harry? Will it make Harry's life better? Will Harry understand it? Will Harry support it? People like Harry are the reason Christ came and the reason He calls you to minister.

Much of your frustration with ministry will be rooted in being physically or emotionally isolated from people. You may be scared or bored by them. Or you may be outright hostile to them. Some pastoral trainers emphasize how irritating people can be. As a result, beginning pastors sometimes suspect people and give them bad vibes. One pastor admitted, "I've been treating people as though they were lucky to have me. But now

I see that it's my privilege to serve them in Jesus' name."

Every congregation has difficult people; your church may have many. But when you're tied with cords of Christian affection to your congregation of generous, devoted, loving people, you can bear even the worst tribulations of ministry.

STEP 9: FUEL PERSEVERANCE WITH PASSION

Someone correctly observed, "The main problem of ministry is that pastors give up a minute, a week or a month too soon."

A fact of ministry is that achievement often results after a fairly long process of doing the right thing for the right reason. And though many pastors believe and preach perseverance, they frequently detest it because of its exacting and continuous demands.

Gritting your teeth, doing your duty and pushing yourself to do what you don't want to do one more time is the popular concept of perseverance. This notion believes that achievement results from doggedly hammering away at a task. So in many minds, perseverance is high on obligation and low on enjoyment.

Perseverance, however, has a more attractive but seldom discussed dimension—an intense and passionate commitment to a cause or task that turns work into fun. Fired-up pastors don't have to force themselves to work. Passionate perseverance rekindles motivation, so ministry is a joy instead of a job, a delight instead of a drag.

Passion produces perseverance. Passion for ministry can make it possible for you to sail right past many risks. While this advice was written for business leaders, the words apply to pastors, too:

If your passion for the project [or ministry] is lower than a seven on a scale of ten, either change it, get yourself more fired up, or forget it. It's too tough out there and there's too much on your plate already to take on something you are not genuinely excited about. A project under a seven will become a burden to you and your people, and you'll only go through the motions with it.[8]

Passionate perseverance makes ministry more interesting, impacts those around us and increases our own stability, resiliency and buoyancy.

STEP 10: TREASURE THE PLEASURE OF GOD

While it's a key concept for healthy ministry, balance is difficult to achieve because it requires carrying on in spite of the endless demands people place upon pastors.

The collision of roles and expectations in the pastorate reminds us of a time when a frightening onset of dizziness sent a friend of ours to the doctor. He expected to receive sophisticated tests and elaborate follow-up treatment. But his doctor offered a surprisingly simple suggestion: "Whenever you feel dizzy, just look at something straight—like a door jam—for a few seconds; then you'll be able to function."

What a useful combination for increasing satisfaction in ministry—*look at something straight.* This idea sounds like Hebrews 12:2, "Let us fix our eyes on Jesus, the author and perfecter of our faith, who for the joy set before him endured the cross, scorning its shame, and sat down at the right hand of the throne of God."

In an ultimate sense, you must please God with a balanced life and a fruitful ministry. And sometimes He defines balance and fruitfulness differently than you do. But rest assured that your best effort always satisfies God. He knows every detail of your life and ministry. And He's a thousand times easier to please than you think.

Remember, you can't permit people in your care to have unrealistic expectations of you, and you can't have unrealistic expectations of yourself. Sure, nearly everyone in your sphere of influence has an opinion about how you should do your work. No two evaluations agree—not even yours and your spouse's. So, joy for your work isn't bound to flow from other people. Rather, you must determine what ministry is to be for you, based on how it pleasures God.

STEP 11: DARE TO LEAD

No one can give a pastor leadership of a church by a one-time appointment or election. Two monumental stumbling blocks that prevent that from happening are

- Leadership is always earned and never bestowed
- No one follows those who don't lead

No call, contract, credential or ecstatic religious experience makes an individual a leader. The most impressive and magnetic characteristic of the effective pastor-leader is single-minded devotion to lead the people into the deeper depths of Christlikeness.

Sometimes it's hard for pastors to accept this concept of leadership because they're called by God, set apart for ministry by ordination and formally installed by a congregation or ecclesiastical official. But a church assignment or a formal rank only means the pastor has permission or

No call, contract, credential or ecstatic religious experience makes an individual a leader.

authority to begin earning leadership. A call to a church is a call to get to work. A wise denominational administrator counseled a green pastor, "Now that you've been invited to pastor a group of people, it means they expect you to lead. If you're to be a leader, you'll have to earn it after you officially become the pastor." The high cost of earning genuine pastoral leadership requires pastors to take ministry into the details of people's lives.

Pastors who think appointment, election or ordination makes them leaders are often bewildered because no one follows them. If that happens, they need to examine their pastoral care of God's flock. No pastor can really lead until he applies the Spirit of Christ to every dimension of church life—efficient organization, solid business principles, strong preaching and sound theology. None of these is adequate without the Spirit of Christ.

That essential element of applying the Spirit of Christ to all dimensions of your work will help your commitment to move from passing interest to increased intensity. Then you and your congregation will be able to move from arm's-length suspicion to wholehearted confidence, working together like a masterful symphony orchestra.

Peter Drucker calls leadership a peak performance by one who is "the trumpet that sounds a clear sound of the organization's goals." Consider his five requirements for doing this:

1. A leader works.
2. A leader sees his assignment as responsibility rather than rank or privilege.
3. A leader wants strong, capable, self-assured, independent associates.
4. A leader creates human energies and vision.
5. A leader develops followers' trust by his own consistency and integrity.[9]

If you use this leadership directive, you can experience a creative surge of satisfaction in your ministry. Then you'll be able to harness the energy you've wasted previously. If you want an unquestioned right to lead, you need to activate these directives in the depths of your personhood and practice them in the details of your work. Strong, capable people stand in the wings in many churches waiting to follow a competent, Christlike leader who dares to lead them to accomplish worthwhile objectives.

STEP 12: EXEGETE YOUR ENVIRONMENT

Good sermons require reliable exegesis. When a pastor faithfully performs this work, he discovers a biblical writer's meaning and brings it into trustworthy dialogue with contemporary life. This work allows a pastor to transfer what he's learned about the text into words his hearers can understand.

Effective biblical preaching is a continuous interplay between the meaning of Scripture, the needs of hearers and the character and competence of the preacher. Expositor Alexander Maclaren cogently abridged the idea, "A true sermon always has humanity within it and Divinity behind it."[10] Exegesis allows Scripture to illuminate and examine and revolutionize real people who live in contemporary situations.

One trainer of preachers suggests that the task of hermeneutics bridges the differences of time, place, culture and meaning between the biblical writer and the modern hearer—and the preacher connects the two.

But another slightly different exegetical skill is important for equipping a pastor to understand, overcome or make use of existing risks in his life and ministry. This essential skill is the lifelong commitment and quest by a pastor to exegete his world—himself, his family, his congregation, his denomination, his town and his culture—so that he develops a thoroughly accurate awareness of the unique dimensions of his assignment.

This new exegetical skill is a commitment by the pastor to discover and rediscover the subtleties of the environment where his ministry will take place. Then he uses that information to shape the details of ministry.

Exegeting the environment for ministry means making a positive gospel response to the conditions and demands of a particular situation. It means asking exegetical questions about the setting: What does this mean? Is my view correct? What do I know about this issue from other settings? Who's in charge? What are they saying? What's happening in my small corner of the world?

It's a lethal delusion to assume every situation is like the previous one, just as it's a miscalculation to think that a specific setting remains static. Settings of ministry, like mountain streams, may look the same year after year. But they're in a constant flux of change, and the familiar appearance is deceiving. No two ministry settings are the same.

Many of the letters we receive at Focus on the Family are filled with distressing disappointment. Some of that aggravation is unnecessary because it grows out of a pastor's inability to understand himself in his surroundings. Many try to do their ministry in the same way in every setting—a kind of one-year effort done over 40 years in several churches.

It seems obvious here: Serving an old established church that was spiritually abused by a previous pastor is very different from gathering people together in a church plant. In each church—and any other situation—the pastor needs to exegete the distinct differences and the congregation's way of looking at its task. Neither church will flourish if the pastor doesn't understand and make use of these variations.

The minister's family situation affects ministry, too. The beginning pastor with preschool children and a working wife will do ministry differently than a pastor whose children are teenagers or another minister whose nest is empty. Exegeting the distinguishing characteristics in his own family helps a pastor cope with, respond to or enjoy the unique qualities of his marriage and family and their affect on his ministry.

Think of denominational and doctrinal differences. The pastor who serves an independent church has a different situation than the pastor who serves in a denominational structure. Clergy leaders find themselves facing many obstacles when they don't factor these issues into their ministry.

Tools for exegeting the environment include awareness, sensitivity, reflection and listening, as well as historical records and key questions of knowledgeable persons in the congregation and community.

Exegeting your environment requires you to know more about your community than anyone else. Pastor Rick Warren of Saddleback Valley Community Church in Southern California advocates, "You cannot reach people unless you understand them first."[11] And he insists that nothing can take the place of a pastor's interviewing 200 or more unchurched people to find out what they think about the Church and the community.

George Hunter III, dean of the E. Stanley Jones School of Evangelism at Asbury Seminary, advises getting intimately acquainted with your environment for ministry by discovering who lives in the community and why, what they think and how they act. He also suggests interviews with school officials, marketing people, regional planning personnel and human services providers in the community.[12]

You might profit from college or university courses in the social sciences such as sociology, anthropology, cross-cultural communication or marriage and family. These can make up for blind spots in your ministry training and help you catch up in quickly changing fields.

Heed the words of modern prophets like Chuck Colson:

> I believe that today in the West, and particularly in America, the new barbarians are all around us. They are not hairy Goths and Vandals, swilling fermented brew and ravishing maidens; they are not Huns and Visigoths storming our borders or scaling our city walls. No, this time the invaders have come from within.[13]

It would be sad to be crippled in your ministry because you refused to exegete the rich treasures of Holy Scripture. But it's equally tragic if you're not able—or worse, if you refuse—to understand your environment.

TAKE CHARGE OF YOUR MINISTRY NOW

These 12 steps will refocus your attention away from the contemporary crises to enormous opportunities at your elbow, down the street or across the world. These steps offer handles to help you respond redemptively to the most astounding possibilities ever experienced by the Christian Church.

The world needs pastors more than ever before in history. In a time when personal and public sins have strangled satisfaction out of life, people are crying for someone like a pastor to put them in touch with the Author of authentic wholeness. In this era of despair when government officials admit that social problems can't be solved with government programs and expenditures, the world needs someone like you to proclaim the reforming work of

Christ for individuals, communities and cultures. At a time when loneliness and isolation have reached epidemic proportions, pastors like you can offer spiritually homeless persons a different status in the family of God. These times demand that pastors like you root and ground people in the new-life realities of Scripture and stimulate their appetites for a personal faith in Christ.

These mammoth miseries offer an unparalleled possibility. How exciting to realize that God placed you in the middle of the action as an agent of reconciliation, hope and righteousness. It's a daring, demanding day. Seize and use it.

Ministry to impact these times will be diverse, complicated and creative. Therefore, it's impossible to describe all the ways you might renew yourself and fall in love again with your calling. But if you can think of your ministry as a work of art that influences all who experience it, then you can use these 12 steps as paint, canvas and brushes, and lessons in texture and color. Of course, nothing in any book faintly replaces divine guidance, renewed passion for souls, fired-up perseverance, Christ-inspired imagination and sacrificial resourcefulness.

Both these puzzling times and the gospel call you to give it your best—one more time. Don't wait for a surge of courage to start again. Get up and get going. Then courage, energy and creativity will follow you into the pulpit, stand by your side in the dark midnights, strengthen you when you want to quit and follow you home to reassure you that you can do it again tomorrow.

Keep close company with God by praying Francis Ridley Havergal's prayer:

Let me, then be always growing,
Never, never standing still;
Listening, learning, better knowing
Thee and Thy most blessed will.[14]

ENDNOTES

Introduction

1. "Pastors Paid Better, but Attendance Unchanged," *Barna Research Online*, March 29, 2001. http://www.barna.org/cgi-bin/pagePressRelease.asp?Press ReleaseID=85&Reference=B (accessed October 26, 2002).

Chapter One

1. Henri J. M. Nouwen, *The Return of the Prodigal Son* (New York: Image Books, 1992), p. 114.
2. Carl S. Dudley and David A. Roozen, "Faith Communities Today: A Report on Religion in the United States Today," *Faith Communities Today*, March 2001. http://fact.hartsem.edu/Final%20FACTrpt.pdf (accessed November 21, 2002).
3. Injoy Ministries, "The State of the Pastor," *Partners in Prayer Report*, quoted in "The State of Ministry Marriage and Morals," *Save America*, n.d. http://www.saveus.org/docs/factsheets/marriage_moral.htm (accessed October 30, 2002).
4. This and the previous six statistics are cited in Fuller Institute of Church Growth, "1991 Survey of Pastors," Fuller Theological Seminary, Pasadena, CA, 1991.
5. Gallup for *USA Today* and CNN, quoted in *Morality in Media Newsletter*, September 1996.
6. Charles Colson, *Against the Night: Living in the New Dark Ages* (Ann Arbor, MI: Servant Publications, 1989), p. 111.

Chapter Two

1. © 2002 Rebecca Barlow Jordan, Used by permission, all rights reserved.
2. George Barna, *Pastor's Weekly Briefing*, June 15, 2001.
3. Kevin Miller, "10 Telling Statistics about Pastors: Research on Money, Sex, and Power," *LeadershipJournal.net*, July 12, 2000. http://www.christianitytoday. com/leaders/newsletter/cln00712.html (accessed October 26, 2002).
4. "A Profile of Protestant Pastors in Anticipation of 'Pastor Appreciation Month,'" *Barna Research Online*, September 25, 2001. http://www.barna.org /cgi-bin/PagePressRelease.asp?PressReleaseID=98&Reference=B (accessed October 26, 2002).
5. "Pastors Paid Better, but Attendance Unchanged," *Barna Research Online*, March 29, 2001. http://www.barna.org/cgi bin/PagePressRelease.asp?Press ReleaseID=85&Reference=B (accessed October 26, 2002).
6. This and the two previous statistics are cited in "New Book Describes the

State of the Church in 2002," *Barna Research Online,* June 4, 2002. http://www.barna.org/cgi-bin/PagePressRelease.asp?PressReleaseID= 114&Reference=B (accessed October 26, 2002).

7. This and the previous statistic are cited in "Americans Are Most Likely to Base Truth on Feelings," *Barna Research Online,* February 12, 2002. http://www.barna.org/cgi-bin/PagePressRelease.asp?PressReleaseID= 106&Reference=B (accessed October 26, 2002).

8. "Americans Are Most Likely to Base Truth on Feelings," *Barna Research Online,* February 12, 2002.

9. Ibid.

10. "Pastors Paid Better, but Attendance Unchanged," *Barna Research Online,* March 29, 2001.

11. Hugh Prather, *Notes on How to Live in the World* (Garden City, NY: Doubleday and Company, 1986), pp. 201-203.

12. "Americans Are Most Likely to Base Truth on Feelings," *Barna Research Online,* February 12, 2002.

13. Source unknown.

14. Elizabeth Skoglund, *Beyond Loneliness* (Garden City, NY: Doubleday and Company, 1980), p. 144.

15. L. Gregory Jones, *Christian Century,* June 15-22, 1994, p. 62.

16. Michael J. Vlach, "Lost in Church," *Intra-Evangelism,* n.d. http://www.intra-evangelism.org/ie/html/lost.asp (accessed November 21, 2002).

17. Guy Greenfield, *The Wounded Pastor* (Grand Rapids, MI: Baker Books, 2001), p. 16.

Chapter Three

1. Paul Wilkes, *Excellent Protestant Congregations* (Louisville, KY: Westminster John Knox Press, 2001), pp. 163-172.

2. Kevin Miller, "10 Telling Statistics About Pastors: Research on Money, Sex, and Power," *LeadershipJournal.net,* July 12, 2000. http://www.christian itytoday.com/leaders/newsletter/cln00712.html (accessed October 26, 2002).

3. John LaRue, "Profile of Today's Pastor: How Prepared Were You for Ministry?" *LeadershipJournal.net,* October 25, 2000. http://www.christianitytoday com/leaders/newsletter/cln01025.html (accessed October 26, 2002).

4. "A Profile of Protestant Pastors in Anticipation of 'Pastor Appreciation Month,'" *Barna Research Online,* September 25, 2001. http://www.barna.org/cgi-bin/PagePressRelease.asp?PressReleaseID=98&Reference=B (accessed October 26, 2002).

5. John C. LaRue, Jr., "Pastors at Work: Where the Time Goes," *Leadership Journal.net,* January 3, 2001. http://www.christianitytoday.com/leaders/ newsletter/2001/cln10103.html (accessed October 26, 2002).

6. John LaRue, "Profile of Today's Pastor: How Prepared Were You for

Ministry?" *LeadershipJournal.net*, October 25, 2000. http://www.christiani tytoday.com/leaders/newsletter/cln01025.html (accessed October 26, 2002).

7. "New Book Describes the State of the Church in 2002," *Barna Research Online*, June 4, 2002. http://www.barna.org/cgi-bin/PagePressRelease.asp? PressReleaseID=114&Reference=B (accessed October 26, 2002).

8. *Pulpit and Pew: Research on Pastoral Leadership.* http://www.pulpitandpew.duke. edu, quoted in "Pulpit and Pew: Selected Findings from National Clergy Survey, *www.Presbyweb.com*, April 10, 2002. http://www.presbyweb.com/ 2002/News/041001PulpitAndPew.htm (accessed November 21, 2002).

9. Adapted from James Hamilton, *The Pair in Your Parsonage* (Kansas City, KS: Beacon Hill Press, 1982), p. 10.

10. Source unknown.

11. Dietrich Bonhoeffer, quoted in Daniel V. Viles, *Pursuing Excellence in Ministry* (New York: The Alban Institute, 1988), p. 43.

Chapter Four

1. Injoy Ministries, "The State of the Pastor," *Partners in Prayer Report*, quoted in "The State of Ministry Marriage and Morals," *Save America*, n.d. http://www.saveus.org/docs/factsheets/marriage_moral.htm (accessed October 30, 2002).

2. A Hartford Seminary study, quoted in "The State of Ministry Marriage and Morals," *Save America*, n.d. http://www.saveus.org/docs/factsheets/ marriage_moral.htm (accessed October 30, 2002).

3. "The State of Ministry Marriage and Morals," *Save America*, n.d. http:// www.saveus.org/docs/factsheets/marriage_moral.htm (accessed October 30, 2002).

4. The Alban Institute, quoted in *pastoralministry.com*, March 28, 2001. http://www.pastornet.net.

5. "Pastors Paid Better, but Attendance Unchanged," *Barna Research Online*, March 29, 2001. http://www.barna.org/cgi-bin/PagePressRelease.asp? PressReleaseID=85&Reference=B (accessed October 26, 2002).

6. This and the two previous statistics are quoted in "The State of Ministry Marriage and Morals," *Save America*, n.d. http://www.saveus.org/docs/ factsheets/marriage_moral.htm (accessed October 30, 2002).

7. Focus on the Family questionnaire, 1997.

8. "I See That Hand: Do You and Your Spouse Believe That Being in the Pastoral Ministry Is Hazardous to Your Family's Well-Being and Health?" *The Parsonage*, November 19, 2000. http://www.family.org/pastor/parson pollarchive.cfm?&showresults=parsonage_001113 (accessed November 3, 2002). Note that online polls of this nature are a good indication of what

pastors are thinking and feeling. In fact, many times the results closely mirror more traditional surveys. However, online polls are just that—indicators. They represent only the views and opinions of those who respond; the results are not scientific.

9. Paul A. Mickey and Ginny W. Ashmore, *Clergy Families: Is Normal Life Possible?* (Grand Rapids, MI: Zondervan, 1991), p. 17.

10. Gordon MacDonald, *Mid-Course Correction* (Nashville, TN: Thomas Nelson, 2000), p. 234.

11. H. Newton Malony and Richard A. Hunt, *The Psychology of Clergy* (Harrisburg, PA: Morehouse, 1991), p. 9.

12. Ibid., p. 36.

Chapter Five

1. "I See That Hand: Does Your Spouse Work Outside the Home?" *The Parsonage*, March 2, 2002. http://www.family.org/pastor/parsonpollarchive. cfm?&showresults=parsonage_020224 (accessed November 3, 2002).

2. This and the previous two statistics are from The Alban Institute, quoted in *pastoralministry.com*, March 28, 2001. http://www.pastornet.net.

3. This and the previous statistic are cited in Focus on the Family questionnaire, 1997.

4. Duane Alleman, *Theology News and Notes*, Fuller Seminary.

Chapter Six

1. "Ministries Today Poll: What Concerns You Most About Your Family?" *MinistriesToday*, 2000. http://www.ministriestoday.com/pollresults.html (accessed November 3, 2002).

2. "I See That Hand: Do You Faithfully Take Off at Least One Full Day Each Week to Spend with Your Family?" *The Parsonage*, October 22, 2000. http://www.family.org/pastor/parsonpollarchive.cfm?&showresults=par sonage_001016 (accessed November 3, 2002).

3. "I See That Hand: Do You and Your Spouse Believe That Being in the Pastoral Ministry Is Hazardous to Your Family's Well-Being and Health?" *The Parsonage*, November 19, 2000. http://www.family.org/pastor/parsonpoll archive.cfm?&showresults=parsonage_001113 (accessed November 3, 2002).

4. "I See That Hand: Do Your Children Enjoy Being Part of a Ministry Family?" *The Parsonage*, July 14, 2001. http://www.family.org/pastor/par sonpollarchive.cfm?&showresults=parsonage_010708 (accessed November 3, 2002).

5. "I See That Hand: Would You Stay at Your Current Pastorate If You Knew It Was Detrimental to Your Family?" *The Parsonage*, September 1, 2001. http://www.family.org/pastor/parsonpollarchive.cfm?&showresults=par sonage_010826 (accessed November 3, 2002).

6. "I See That Hand: What Time of the Day Is the Most Stressful in Your Home?" *The Parsonage*, October 13, 2001. http://www.family.org/pastor/parsonpollarchive.cfm?&showresults=parsonage_011007 (accessed November 3, 2002).

7. "I See That Hand: Do You and Your Family Feel Pressure to Model the Ideal Family to Your Congregation and Community?" *The Parsonage*, April 13, 2002. http://www.family.org/pastor/parsonpollarchive.cfm?&showresults=parsonage_020407 (accessed November 3, 2002).

8. "I See That Hand: How Do You Typically Spend Your Time Off from Your Pastoral Duties?" *The Parsonage*, August 10, 2002. http://www.family.org/pastor/parsonpollarchive.cfm?&showresults=parsonage_020810 (accessed November 3, 2002).

Chapter Seven

1. "I See That Hand: Have You Ever Experienced Depression or Burnout to the Extent That You Needed to Take a Leave of Absence from the Ministry?" *The Parsonage*, April 6, 2002. http://www.family.org/pastor/parsonpollarchive.cfm?&showresults=parsonage_020331 (accessed November 3, 2002).

2. "The State of Ministry Marriage and Morals," *Save America*, n.d. http://www.saveus.org/docs/factsheets/marriage_moral.htm (accessed October 30, 2002).

3. "I See That Hand: Do You Have a Regularly Scheduled and Implemented Exercise Routine (Walking, Sports, Aerobics, Exercise Equipment, Gym)?" *The Parsonage*, May 11, 2002. http://www.family.org/pastor/parsonpollarchive.cfm?&showresults=parsonage_020505 (accessed November 3, 2002).

4. *The Bridge*, Clergy Center of Pastors Institute and Department of Family and Child Services at Florida State University, February 28, 2001.

5. John C. LaRue, Jr., "Pastors at Work: Where the Time Goes," *LeadershipJournal.net*, January 3, 2001. http://www.christianitytoday.com/leaders/newsletter/2001/cln10103.html (accessed October 26, 2002).

6. *Pulpit and Pew: Research on Pastoral Leadership*. http://www.pulpitandpew.duke.edu, quoted in "Pulpit and Pew: Selected Findings from National Clergy Survey, www.*Presbyweb.com*, April 10, 2002. http://www.presbyweb.com/2002/News/041001PulpitAndPew.htm (accessed November 21, 2002).

7. John A. Sanford, *Ministry Burnout* (New York: Paulist Press, 1982), p. 18.

8. Ibid.

9. Lloyd J. Ogilvie, *Making Stress Work for You* (Waco, TX: Word Books, 1984), p. 125.

Chapter Eight

1. "I See That Hand: How Many Days Off Do You Regularly Get Each Week?" *The Parsonage*, October 19, 2002. http://www.family.org/pastor/

parsonpollarchive.cfm?&showresults=parsonage_021019 (accessed November 3, 2002).

2. "I See That Hand: Do You Feel You Receive Sufficient Vacation Time Each Year, Including Several Weekends?" *The Parsonage*, October 26, 2002. http://www.family.org/pastor/parsonpollarchive.cfm?&showresults=par sonage_021026 (accessed November 3, 2002).

3. "A Show of Hands: Has Your Pastor Had a Vacation in the Past Year?" *family.org*, October 28, 2002. http://www.family.org/focuspollarchive.cfm?&showresults=HP/pastorsvacation (accessed November 3, 2002).

4. "I See That Hand: What Is Your Favorite Means of Relaxing, Letting Go, Escaping, and Releasing—of Taking Care of Yourself?" *The Parsonage*, May 19, 2001. http://www.family.org/pastor/parsonpollarchive.cfm?&showre sults=parsonage_010513 (accessed November 3, 2002).

5. Kevin Miller, "What Pastors Are Saying," *LeadershipJournal.net*, December 5, 2001. http://www.christianitytoday.com/leaders/newsletter/2001/cln11205.html (accessed November 22, 2002).

6. *Pulpit and Pew: Research on Pastoral Leadership*. http://www.pulpitandpew.duke.edu, quoted in "Pulpit and Pew: Selected Findings from National Clergy Survey," *www.Presbyweb.com*, April 10, 2002. http://www.presby web.com/2002/News/041001PulpitAndPew.htm (accessed November 21, 2002).

7. Philip Yancey, "Replenishing the Inner Pastor," *Christianity Today* (May 21, 2001), p. 104.

8. Georges Bernanos, *The Diary of a Country Priest* (New York: Carroll and Graf Publishers, 1937), p. 117.

9. Washington Bureau of Scripps Howard News Service, March 10, 1990.

Chapter Nine

1. "I See That Hand: What Is the First Thing You Put on Your Schedule Each Week?" *The Parsonage*, September 22, 2001. http://www.family.org/pastor/parsonpollarchive.cfm?&showresults=parsonage_010916 (accessed November 3, 2002).

2. Ed Rowell, "How Does Your Week Measure Up?" *LeadershipJournal.net*, Spring 1998. http://www.christianitytoday.com/le/812/812089.html (accessed October 26, 2002).

3. John C. LaRue, Jr., "Pastors at Work: Where the Time Goes," *LeadershipJournal.net*, January 3, 2001. http://www.christianitytoday.com/leaders/newsletter/2001/cln10103.html (accessed October 26, 2002).

4. Ibid.

5. Richard A. Swenson, *Margin: Restoring Emotional, Physical, Financial, and Time Reserves to Overloaded Lives* (Colorado Springs, CO: NavPress, 1995), pp. 91-92.

Chapter Ten

1. "The State of Ministry Marriage and Morals," *Save America*, n.d. http://www. saveus.org/docs/factsheets/marriage_moral.htm (accessed October 30, 2002).
2. "I See That Hand: How Much Time Do You Spend on the Internet Each Week?" *The Parsonage*, May 18, 2002. http://www.family.org/pastor/parson pollarchive.cfm?&showresults=parsonage_020512 (accessed November 3, 2002).
3. "The State of Ministry Marriage and Morals," *Save America*, n.d. http://www. saveus.org/docs/factsheets/marriage_moral.htm (accessed October 30, 2002).
4. Kevin Miller, "10 Telling Statistics About Pastors: Research on Money, Sex, and Power," *LeadershipJournal.net*, July 12, 2000. http://www.christian itytoday.com/leaders/newsletter/cln00712.html (accessed October 26, 2002).
5. The editors of *Leadership Journal*, "The Leadership Survey: Pastors Viewing Internet Pornography," *LeadershipJournal.net*, Winter 2001. http://www.chris tianity today.com/le/2001/001/12.89.html (accessed October 26, 2002).
6. Christine J. Gardner, "Tangled in the Worst of the Web," *Christianity Today* (March 5, 2001), pp. 44-45.
7. The editors of *Leadership Journal*, "The Leadership Survey: Pastors Viewing Internet Pornography," *LeadershipJournal.net*, Winter 2001.
8. Stephen Arterburn and Fred Stoeker, *Every Man's Battle* (Colorado Springs, CO: Waterbrook Press, 2000), p. 29.
9. Patrick J. Carnes, "Abused Children, Addicted Adults," *Changes* (June 1993), p. 81.
10. Ted Roberts, *Pure Desire* (Ventura, CA: Regal Books, 1999), pp. 255-256.
11. C. S. Lewis, *Mere Christianity*, as quoted in *Romance*, compiled by Ellyn Sanna (Uhrichsville, OH: Barbour Publishing, 1999), p. 56.
12. Steven Fetrow, "Bold Next Steps," *pureintimacy.org*, 2000. http://www.pure intimacy.org/online1/essays/a0000028.html (accessed November 20, 2002).
13. Arterburn and Stoeker, *Every Man's Battle*, pp. 65, 68.
14. Ibid., p. 70.

Chapter Eleven

1. This and the previous statistic are from "I See That Hand: What Do You See as Your Number One Priority?" *The Parsonage*, August 25, 2001. http://www.family.org/pastor/parsonpollarchive.cfm?&showresults=par sonage_010819 (accessed November 3, 2002).
2. "I See That Hand: Are You a Member of a Small Group That Provides You with Support and Holds You Accountable?" *The Parsonage*, January 28, 2001. http://www.family.org/pastor/parsonpollarchive.cfm?&showresults=par sonage_010122 (accessed November 3, 2002).

3. "I See That Hand: What Activity Provides Sustained Renewal in Your Spirit?" *The Parsonage,* October 20, 2001. http://www.family.org/pastor/parsonpollarchive.cfm?&showresults=parsonage_011014 (accessed November 3, 2002).

4. This and the previous statistic are from "I See That Hand: If You Felt the Need for Personal Counseling, to Whom Would You Go?" *The Parsonage,* August 24, 2002. http://www.family.org/pastor/parsonpollarchive.cfm?&showresults=parsonage_020824 (accessed November 3, 2002).

5. "The State of Ministry Marriage and Morals," *Save America,* n.d. http://www.saveus.org/docs/factsheets/marriage_moral.htm (accessed October 30, 2002).

6. Leonard Griffith, *We Have This Ministry* (Waco, TX: Word Books, 1973), p. 16.

7. Henri J. M. Nouwen, *Reaching Out* (Garden City, NY: Doubleday and Company, 1975), p. 97.

Chapter Twelve

1. Eugene H. Peterson, *Working the Angles* (Grand Rapids, MI: Eerdmans, 1987).

2. Leonard Griffith, *We Have This Ministry* (Waco, TX: Word Books, 1973), p. 87.

3. Stephen R. Covey, *The Seven Habits of Highly Effective People* (New York: Simon and Schuster, 1989), p. 97.

4. Ibid., p. 219.

5. Robert J. Kriegel and Louis Patler, *If It Ain't Broke . . . Break It!* (New York: Warner Books, 1991), p. 85.

6. John Akers, quoted in Kriegel and Patler, *If It Ain't Broke . . . Break It!,* p. 169.

7. Alan Jones, *Sacrifice and Delight: A Spirituality for Ministry* (San Francisco, CA: HarperCollins Publishers, 1992), p. 34.

8. *Forbes* (2 October 1989), p. 31.

9. Peter F. Drucker, *Managing for the Future* (New York: Dutton, 1992), pp. 119-123.

10. Alexander Maclaren, quoted in A.W. Blackwood, *Expository Preaching for Today* (Nashville, TN: Abingdon Press, 1953), p. 25.

11. Rick Warren, quoted in George Hunter III, *How to Reach Secular People* (Nashville, TN: Abingdon Press, 1992), p. 154.

12. George Hunter III, *How to Reach Secular People,* p. 155.

13. Charles Colson, *Against the Night: Living in the New Dark Ages* (Ann Arbor, MI: Servant Publications, 1989), p. 23.

14. Francis Ridley Havergal, quoted in "Growing in Grace," *AGS Consulting,* April 18, 2002. http://www.agsconsulting.com/htdbnon/r808c.htm (accessed November 21, 2002).

CONTRIBUTORS

Dr. James C. Dobson is founder and president of Focus on the Family, a nonprofit organization that produces his internationally syndicated radio program heard by more than 200 million people daily on over 4,200 radio stations and publishes 11 magazines sent to more than 3 million people each month.

Dobson is author of numerous best-selling books dedicated to the preservation of the family including *Bringing Up Boys, Love for a Lifetime* and, with his wife, Shirley, *Night Light: A Devotional for Couples.*

Dr. Dobson served on the faculty of the University of Southern California School of Medicine for 14 years and on the attending staff of Children's Hospital of Los Angeles for 17 years. He has been active in governmental affairs and has advised three U.S. presidents on family issues. He earned his Ph.D. from the University of Southern California in the field of child development.

Gordon and Gail MacDonald have shared ministry in four congregations across more than 40 years. Presently they are serving the next generation of ministry couples through writing, teaching in seminaries and speaking to various conferences all across the United States. Gordon's books include *Ordering Your Private World,* a religious best-seller that impacted thousands, and his more recent books *Mid-Course Correction* and *Secrets of the Generous Life.* Gail's books include *High Call, High Privilege, A Step Farther and Higher* and *In His Everlasting Arms—Learning to Trust God in All Circumstances.*

An interview with seven women, each either a pastor's wife or well experienced in helping ministers' wives, provides the foundation for chapter 5.

Pam Farrel, who has served as a pastor's wife, is cofounder and codirector with her husband of Masterful Living—an organization dedicated to strengthening marriage relationships. They have a premarital counseling ministry and work extensively with couples at Valley Bible Church in San Marcos, California.

Janell Repp serves with her husband at Minnesota Renewal Center in Shoreview, Minnesota. Their organization provides renewal counseling, healing, consultation and training of pastors and missionaries.

Linda Riley, a pastor's wife, is founder and director of Called Together Ministries (CTM) of Torrance, California. CTM is a resource organization for pastors' wives that seeks to provide learning, inspiration and fellowship.

Jane Rubietta, teacher and author, serves with her husband at Abounding Ministries in Grays Lake, Illinois. Her latest book is *How to Keep the Pastor You Love*.

Linda Swanson serves with her husband in counseling and helping ministry couples find renewal at Fair Haven Retreat Center located in the Blue Ridge Mountains of Tennessee.

Kandy Veenker, executive director of Mountain Learning Center in June Lake, California, serves with her husband to provide clergy couples opportunities to find restoration and clarify perspectives.

Kay Warren, pastor's wife, Bible teacher and conference speaker for women's groups, is deeply involved in the life of Saddleback Valley Community Church in Lake Forest, California. She and her husband started Saddleback Church in their home in 1980 with seven people. She is coauthor of *Life Perspectives*.

Archibald Hart is professor of psychology at Fuller Theological Seminary in Pasadena, California. He is a licensed psychologist, certified biofeedback practitioner and board-certified diplomat fellow in psychopharmacology. A former dean of the graduate School of Psychology at Fuller, he has demonstrated strong professional interests in clergy stress issues including burnout, depression and family relationships. As a prolific researcher and writer, his list of books include *Unmasking Male Depression*, *The Anxiety Cure*, *The Sexual Man* and *Unveiling Depression in Women*.

Bob and Sandy Sewell are counselors and teachers at SonScape Re-Creation Ministries—a retreat center located in Woodland Park, Colorado, for ministers and their spouses, which they founded in 1984. Their goal at the retreat center is to either prevent or help heal burnout through spiritual formation—the process of being conformed to the image of Christ for the sake of others. As wounded healers, they teach the "Holy Rhythm of Life."

Following five years of private practice, **Dr. Richard A. Swenson** accepted a teaching position at the University of Wisconsin Medical School. His revolutionary ideas about time management for the pastor form the basis for chapter 9. As a physician, Swenson's current focus is cultural medicine—the intersection of health and culture. As a futurist, his emphasis is fourfold: the future of the world, society, faith and health care. His books include *Margin—Restoring Emotional, Physical, Financial, and Time Reserves to Overloaded Lives*; *The Overload Syndrome*; *Hurtling Toward Oblivion*; *Restoring Margin to Overloaded Lives*; and *More Than Meets the Eye*.

Ted Roberts is senior pastor of East Hill Foursquare Church in Gresham, Oregon. He has led his congregation to become a world leader in developing small-group ministries for those victimized by drugs and alcohol, divorce, dysfunctional families and sexual addiction. His book *Pure Desire* addresses the difficult issues of sexual addiction and pornography and restoration through the healing love of Christ.

Jerry Bridges has been on the staff of Navigators since 1955. He served as vice president for corporate affairs from 1979 through 1994. Since then he has been involved in staff training and serves as a resource person to those who minister on university campuses. In addition to his work in the college ministries at Navigators, he also speaks at numerous conferences and retreats in the United States and overseas. His books include *The Pursuit of Holiness*, *The Practice of Godliness*, *Trusting God*, *Transforming Grace*, *The Discipline of Grace*, *The Crisis of Caring* and *The Joy of Fearing God*.

ADDITIONAL RESOURCES FOR PASTORS AND CHURCHES

PASTORAL RESOURCES AND SERVICES AVAILABLE FROM THE PASTORAL MINISTRIES DEPARTMENT OF FOCUS ON THE FAMILY

The resources listed in this section are available by calling 1-800-A-FAMILY or visiting www.parsonage.org.

Website

The Parsonage (www.parsonage.org)—a home page for ministers and their families.

Toll-Free Phone Line

The Pastoral Care Line (1-877-233-4455)—a listening ear or word of advice from our staff of pastors for ministers, missionaries, chaplains and their families.

Audiocassettes

Pastor to Pastor—an audiocassette series available as a bimonthly subscription or individual sets. Features H. B. London interviewing Christian experts on topics pertaining to the personal and family lives of pastors, such as pastors in crisis, keeping romance alive, overcoming weariness, retaining your own identity as a pastor's wife, dangers of the Internet and pastors as parents.

Newsletter

The Pastor's Weekly Briefing—a quick look at current events of interest to pastors, their families and their congregations. Available by fax or e-mail or at the website.

Congregational Booklets

The Pastor's Advocate Series—a set of booklets designed to help congregations better understand pastors and their families, better care for them and better join them in ministry.

Resource Directory

The Pastoral Care Directory—an invaluable list of ministries specializing in care for pastoral families, plus the best in books, audiocassettes, videos, publications and other resources (available both in print and online).

BOOKS BY THE AUTHORS

London, H. B., Jr. *Refresh, Renew, Revive: How to Encourage Your Spirit, Strengthen Your Family, and Energize Your Ministry*. Colorado Springs, CO: Focus on the Family, 1996.

London, H. B., Jr., and Neil B. Wiseman. *Becoming Your Favorite Church*. Ventura, CA: Regal Books, 2002.

———. *The Heart of a Great Pastor: How to Grow Strong and Thrive Wherever God Has Planted You*. Ventura, CA: Regal Books, 1994.

———. *Married to a Pastor: How to Stay Happily Married in the Ministry*. Ventura, CA: Regal Books, 1999.

———. *They Call Me Pastor: How to Love the Ones You Lead*. Ventura, CA: Regal Books, 2000.

London, H. B., Jr., and Stan Toler. *The Minister's Little Devotional Book*. Tulsa, OK: Honor Books, 1997.

Wiseman, Neil B. *Come to the Water Brook.* Kansas City, MO: Beacon Hill Press, 1997.

———. *Conditioning Your Soul.* Kansas City, MO: Beacon Hill Press, 1999.

———. *Hunger for the Holy—71 Ways to Get Closer to God.* Grand Rapids, MI: Baker Books, 1996.

———. *Maximizing Your Church's Spiritual Potential.* Kansas City, MO: Beacon Hill Press, 1999.

———. *The Untamed God—Unleashing the Supernatural in the Body of Christ.* Kansas City, MO: Beacon Hill Press, 1996.

PASTOR CONFERENCES AND SEMINARS

H. B. London and Neil B. Wiseman are available to speak at conferences, conventions and organizations concerning the ideas described in this book, pastoral renewal, the inner life of the Christian and the renewal of the supernatural in the Body of Christ. Wiseman, who has led the Small Church Institute since 1991, also does consulting with denominational leaders concerning issues facing smaller congregations.

INTERNET CONTACT INFORMATION

H. B. London: http://www.parsonage.org

Neil B. Wiseman: nbwiseman@aol.com

Also from H. B. London, Jr., and Neil B. Wiseman

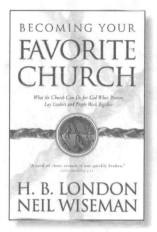

Becoming Your Favorite Church
What the Church Can Do for God
When Pastors, Lay Leaders and
People Work Together
Paperback • ISBN 08307.29046

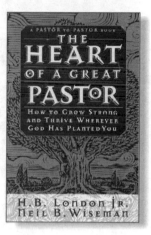

The Heart of a Great Pastor
How to Grow Strong and Thrive
Wherever God Has Planted You
Paperback • ISBN 08307.16890

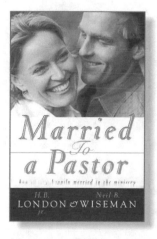

Married to a Pastor
How to Stay Happily Married in the Ministry
Paperback • ISBN 08307.25059

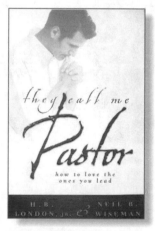

They Call Me Pastor
How to Love the Ones You Lead
Paperback • ISBN 08307.23900

More Ways for Churches to Move Up and Reach Out

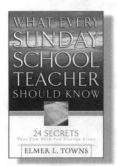

What Every Sunday School Teacher Should Know
24 Secrets That Can Help You Change Lives
Elmer L. Towns
Mass
ISBN 08307.28740

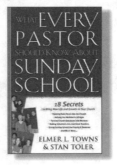

What Every Pastor Should Know About Sunday School
18 Secrets to Bring New Life and Growth to Your Church
Elmer L. Towns & Stan Toler
Paperback
ISBN 08307.28597

Habits of Highly Effective Churches
Being Strategic in Your God-Given Ministry
George Barna
Paperback
ISBN 08307.18605

The Five-Star Church
Serving God and His People with Excellence
Stan Toler and Alan Nelson
Paperback
ISBN 08307.23501

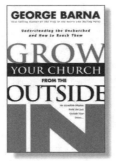

Grow Your Church from the Outside In
Understanding the Unchurched and How to Reach Them
George Barna
Hardcover
ISBN 08307.30877

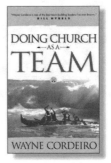

Doing Church as a Team
The Miracle of Teamwork and How It Transforms Churches
Wayne Cordeiro
Paperback
ISBN 08307.26527